Divorce in Transnational Families

Iris Sportel

Divorce in Transnational Families

Marriage, Migration and Family Law

palgrave
macmillan

Iris Sportel
Lichtenberg-Kolleg / Historic Observatory
University of Göttingen
Göttingen, Germany

ISBN 978-3-319-34008-1 ISBN 978-3-319-34009-8 (eBook)
DOI 10.1007/978-3-319-34009-8

Library of Congress Control Number: 2016953476

Printed on acid-free paper

This Palgrave Macmillan imprint is published by Springer Nature
The registered company is Springer International Publishing AG Switzerland

Acknowledgements

This research project was part of a larger programme entitled Transnational Families between Dutch and Islamic Family Law at the Radboud University Nijmegen, coordinated by Betty de Hart and funded by a NWO-VIDI grant. Betty de Hart has been and continues to be a great mentor. I have also learned much from working with Friso Kulk and Jessica Carlisle; I feel privileged to have been part of such a great team. I am also very grateful to Willy Jansen and Ashley Terlouw for their continual guidance, thoughtful comments and thought-provoking questions.

I am deeply indebted to all who have contributed to this study. First and foremost, the people who were willing to share sometimes painful stories about a very intimate subject and without whom this research project would not have been possible. I would also like to thank all NGO representatives, lawyers, translators and other professionals who have agreed to spend time with me and answer my many questions. Joke Verkuijlen of Stichting Steun Remigranten (SSR), the staff of the Steunpunt in Berkane and Noor Stevens of Bezness Alert were particularly helpful. The court in The Hague and the *Raad voor de Rechtspraak* enabled me to do research at the court. The Dutch institutes in Rabat (NIMAR) and Cairo (NVIC) supported me during my fieldwork.

Many thanks also go to my colleagues at the Institute for Gender Studies, Centre for Migration Law and Institute for Sociology of Law at the Radboud University of Nijmegen, the Faculty of Law at Maastricht

University and the Lichtenberg Kolleg of the Georg-August University in Göttingen. I would like to especially mention Anita Böcker, Anoeshka Gehring, Esther van Eijk and Pauline Kruiniger. Susan Rutten and Nadia Sonneveld kindly used their expertise on Dutch, Moroccan and Egyptian law to correct some of the legal parts of this book. The Lichtenberg Kolleg of the Georg-August University Göttingen provided funding to finish this book.

Lastly, I would like to thank my family and friends for their interest, support and their acceptance of my absence when doing fieldwork and writing. Thank you for being at my side.

Contents

1

Introduction

Malika, a single mother working in government service in the Moroccan city of Casablanca, met Dutch businessman Martin when he was visiting Morocco for work. They fell in love and got married. For both it was their second marriage. The couple decided that, after their marriage in Morocco, they would live in the Netherlands, where Martin had his business, and that they would return to live in Morocco after Martin's three adolescent children would have left home. Malika also had a daughter, aged seven, whom she would bring to the Netherlands. After their marriage, it took the couple almost a year to navigate the complex Dutch migration procedures to get permission for Malika and her daughter to settle in the Netherlands. Malika used this time to sell her apartment, quit her job, and prepare for migration.

Upon her arrival in the Netherlands, Malika started to look for new employment. At first she felt 'handicapped' for not being able to speak Dutch, and while she studied to learn the language, she found a small, freelance job. Malika also did all of the housework, while Martin worked long hours in his business. As Malika felt marriage is all about sharing, she freely spent her savings from selling her Moroccan property on the communal household. Her freelance work brought only very little money. Martin tightly controlled his earnings from his successful business as he felt Malika should take responsibility for paying for her and her daughter's upkeep.

I. Sportel, *Divorce in Transnational Families*,
DOI 10.1007/978-3-319-34009-8_1

> The marriage was not a happy one. In fights Martin regularly told Malika to pack up and go back to Morocco, and after a while he became abusive. Malika did not know he was serious about divorce until she received a letter from his lawyer, just before she would have been living in the Netherlands long enough to be entitled to an independent residence permit. At the moment of the interview, Malika and Martin were entangled in a series of court cases involving property and maintenance disputes. Malika felt that, as a Moroccan migrant, she was less likely to be believed by the Dutch authorities and court than Martin. After finishing the Dutch divorce Malika aimed to arrange the Moroccan divorce as soon as possible, as their marriage was still registered there. This means she would probably have had to start another divorce case in Morocco.

Transnational divorces follow marriages in which one of the spouses, like Malika, has migrated. In doing so, spouses have crossed borders: state borders but possibly also religious, cultural, or ethnic borders. In this study, I focus on divorce in Dutch-Moroccan and Dutch-Egyptian transnational families, living in the Netherlands, Morocco, or Egypt. As border-crossers, transnational family members provide a lens for studying social norms and relations on a variety of issues. What is specific about state interventions in transnational families? What does it mean for families to have connections to two states? What can state interventions through migration law tell us about the 'proper' family? What differences determine whether a marriage is considered mixed? How does this mixedness inform the experiences of family members? How do migration and citizenship influence the gendered division of labour and power relations in the family? How is the legal regulation of intimate relations experienced by family members? How can knowledge of these individual experiences contribute to our understanding of normative issues, such as legal pluralism in family law?

Malika's story illustrates how transnational families may get into contact with multiple state legal systems. While the interactions of transnational families with migration law have been extensively studied, the role of family law in transnational family life has so far gained only limited academic attention, despite its importance for the everyday life of transnational families. Most major life events, such as marriage, birth, and death have a legal dimension. While this legal dimension tends to remain almost invisible in the absence of conflict, in transnational family life state intervention is often more pronounced. Matters like establishing parenthood and custody over a child, proving a marriage, or claiming an inheritance can take years of complicated work while dealing with multiple and interacting state bureaucracies. Due to the interconnectedness of migration law and family law (van Walsum 2008), family law can be especially important for transnational families, as even the possibility of living together in the same country can depend on the legal validity of family ties.

Spouses in transnational marriages can be married in one legal system and divorced under another, exploit differences between the legal systems, or arrange everything locally in their country of residence. The considerable differences, as well as unexpected similarities, in marriage and divorce regulations between the Netherlands, Morocco, and Egypt may create all kinds of problems for members of transnational families as well as possibilities for strategic action, especially during divorce. In Malika and Martin's marriage, control over money was a problematic issue. During the divorce process of Martin and Malika, these conflicts translated into a legal conflict over the applicable marital property regime. Martin thought Moroccan family law should be applicable to their marriage, as he married Malika in Morocco. This means that all property would remain separated and that he could simply put Malika out of the marital home, which he owned. Malika, having spent all her savings on the communal household—while in Moroccan family law Martin would have been responsible for maintaining her—then would return to Morocco penniless. During the court case, Malika's lawyer argued that Dutch marital property law should be applicable, as the Netherlands was their first country of communal residence. In a Dutch marital property regime, all property and debts are considered to be communal. This would mean that Malika would get half of all Martin's property, including a share of his business and the marital home. Moreover, Martin would have to pay maintenance to Malika. If Moroccan law would be applied to their divorce and marital property, Malika would have gotten the worst of the differences between the two legal systems, having no claim to Martin's property, while having spent her own property on household costs Martin should have paid.

In addition to analysing disputes relating to divorce, this research project aims to study the meaning and working of family law in the everyday life of transnational families. For this purpose, I will draw on the work of Merry (1986, 1990) and Ewick and Silbey (1998). Ewick and Silbey have studied law in everyday life by looking at breaches from normal routine. Divorce is therefore a good opportunity to observe the working and meaning of family law in daily life. It was not until the moment of divorce that Malika and Martin reframed their conflicts about money in expectations based on family law. Even though marital property law is already applicable during the marriage, the legal ownership of Martin's business and home and Malika's savings only became relevant at the moment of divorce. This redefinition of daily life in legal terms at the moment of divorce can be shocking for the people involved.

Gender, ethnicity, and social class can be important factors contributing to the way partners experience and narrate marriage and divorce (Walzer and Oles 2003; Hopper 2001). In custody disputes, both parents can get the impression that law is gender-biased to the advantage of the other party (Kaganas and Day-Sclater 2004). In transnational marriages, religion and conceptions of religious and cultural differences can also play a role. During the legal process, one partner may find a recognition of rights that they had not experienced before, while the other may feel deprived, based on perceived power relations during the marriage (Merry 2003).

Transnational Marriage and Divorce

Literature on transnational marriages tends to be either on mixed marriages, marriages between partners from different ethnic backgrounds, or on marriages of migrants with a partner from their country of origin, so-called migration marriages. What is seen as a mixed marriage depends on the context and the perceived distance between the partners. In the Dutch context, mainly marriages between partners of different ethnic backgrounds tend to be seen as mixed. Whereas until the 1970s the term mixed marriages was mostly used to describe marriages between persons of different Christian denominations (Hondius 1999), religious differences are nowadays connected to and regarded as a part of ethnicity or culture. Marriages between partners of the same ethnic background but with different religions are unlikely to be seen as mixed. Similarly, because of this focus on ethnicity and culture, marriages of—second-generation—migrants with partners from their country of origin are seldom seen as mixed marriages, even though the spouses have been raised in different countries. This research combines both groups, using the term transnational marriages.

The empirical literature on transnational marriages seems to be focused mostly on the beginning of the transnational relationship. Research on later stages of the relationship is far more limited, and consists mostly of life stories of migrant women (Rozema 2005; van der Zwaard 2008; Walby 2010; Luyckx 2000; Buitelaar 2000) and intercultural communication in mixed marriages (Speelman 1993, 2001; Ask 2006; Hondius 1999; Waldis 1998, 2006; Waldis and Byron 2006).

A main issue in research on mixed marriages is the explanation or description of the coming about of the marriage. Some authors try to find explanations in circumstances. According to Bacas, for example, socio-economic processes contributed to the possibility of transnational mixed relationships. Globalised markets, modernised transport, and communication systems together with a growing tourist industry offer more and better opportunities for cross-border contacts. Furthermore, because of processes of individualisation in Western Europe, women have fewer constraints placed on them with regard to marriage choices (Bacas 2002). Transnational marriages of migrant minorities are often interpreted in terms of integration. Whereas mixed marriages between migrants and the native population of a country are often seen as a sign of and contributor to the integration of ethnic minorities, marriages with partners from the country of origin are seen as problematic and as a sign of poor integration (de Hart 2003; van der Zwaard 2008; Sterckx 2014). In addition to the explanation for migration marriages being a lack of integration in the new country of residence, a second explanation for the high number of transnational marriages with partners from the country of origin by some groups of migrants is marriage as a strategy to obtain sought-after legal residence in a European country. This explanation is especially popular among policymakers. According to Charsley (2005), this factor does play a role in explaining the very high number of cousin marriages in transnational marriages of Pakistani people in the UK. A possibility of migration can be seen as capital that needs to be kept in the family. However, strategic interests are not the only reason. Pakistani parents also try to limit the risk of divorce, and thus look for a partner they think is best suited for their child in their network in their country of origin. Because of the distance, monitoring potential candidates is difficult. Transnationalism therefore enhances the need for marriages with close relations (Charsley 2005: p. 385). Based on their study of partner choice of second-generation Moroccan and Turkish migrants in the Netherlands, Sterckx and Bouw (2005) add some further explanations why many of them choose a partner from their parents' country of origin. For example, parents tend to be more relaxed during holidays in their country of origin, giving their children more freedom and therefore the opportunity to meet potential partners. On the other hand, potential partners have to meet all kinds of demands concerning background, education, and religion. The pool of possible candidates in Morocco or Turkey is simply bigger than in the Netherlands, even when marrying transnationally was not the initial intention (Sterckx and Bouw 2005: p. 47).

Other authors have tried to find explanations for mixed marriages in characteristics of persons who contract such a marriage. The eldest and most famous explanation of this kind is the status-exchange hypothesis, first described by Merton and Davis in 1941. According to this theory, in a mixed marriage there is an exchange of socio-economic resources and status. Members of groups of low status, for example, ethnic minorities, compensate their lower status with higher socio-economic resources, for example, when marrying a poor member of a group of high status. Kalmijn & van Tubergen have tested this hypothesis in the Netherlands, but found little evidence for status exchange (Kalmijn and van Tubergen 2006). A more personal explanation is given by Appel (1994). She interviewed German women about their choice for a foreign, Islamic, husband. These women shared a longing for strong family values and relations which they found in their Islamic husbands. Appel sees these marriages as a reaction to the decline of certain traditional marriage and family values in Germany. On the other hand, a mixed marriage to an Islamic man offers possibilities to fulfil certain modern demands such as the development of an individual identity and self-fulfilment (Appel 1994).

Although there is, as Hondius (1999: p. 83) claims, 'a universal concern for the stability and durability of mixed marriages', literature on transnational divorce is very limited, in the Netherlands as well as internationally, with the notable exceptions of Liversage (2013) writing on Turkish migrant couples and divorce in Denmark, and Rosander (2008) writing on Moroccan migration marriages and divorce in Spain. Literature available on transnational divorce consists mostly of statistical studies on the divorce risks of certain groups (e.g. van Huis and Steenhof 2003; Kalmijn and van Tubergen 2006; Kalmijn et al. 2005). Van Huis and Steenhof found that especially couples consisting of a non-Western man[1] (including Moroccans and Egyptians) married to a Dutch woman have a much higher divorce risk than Dutch–Dutch couples. After ten years, 17 % of Dutch–Dutch marriages have been dissolved, while 30 % of marriages between a Dutch man and a non-Western foreign woman and 54 % of marriages between Dutch women and non-Western foreign men have ended in divorce. Divorce rates of second-generation non-Western migrants with a foreign partner are slightly lower. Native Dutch women with a Moroccan husband have the highest divorce risk. Seventy-four percent of these marriages are dissolved after ten years. A marriage between two Moroccan first-generation migrants has a divorce risk of 30 % and a marriage between a second-generation Moroccan wife and a first-generation Moroccan husband has a divorce risk of 43 %[2] (van Huis and Steenhof 2003: p. 10–11). Kalmijn et al. did research on divorce rates in transnational marriages as well, but using different methods and taking nationality as a main criterion. In this study, both Moroccan women married to Dutch men as well as Moroccan men married to Dutch women had a far higher percentage of divorce, 63.6 % and 52.2 %, respectively, than Dutch–Dutch (11.4 %) and Moroccan–Moroccan (1.6 %) marriages. They also noted that, although the divorce

[1] Although I do not approve of the vague and problematic term 'non-western', the categories 'western' and 'non-western' immigrants are used by the Centraal Bureau voor de Statistiek (CBS), the Dutch statistics bureau, which provided the data Van Huis and Steenhof used for their analysis. Non-Western countries include Africa, Asia, except Japan and Indonesia, South America and Turkey. Western countries include all countries in Europe, except Turkey, North America, Indonesia, Japan, and Oceania (van Huis and Steenhof 2003: p. 2).

[2] The divorce risk of a Dutch man married to a Moroccan woman could not be calculated because of the small numbers involved (van Huis and Steenhof 2003).

risks in nationality-mixed marriages were indeed higher, these declined over time. In the first five years, the risk of divorce was four to five times as high,[3] and afterwards it went down to 1.5–2 times as high (Kalmijn et al. 2005: p. 81–82).

Some researchers, and especially policymakers, explain the high divorce rate of some kinds of transnational marriages by considering the divorce as signalling that those marriages were marriages of convenience. Because a marriage or family bond with a legal resident is one of the few ways for non-European Union (EU) nationals to obtain legal residence in the Netherlands, the fear of marriages of convenience, for example, to give a foreigner access to the Dutch labour market and social services, is persistent. Although research has shown there is little or no evidence to justify this claim of large-scale marriages of convenience (Strik et al. 2013; Hondius 1999; de Hart 2003; EMN 2012), it continues to be mentioned as an explanation for high divorce rates (e.g. van Huis and Steenhof 2003). But as Hondius rightly remarks, one cannot draw conclusions about motives based on marriage or divorce statistics (Hondius 1999: p. 83–96).

Transnational Families and Law

Most of the international literature on transnational families and law focuses on the impact of Islamic law or cultural and religious claims of Muslims on legal procedures in the West (Bano 2007; Charsley 2005, 2007; Charsley and Shaw 2006; Keshavjee 2007; Khir 2006; Mehdi 2003, 2005; Shah 2007; Yilmaz 2002; Berger 1992; Rutten 1988, 1999, 2011; Fournier 2006; Fournier and McDougall 2013; van Rossum 2007; Foblets 1994, 1998, 2002). A substantial part of this literature is from the British context, where a variety of community-based alternative dispute resolution (ADR) options are available for members from religious and ethnic minority groups.

Most of this literature is written from a legal pluralism perspective. While the concept of legal pluralism had its roots in legal anthropology

[3] Compared to the highest level of divorce between non-mixed marriages in the two groups both partners come from (Kalmijn et al. 2005: p. 82).

in colonial times, studying the interactions of native populations' norm systems and colonial state law, it has in recent times also been used to study the interactions between migrants'—especially Muslims'—norm systems and their state of residence. Typically, studies of legal pluralism use a broad definition of law, including multiple forms of legal ordering outside of state law. As such, the focus is often on the differences and tensions between cultural or religious minority norms and values and the state.

However, these analyses mostly focus on legal pluralism within the context of a single state. In a way, such studies could be seen to suffer from methodological nationalism (Wimmer and Glick Schiller 2002). Even though some studies also mention legal pluralism in the sense of courts dealing with multiple sets of legal sources, e.g. through private international law (PIL) or legally recognised indigenous laws (Hoekema 2004), these studies mostly still focus on situations within the borders of the nation-state (with the notable exception of: Glick Schiller 2005). However, as will be demonstrated in this book, transnational families do not just deal with the state law in their country of residence, but may also deal with state legal institutions in other countries. Thus, they do not just deal with multiple sets and sources of norms, but also with multiple states.

This interaction of multiple state legal systems adds an extra complication to analyses of legal pluralism, which generally describe hierarchical interactions of norms. The concept of legal pluralism draws valuable attention to the importance of other social fields, norms, and values in determining people's behaviour. However, especially for transnational families, state law holds real power, with which family members need to deal with in order to live their life. When failing to meet the standards of migration policies and bureaucracy, transnational families may be forcibly separated across borders. Without aiming for 'legal centralism' as criticised by the legal pluralism paradigm, I wish to draw attention to the importance of the interaction of multiple legal systems and the meanings of these interactions for transnational families.

Furthermore, while writers from the field of legal pluralism tend to assume that minorities want recognition of their cultural and religious norms in family law matters; this assumption has rarely been empirically studied. As we have seen in the story of Malika at the beginning of this chapter, cultural or religious norms played only a limited role in her struggle over which legal system should be applied. This study will offer a bottom-up, empirical perspective based on interviews with spouses divorced from a transnational marriage. What are the difficulties they face, what are their issues of concern and what normative issues are they confronted with when their marriage ends? How do they navigate between two family law systems and with what results?

Divorce in the Netherlands, Morocco, and Egypt

The number of empirical, especially qualitative, studies on legal disputes and divorce in the Netherlands is limited, dating mostly from the 1980s (van der Werff et al. 1987; Weeda 1983a; Griffiths and Hekmen 1985; Griffiths 1986; Weeda 1983b; Ruiter et al. 1984; van Wamelen 1987; van der Werff and Docter-Schamhardt 1987). Because over 30 years have passed since this research was published, this study does not only provide information on transnational divorce, but it will also present new insights on contemporary divorce practices in the Netherlands.

More recent work on divorce mostly focuses on the effects of divorce on children instead of the experiences of divorcing couples. Notable exceptions are the work of Dijksterhuis (Dijksterhuis and Vels 2011; Dijksterhuis 2008) on child maintenance issues and the research project of Kalmijn et al. (2001a) who did survey research in 1998 including issues such as divorce motives (de Graaf and Kalmijn 2001), employment and divorce (Kalmijn et al. 2001b), and the economic consequences of divorce for men and women (Poortman and Fokkema 2001). These studies use mostly quantitative analyses. This research project will focus on divorce from a qualitative, in-depth perspective, analysing the stories, meanings, and interpretations of respondents.

Internationally, especially in the UK, US, and Canada, divorce is a more common research topic, resulting in a more extended body of literature, especially on custody cases (e.g. Madden-Derdich and Leonard 2002; Kaganas and Day-Sclater 2004; Hopper 2001; Collier and Sheldon 2008; Rhoades 2002; Boyd 2004; Williams 2004). Specifically, some attention has been paid to the role of gender, ethnicity, and social class play in divorce, notably during custody cases, but there has not been much explicit attention paid to transnational families (e.g. Fox and Kelly 1995; Williams 2004).

There is also a wide range of literature available on Islamic family law, both from Western and Arab writers. Dupret (2012, 2007) and Voorhoeve (2012) have raised important questions with regard to the academic discussion of Islamic family law as being Islamic. They claim that, through the focus on the Islamic aspects of law in the Middle East and North Africa (MENA) region, 'Islam's influence was overemphasised, while the impact of socio-political transformation was neglected' (Dupret and Voorhoeve: p. 1). They argue instead for a study of what people do with the law and legal institutions. A body of literature on divorce in Islamic countries, based on empirical research, is available, including the implementation of laws regarding divorce in courts in Morocco (Zeidguy 2007; Mir-Hosseini 2000), Tunesia (Voorhoeve 2009), Syria (Carlisle 2007; van Eijk 2013), and Egypt (Sonneveld 2012a). Recently, Lindbekk and Sonneveld have studied the developments in Egyptian debates on family law since the 2011 revolution (Sonneveld and Lindbekk 2015). However, all of these studies focus on the national context, and none pay attention to transnational families. This study will provide a law in everyday life analysis of Egyptian and Moroccan family law from the perspective of transnational families.

Gender, Ethnicity, and Social Class: An Intersectional Approach

> Family law is central to the reproduction of the social and cultural order: it arranges for the transfer of material resources from one generation to the next (succession), it organises care for, and socialization of, the next generation (custody and guardianship), and it regulates sexual relations (marriage and its effects). As these various fields are strongly gendered, debates about family law tie in with those on gender relations and 'the position of women', another highly controversial topic in both the colonial and post-colonial periods, often framed in terms of the desirability of westernization versus the call for cultural authenticity (Moors 2003: p. 2).

When speaking about Islamic family law, gender—mostly in terms of the oppression of women—is often the first issue that comes to mind. An important part of the literature on Islamic family law and the Middle East, including literature on Morocco and Egypt, is also from a normative, women's rights perspective, discussing the position of women in family law and contested topics such as polygamy and repudiation. Mainstream media and some academic writings depict Muslim women as the victims of patriarchal Islamic family laws that grant them little claim to legal rights. This picture leaves little room for women's agency as well as effects in everyday life. According to Hirsch, these images are based on a simplistic dichotomy of Muslim women (silenced through law) as the 'silenced Others' of Western women (liberated through law) (Hirsch 1998, p. 2). In Islamic family law, men and women are openly assigned different roles and positions in divorce, for example, with regard to child custody. However, although Dutch family law claims to be based on equality, it also contains and produces gender differences, although these are often more concealed and indirect, described by Boor (1999) as the 'hidden morals' of family law (Boor 1999: p. 34–35; Lünnemann et al. 1999).

Critical analyses of Western and Islamic family law rarely meet. Nader (1989) has argued that both Orientalist and Occidentalist discourses frequently focus on the position of women. By commenting on the position of women in the other society, both the West and the East obscure similar gender inequalities in their own society, implicitly placing the speaker in a superior position (Nader 1989: p. 323–325). This especially holds true for many studies on Muslim family law. This study will pay attention to gender, ethnicity, and social class and their intersectionality in the analysis of regulations of marriage and divorce and their implementation in the Netherlands, Morocco, and Egypt. I aim to analyse family law beyond stereotypes and dichotomies like the passive Muslim woman, the liberated Western woman and the powerful Muslim man, applying a critical gender perspective to Egyptian and Moroccan family law as well as to Dutch family law.

In the context of this research, it is important to make a distinction between ethnicity and nationality. These two concepts are often connected and can overlap but do not necessarily do so. In this study, I will use the term nationality as a legal term, which people can hold or be entitled to after fulfilling certain demands. Ethnicity, however, is about identification rather than legal rights to membership. Ethnicity originates by delineating between 'us' and 'them' and has meaning only in a context involving others (Cornell and Hartmann 1998: p. 18–21). Ethnic identity can be the same as national identity, but it does not have to be so. Migrants and even children of migrants are often identified in the Netherlands in terms of their origin, even though they may have only Dutch nationality, especially when visible signs of difference are present.

Neither ethnic identification nor nationality is fixed and exclusive; they can be changed during a lifetime and people can have multiple ethnicities and nationalities. When marrying transnationally, for example, it is often possible to adopt the nationality of the spouse as a new nationality, either giving up the original one or as a second nationality. Ethnic identifications can change and shift as well, especially in a transnational marriage. Hondius, for example, describes how partners in mixed marriages sometimes 'take over' the ethnic identification of their spouse; even if they stay in the Netherlands they become 'Moroccan' or 'Spanish' as well as Dutch (Hondius 1999: p. 287). Ethnicity is thus related to both self-identification and assignment to an ethnic category by others.

Similar to the way relations of gender and ethnicity are also expressions of inequality (Shields 2008: p. 302), class is closely connected to inequality and power. In a transnational context, class is a complicated subject, closely intersected with ethnicity and gender. Migration can change class positions fundamentally, and assessing the class positions of others in a new context can be difficult. Class has economic aspects, such as employment, income, and ownership of economic resources, but these aspects only partly define class. Other sources of capital defining class include cultural, social, and symbolic capital (Seron and Munger 1996: p. 198–199, Bourdieu 1986). These forms of capital can also change as a result of migration.

The interaction between social identities also means intersectional positions are connected to inequality and power in a more complex way. One can be privileged relative to one group but disadvantaged to another (Shields 2008: p. 302). Verloo (2006), however, warns that 'different inequalities are dissimilar because they are differently framed'. They differ in dimensions such as choice or visibility; religion can be changed, but age cannot; sexuality can be hidden but race cannot. Moreover, social categories themselves 'can be unstable and contested: what counts as race or ethnicity in specific contexts, what counts as young or old, is intertwined with power in many ways' (Verloo 2006: p. 221). In this study, social identities such as gender, ethnicity, and social class will therefore be studied from the perspective of intersectionality (Crenshaw 1991). This perspective implies that in transnational marriages gender, ethnicity, and social class are interconnected and intersected, meaning, for example, that gender can work differently for Moroccan, Egyptian, or Dutch women and that class does not necessarily work the same for Dutch men and women.

Legal Consciousness

To understand how people divorced from a transnational marriage talk about the law and experience the law in their everyday lives, I will make use of the concept of legal consciousness. Legal consciousness is not only the way people think about the law but also the way this unconsciously influences decisions (Nielsen 2000: p. 1058). It is 'the ways people understand and use law', not only in conscious actions but also in habits (Merry 1990: p. 5). Legal consciousness is not static but changing from one situation to another. It is shaped by experience, which is connected to the social position of people (Nielsen 2000: p. 1087), meaning it can be connected to gender, social class, and ethnicity.

Merry distinguishes three different discourses in her study on working-class Americans; a legal, moral, and a therapeutic discourse. The use of these different discourses is linked to social status aspects such as gender, ethnicity, and social class. She found that, while men tended to use more legal discourse, women used more therapeutic discourse. In court cases on marital problems, moral discourses of guilt and obligations in relationships were used most often (Merry 1990: p. 112). Before people come to court, they have often already framed their problem in a certain discourse, which is most of the time a legal discourse. If a certain discourse is unsuccessful, people may try to switch to another discourse. In Merry's study, judges, mediators, and court clerks tended to reframe legal claims into moral or therapeutic discourse, depending on the case, but litigants can try to resist this reframing (Merry 1990: p. 112–115).

Legal consciousness can be divided into several types. In this study, I will use Merry's (1986, 1990) division of legal consciousness in two ideologies: 'formal justice' and 'situational justice'.[4] While the first is more connected to the dominant political ideology, the second is a bottom-up perspective. Merry defines the ideology of formal justice as:

> Working-class court users typically see themselves endowed with a broad set of legal rights, loosely defined, which shade into moral rights. [...] These rights are routinely enforced by the state through a system of police and courts that are accessible to all. The state takes infractions of the legal rights of its citizens seriously. To be accused of a violation of the law is a serious and frightening event, and to make accusations of others is to invoke a powerful weapon. The court itself is regarded with awe and fear and a court appearance is a scary experience. In this ideology, persons are legally defined as equals and enforcement is predictable and firm. (Merry 1986: p. 257)

Situational justice leaves this presumption of the universal and equal rights of citizens. Instead:

> In the ideology of situational justice, the person is socially constructed by his or her history, character, rank, and social or ethnic identity. [...] Instead of flowing inevitably from a violation of the law, enforcement is viewed as dependent on the social identities of the parties and their relationship. The law is a set of rules that are enforced partially and only when someone complains. Interpersonal disputes are not seen as real 'crimes' but as less important, 'garbage' cases because of their social context. Enforcement can be manipulated depending on how the problem is presented. (Merry 1986: p. 258)

While formal justice is based on a political view of the legal system, the formal perspective, removed from knowledge of any specific laws, situational justice is a perspective acquired by experience on how the informal

[4] Another classification was made by Ewick and Silbey. They introduced three types of legality: 'before the law', 'with the law', and 'up against the law' (Ewick and Silbey 1998).

side of the court works. It takes into account the mobilisation of laws. However, both discourses equally reflect 'a kind of truth about how the legal system works' (Merry 1986: p. 258).

So far, there are only a few studies of legal consciousness in the context of migration. Little is known of how people connect to at least *two* legal systems instead of just one, as in most previous studies. Furthermore, as de Hart (2003) has demonstrated, 'native' spouses in mixed marriages can be shocked when, through their marriage, they are confronted with migration law. While formerly members of a privileged group, by marrying a foreign spouse they gain new experiences with the law, which can transform their legal consciousness. This study will investigate legal consciousness in the context of transnational marriages, and test the connection between legal consciousness and legal action. Can people have multiple legal consciousnesses? How do experiences in one legal system influence the way people see and experience another legal system? How do the state interventions in transnational families through migration law influence legal consciousness? How do negative discourses on Muslims and Islamic family law impact on how transnational families deal with *shari'a*-based family law systems?

Texts and Talk: Studying Law as an Anthropologist

This ethnographic research project is based on three main sources: (1) an analysis of texts, both legal and non-legal, (2) interviews with spouses divorced from transnational Dutch-Moroccan and Dutch-Egyptian marriages, and (3) interviews and participant observation with organisations and actors involved professionally in transnational divorce. Most material was gathered during fieldwork in the Netherlands (2008–2012), Egypt (November 2010–January 2011), and Morocco (September–December 2009, May 2011).

During this research project, I struggled with studying law, for which I had no formal training. Being daunted at first by the prospect of reading actual law, I started by reading manuals, and asking experts about the law. At first I was surprised when doing interviews at the court that even judges look up specific legal information before handling a court case. Gradually I learned that being a lawyer is mostly about *knowing how and where to find and interpret law*. While interviews and discussions with lawyers were indispensable in finding and navigating applicable legal texts and learning about court practice and experiences, it turned out that interviewing lawyers without studying the law itself—or reading social science literature containing legal information solely based on such interviews—often produces an incomplete or incorrect picture, as so much information is 'lost in translation'. Especially in the complex field of transnational marriages, where many exceptions and obscure rules apply, studying the original texts was crucial for a full understanding of the law. Moreover, laws and legal texts are also a valuable source to study concepts and ideas about the family, gender, migration, and other important themes for this research.

With the invaluable help of my colleague and friend Friso Kulk and his ever-growing collection of Arabic-language legal texts, I learned to navigate legal texts: law books but also dissertations, commentaries, and jurisprudence.[5] I also analysed parliamentary debates—especially the preambles of laws—but also brochures, websites, information booklets, and reports of meetings. Dutch law and jurisprudence are easily accessible through the internet, which also holds true for the Moroccan *Moudawana*. Egyptian family law is a more complicated matter. It is only published on paper and not completely codified. For example, only after a remark in a newspaper article, I found out that the age limit for *hadana* (child custody) had been raised in 2005. None of the law books I bought in Cairo in 2011 as being 'the newest versions' included this reform, nor was it mentioned by any of my informants.[6] Moreover, not every legal

---

[5] For quoting Moroccan family law, I mainly used the (unofficial) English translation of the *Moudawana* by HREA, in addition to the official Arabic version and its French translation, and the Dutch translation (Berger 2004). The main source for the interaction of Dutch and Moroccan family law was the work of Jordens-Cotran (Jordens-Cotran 2007). Both Berger and Jordens-Cotran are also used in Dutch courts. For quoting Egyptian family law, I used an English translation made by el-Alami of law no. 100 of 1985 (El-Alami 1994) in addition to the original Arabic texts. For Dutch law, judgements, and parliamentary discussions no translations were available, so I used the original texts and translated them into English myself.

[6] It must be noted that I did my interviews just before the revolution in early 2011. As has been described by Lindbekk and Sonneveld (2015), child custody and visitation laws have since become a matter of much public debate.

provision regulating transnational marriage and divorce can be found in family law; they can also be located in, for example, the law on civil registry.

In this book, I present a picture of the law to the best of my abilities. However, I was trained as an anthropologist, not as a lawyer, and this book is not a legal manual or a source of law. I may have missed things, made mistakes, and laws and legal practices change over time. Furthermore, the law I describe in this book covers only the main points, it does not cover every possible (or impossible) case.

Interviews with Divorced Spouses

In total, I interviewed 26 spouses divorced from transnational marriages, 5 men and 21 women. This sample includes 11 spouses divorced from Dutch-Egyptian marriages and 15 from Dutch-Moroccan marriages. There were 13 native Dutch spouses, 9 Moroccan spouses, 2 Egyptians, and 2 Dutch-Moroccans. Seventeen marriages were mixed, 9 were migration marriages. When quoted in the text, interviewees will be described by their gender, country of origin—in order to distinguish between Dutch and Egyptian or Moroccan partners and between mixed and migration marriages—and (main) country of residence *during* the marriage. To protect the privacy of interviewees, all names and sometimes also other identifying details have been changed or omitted. Spouses born or raised in the Netherlands with Moroccan or Egyptian migrant parents will be described as Dutch-Moroccan or Dutch-Egyptian, as their background is important for this research, all others will be described as 'Dutch', 'Moroccan' or 'Egyptian' if they have grown up in the Netherlands, Morocco, or Egypt, respectively. It is important to note that these are not unified categories, and they contain people from a diversity of backgrounds and self-identifications, such as Moroccan Berbers and Arabs; Egyptians of European origin and Bedouins; Dutch with roots in former colonies such as Suriname or Indonesia or migrant backgrounds. As will be discussed in the legal chapter, the diverse categories of Dutch, Egyptian, and Moroccan interviewees can also contain people of multiple nationalities, especially after migration.

For the selection of respondents, transnational marriages were defined as marriages in which one partner was raised in—meaning having been born in or as a child having migrated to—the Netherlands, while the other was raised in Morocco or Egypt. I aimed for diversity with regard to mixed and migration marriages, gender, and country of residence. The interviewees were of widely different backgrounds regarding age, ranging from early 20s to late 70s, education and social class. They were also in different stages of the divorce process; some did not even start a formal divorce procedure yet while the oldest divorce was finalised over 20 years ago. In all cases, only one partner of a former transnational couple was interviewed, to permit interviewees to speak freely.

Finding people divorced from transnational marriages, especially men, turned out to be the main, and sometimes frustrating, difficulty of this research project. However, when a possible respondent was approached, most were willing to participate in the research. I approached respondents in a variety of ways. First of all, I made use of my own networks and those of my colleagues, family, and friends. Secondly, throughout the research I contacted organisations, such as NGOs and social networks, migrant organisations, *bureaus inburgering*, translators, the embassies, and specialised lawyers.[7] Especially the Stichting Steun Remigranten (SSR) office in Berkane was a great help in finding and contacting potential interviewees in Morocco. Thirdly, a call for respondents was made, published, and spread through relevant mailings lists, websites of organisations, and internet forums. Fourthly, I approached the lawyers of recently published court cases of Dutch-Moroccan and Dutch-Egyptian divorces. In a similar way, I found some interviewees through internet forums by directly approaching members asking questions or sharing stories related to transnational divorce. Lastly, I also spent time at locations and events relevant to transnational couples: such as visiting the 'Orange café' in Hurghada, activities and lectures of the Dutch institutes in Rabat and Cairo, and volunteering at the annual *Sinterklaas* celebration of the Dutch embassy in Morocco. Apart from meeting possible interviewees, hanging around at such locations also presented valuable opportunities for small talk (Driessen and Jansen 2013).

[7] *Bureaus Inburgering* or integration bureaus handle the obligatory courses in Dutch language and culture for new migrants.

Interestingly, snowball sampling turned out to be of little use when finding new respondents, most respondents stated not to know anyone else who had divorced from a transnational marriage. While this might be explained by the controversial subject, I also believe that it can be related to the social consequences of divorce. Social networks of the marriage may lessen or be lost after a divorce, especially if a transnational divorce involves return migration. Furthermore, after divorce, former spouses in mixed couples lose their visibility as being part of a mixed couple. This lack of snowball sampling means that almost all of the people interviewed came from different social networks and they did not know each other.

In order to answer questions about the role of law in everyday life, it is important that respondents are free to mention or not mention legal issues. In their research on law in everyday life, Ewick and Silbey

> [...] did not directly ask about law; they asked about people's lives and waited to hear when the law emerged, or did not emerge, in the accounts people provided of an enormous array of topics and events that might pose problems or become matters of concern or conflict. [...] The method did not assume the importance or centrality of law, although the object of the analysis was to create an account of hegemonic legality. It was simply the target of the research, the analysts' construction of the research problem. Thus, the work focused on everyday life, did not adopt a law-first perspective, and waited to see if, when, and how legal concepts, constructs, or interpretations emerged. (Silbey 2005: p. 347–348)

In this research, I maintained a similar approach by letting people tell the story of the relationship, generally with the question: 'how did you meet your former spouse?', although the subject of the research was mentioned when making an appointment for an interview. The stories interviewees told were not always easy and included difficult, emotional topics such as domestic violence, loneliness, loss, and betrayal. Regularly, interviewees did not remember the legal details. Others showed documents during the interview and, in a few cases, gave or sent copies from legal files to me afterwards. This approach did not work in all cases; some interviewees, who had been frustrated by prolonged legal procedures against their former spouse, started telling about legal procedures before I had the chance to ask any questions about their relationship.

Interviewees regularly told very painful and negative stories about their former spouse, sometimes generalising those to the ethnic group of their spouse or mixed marriages in general. I have tried to handle and analyse all stories with respect, regardless of my own opinion or perspective, although some stories were easier for me to empathise with than others. A thought-provoking question Razack asked in her provocative article on the Ontario Sharia law debate is: 'how might feminists have avoided being drawn into the framework of superior, secular women saving their less enlightened and more imperiled sisters from religion and community and still responded to the dangers at hand' (Razack 2007: p. 16). In this research, I have tried to avoid these pitfalls by collecting narratives of a wide range of people from different contexts and backgrounds and presenting them together on an equal level.

The interviews were held in the best common language of researcher and interviewee. In most cases, this was Dutch, sometimes mixed with English, French or Moroccan or Egyptian Arabic. Two interviews were held in a mixture of French and (Moroccan) Arabic. In two other interviews taking place in the North-East of Morocco, I made use of a local teacher of Dutch as a translator. Two interviewees were not available for an interview in person and I interviewed them by phone or using Skype.

The interviews lasted between 40 minutes and 4 hours, with an average of 1.5–2 hours. Most interviews were tape-recorded and transcribed. If the interviewee did not consent in tape-recording, notes were made during the interview. After the interview, most interviewed spouses were given the opportunity to react to or edit their stories, and only a few did so. I made use of ATLAS.ti to facilitate the organisation and analysis of the research material.

Interviews with Professional Actors and Courts

In addition to the interviews with divorcees, members of interest groups, migrant organisations, NGOs, social workers, lawyers, and legal experts in the fields of divorce and transnational relationships were interviewed about their experiences with transnational divorce. Formal semi-structured interviews were held with 34 representatives of 28 organisations involved in transnational divorce, such as NGOs and migrant organisations (11, both in the Netherlands and in Morocco), translators (2), lawyers (6 in the Netherlands, two in Morocco and 3 in Egypt), and the Dutch embassies in Rabat (multiple interviews) and Cairo.[8] I also interviewed officials from the Dutch Ministry of Foreign Affairs. Most interviews were done in person and a few were done using Skype or telephone. Additionally, a Dutch translator in Egypt and the Egyptian embassy in the Netherlands answered questions by email. I continued to interview new professionals until I reached the point of saturation.

Further information was gathered doing participant observation and informal interviews at meetings related to the topic in both the Netherlands and Morocco. I participated in expert meetings, project presentations, and NGO conferences. I joined a group of volunteers being trained to provide education and advice about Moroccan and Turkish family law and observed during consultations of the SSR office in Berkane. I also collected information doing informal interviews and participant observation during contacts with Dutch and other Europeans living in Egypt or Morocco and by participating in an internet discussion forum for Dutch people in Egypt. I conducted formal and informal interviews with employees of the Dutch institutes in Cairo and Rabat, Dutch journalists living in Morocco, and local scholars of family law in the Netherlands and Morocco.

As part of this research project, I intended to observe transnational divorce cases in courts in all three countries. In Morocco, in 2009, my colleague Friso Kulk and I spent considerable time and effort in gaining a research permit and access to Moroccan courts, but we did not succeed. We visited the court in Rabat once and spent some time speaking to court officials and lawyers, but after a while we were sent out of the building when court officials found out we did not have a research permit. In the Netherlands, I did manage to gain access to the court in The Hague. The entire procedure to gain access in the Netherlands took about a year and a half, and it seemed to be just as bureaucratic and complicated as the Moroccan process. It also entailed making use of contacts. Due to organisational constraints I never managed to witness an actual

[8] About half of these interviews were held together with my colleague Friso Kulk.

court case, although I did multiple interviews with one of the family law judges, one lawyer, and a divorcee while spending time at the court.[9] After these experiences of court bureaucracy, I decided not to try again in the Egyptian courts.

Layout of the Book

Chapter 2, *The Contexts of Transnational Divorce*, will provide an introduction to several elements of the contexts of transnational marriages which will be important to understand the stories of transnational marriage and divorce in this research. In this chapter, I will outline these contexts, distinguishing between the dimensions of *time*, *place*, and *distance*. Subsequently, Chapter 3, *Legal Aspects of Divorce*, contains an analysis of Dutch, Moroccan, and Egyptian divorce law and private international law. It outlines and compares the legal provisions for transnational couples with regard to divorce, maintenance, division of property and child custody, and contact in the three countries with specific attention to the effects for transnational families. It is argued that in Dutch, Moroccan, and Egyptian family law, marriage and divorce are based on the same ideas and assumptions about the family in gender-based roles of homemaker and breadwinner. However, the three legal systems provide different solutions in arranging the financial consequences of this gender-based division of labour.

Chapter 4, *The Transnational Divorce Process*, is the first chapter mainly based on interview material. During the transnational marriage and divorce process, couples are faced with many choices and decisions. While some couples in this study made a lot of effort to arrange the legal aspects of their marriage, most made such decisions as they went along, navigating between practical and financial concerns. This chapter shows how spouses during the transnational marriage and divorce process can develop a different legal consciousness for each legal system they get

[9] The court could only provide me with information about transnational divorce cases a few days beforehand, which never left me enough time to get the required permission of both parties and their lawyers.

into contact with. Furthermore, it demonstrates how legal consciousness is not only informed by formal experience with the courts in the field of family law but also by other, seemingly unrelated experiences with the 'people of the law', such as chaotic bureaucracy, discrimination, and messy procedures.

Chapter 5, *Marital power and the Law*, discusses the power relations between the spouses. Although transnational marriage can be connected to a range of intersecting power-related issues, such as the division of labour during the marriage, access to divorce and dependent residence status, little is known about the power relations in transnational marriages or their impact on divorce. In this chapter, I will provide a theoretical framework and focus on two power-related issues: the division of labour in marriage and domestic violence. As we will see, these two issues are of great importance for power relations in transnational marriages, due to shifts in gender roles related to migration, and state interventions through migration law.

In Chapter 6, *Taking Care of the Children. Organising Child Care After Divorce*, I will demonstrate the importance of gendered notions of good and bad parenthood for how parents talk about care for children after divorce. In this study, the child welfare discourse seems to be nearly universal, present in all three countries and in all interviews with parents. Furthermore, when arranging child maintenance, child residence, or contact privately with the non-resident parent, this was generally not the result of explicit bargaining 'in the shadow of the law'. Instead, the outcome was either taken for granted, or one of the parents took matters in his or her own hands, which made marital power an important factor. As we will see in this chapter, migration law can be a powerful tool for parents in transnational divorce, made visible in issues such as international child abduction and involuntary abandonment in the country of origin.

Chapter 7, *Financial Aspects of Divorce*, discusses that apart from legally arranging the relationship between spouses and their children, marriage and divorce are also—maybe even foremost—financial matters, entailing rights, and obligations for the spouses as well as the household property. As the legal systems provide different solutions for arranging the financial consequences of a gender-based division of labour during the marriage, their interactions can have severe negative consequences for spouses, but also provide options for strategic behaviour. Financial matters are especially suited for so-called forum shopping. However, even though financial matters are at first sight 'simply about money', issues such as maintenance and alimony are infused with moral matters such as fairness. Instead of strategic action, exploiting the collision of legal systems to maximise financial gain, gendered moral discourses informed the position of the interviewees, while actual legal provisions played only a minor role in their stories.

In Chapter 8, *Support in Transnational Divorce: Actors, Norms, and their Influence*, the social environment is central. Divorcing couples may receive support and advice from their networks, friends, and family, and they may also get into contact with all kind of professionals providing legal or social aid. Complicated legal issues related to transnational divorce, such as the involvement of migration law, may require specific forms of support from both professionals as well as private networks. While the concept of social capital has strong positive connotations, I aim to demonstrate how the support of private and professional actors can also entail constraints. As will become clear in this chapter, this is due to the production and enforcement of norms on, for example, conducting a transnational marriage or handling the law in transnational divorce. These norms are created in transnational legal space.

In Chapter 9, *Conclusions*, I will present the conclusions of this study on transnational Dutch-Moroccan and Dutch-Egyptian divorce. I will discuss four main themes: (1) an analysis of Dutch, Egyptian, and Moroccan family law; their interactions and consequences for transnational families; and how the spouses in this research arranged their divorce in one or both legal systems, (2) the issue of marital power relations and extend the perspective of power relations between spouses with a discussion of the power of the law in intimate relationships, (3) transnational legal space and the kinds of support organisations and private networks provide in transnational divorce cases, and (4) the meaning of family law in the everyday life of transnational families. Lastly, I will reflect on how 'transnational' transnational families actually are and how they are the same as or differ from 'normal', non-transnational families in the three countries.

References

Appel, Sabine. 1994. Liebe und Partnerschaft zwischen deutschen Frauen und Ausländern. *Psychosozial* 55(1): 17–25.

Ask, Jenny. 2006. Challenges and Choices: An Analysis of Gender Strategies among Women in Cross-Cultural Marriages. In *Migration and Marriage. Heterogamy and Homogamy in a Changing World*, eds. Barbara Waldis and Reginald Byron. Berlin: Lit Verlag.

Bacas, Jutta Lauth. 2002. Title. Transnational Communities Programme Working Paper Series 1998–2002.

Bano, Samia. 2007. Islamic Family Arbitration, Justice and Human Rights in Britain. *Law, Social Justice & Global Development* 1.

Berger, Maurits S. 1992. Het afdwingen van een verstoting bij de Nederlandse rechter. *Recht van de Islam* 9: 79–91.

Berger, Maurits S 2004. *Mudawwana. Marokkaanse familiewet.* Nijmegen: Ars Aequi Libri.

Boor, Elsbeth. 1999. De verborgen moraal in het familierecht. Mechanismen van in- en uitsluiting naar sekse binnen het naam- en gezagsrecht. In *De onzichtbare standaard in het recht.* In *In- en uitsluiting van vrouwen, etnische minderheden en homoseksuelen in het familierecht, arbeidsrecht en strafrecht*, eds. K.D. Lünnemann, M.L.P. Loenen, and A.G. Veldman. Deventer: Gouda Quint.

Bourdieu, Pierre. 1986. The Forms of Capital. In *Handbook of Theory of Research for the Sociology of Education.*

Boyd, Susan B. 2004. Backlash Against Feminism: Canadian Custody and Access Reform Debates of the Late Twentieth Century. *Canadian Journal of Women and the Law* 16(2): 255–290.

Buitelaar, Marjo. 2000. Het liefst gewoon een Marokkaan? Over de partnerkeuze van hoogopgeleide vrouwen van Marokkaanse afkomst in Nederland. In *Liefst een gewoon huwelijk? Creatie en conflict in levensverhalen van jonge migrantenvrouwen*, ed. Kristel Luyckx, 139–180. Leuven: Acco.

Carlisle, Jessica. 2007. Mother Love: A Forced Divorce in Damascus. *Anthropology of the Middle East* 2(1): 92–105.

Charsley, Katharine. 2005. Vulnerable Brides and Transnational Ghar Damads: Gender, Risk and 'Adjustment' among Pakistani Marriage Migrants to Britain. *Indian Journal of Gender Studies* 12(2&3): 381–406.

———. 2007. Risk, Trust, Gender and Transnational Cousin Marriage Among British Pakistanis. *Ethnic and Racial Studies* 30(6): 1117–1131.

Charsley, Katharine, and Alison Shaw. 2006. South Asian Transnational Marriages in Comparative Perspective. *Global Networks* 6(4): 331–344.

Collier, R., and S. Sheldon. 2008. *Fragmenting fatherhood: A socio-legal study*. Portland, OR: Hart Pub.

Cornell, Stephen, and Douglas Hartmann. 1998. *Ethnicity and Race. Making Identities in a Changing World*. London: Pine Forge Press.

Crenshaw, Kimberle. 1991. Mapping the Margins: Intersectionality, Identity Politics, and Violence Against Women of Color. *Stanford law review*: 1241–1299.

de Graaf, Paul M., and Mattijs Kalmijn. 2001. Scheidingsmotieven in Nederland sinds de jaren vijftig. *Tijdschrift Sociale Wetenschappen* 44(2): 16–33.

de Hart, Betty. 2003. *Onbezonnen vrouwen. Gemengde relaties in het nationaliteitsrecht en het vreemdelingenrecht., Migratie- en Etnische studies*. Amsterdam: Aksant.

Dijksterhuis, Bregje Monique. 2008. *Rechters normeren de alimentatiehoogte : een empirisch onderzoek naar rechterlijke samenwerking in de Werkgroep Alimentatienormen (1975–2007)*. Amsterdam: Leiden University Press.

Dijksterhuis, Bregje Monique, and Nina Vels. 2011. *Samenvatting van het HvA-LBIO-rapport alimentatieberekening*. HvA/LBIO: Onderzoek naar de mening van burgers over de berekening van kinderalimentatie.

Driessen, Henk, and Willy Jansen. 2013. The Hard Work of Small Talk in Ethnographic Fieldwork. *Journal of Anthropological Research* 69(2): 249–263.

Dupret, Baudouin. 2007. What Is Islamic Law? *Theory Culture & Society* 24(2): 79–100. doi:10.1177/0263276407074997.

Dupret, Baudouin, and Maaike Voorhoeve. 2012. Introduction. In *Family Law in Islam: Divorce, Marriage and Women in the Muslim World*, ed. Maaike Voorhoeve, 1–10. London/New York: IB Tauris.

El-Alami, Dawoud S. 1994. Law no. 100 of 1985. Amending Certain Provisions of Egypt's Personal Status Laws. *Islamic Law and Society* 1: 116–136.

EMN. 2012. *Marriages of convenience and false declarations of parenthood*. Luxembourg: Publications Office of the European Union.

Ewick, Patricia, and Susan S. Silbey. 1998. *The common place of law. Stories from everyday life*. Chicago-London: University of Chicago Press.

Foblets, Marie-Claire. 1994. *Les familles maghrébines et la justice en Belgique: anthropologie juridique et immigration*. Paris: Karthala Editions.

———. 1998. *Marokkaanse migrantenvrouwen in gezinsgeschillen: wat zijn passende juridische oplossingen?* Antwerpen: Maklu.

———. 2002. Muslims, a new transnational minority in Europe? Cultural pluralism, fundamental liberties and inconsistencies in the law. documento presentado en la conferencia Mobile People, Mobile Law: Expanding Legal Relations in a Contracting World, Max Planck Institute for Social Anthropology, Halle, Germany, del.

Fournier, Pascale. 2006. In the (Canadian) Shadow of Islamic Law: translating Mahr as a Bargaining Endowment. *Osgoode Hall Law Journal* 44: 649.

Fournier, Pascale, and Pascal McDougall. 2013. False Jurisdictions? A Revisionist Take on Customary (Religious) Law in Germany. *Texas International Law Journal* 48(3): 435–463.

Fox, Greer Litton, and Robert.F. Kelly. 1995. Determinants of Child Custody. Arrangements at Divorce. *Journal of Marriage and the Family* 57: 693–708.

Glick Schiller, Nina. 2005. Transborder citizenship: An outcome of legal pluralism within transnational social fields. In *Mobile People, Mobile Law: Expanding Legal Relations in a Contracting World*, eds. Franz Bender Beckman and Keebit Bender Beckman, 48–81. London: Ashgate.

Griffiths, John. 1986. What do Dutch Lawyers Actually do in Divorce Cases? *Law & Society Review* 20(1): 135–175.

Griffiths, John, and E.G.A. Hekmen. 1985. *De totstandkoming van een bezoekregeling na echtscheiding*. Den Haag: Coördinatiecommissie wetenschappelijk onderzoek kinderbescherming.

Hirsch, S. F. (1998). Pronouncing & Persevering. Gender and the Discourses of Disputing in an African Islamic Court. Chicago, The University of Chicago Press.

Hoekema, A. J. (2004). *Rechtspluralisme en interlegaliteit*. Amsterdam, Vossiuspers UvA.

Hondius, Dienke. 1999. *Gemengde huwelijken, gemengde gevoelens. Aanvaarding en ontwijking van etnisch en religieus verschil sinds 1945*. Den Haag: Sdu uitgevers.

Hopper, Joseph. 2001. The Symbolic Origins of Conflict in Divorce. *Journal of Marriage and the Family* 63: 430–445.

Jordens-Cotran, Leila. 2007. *Nieuw Marokkaans Familierecht en Nederlands IPR*. Den Haag: SDU Uitgevers.

Kaganas, Felicity, and Shelley Day-Sclater. 2004. Contact Disputes: Narrative Constructions of 'Good' Parents. *Feminist Legal Studies* 12: 1–27.

Kalmijn, M., et al. (2001a). Oorzaken en gevolgen van echtscheiding: Een landelijk onderzoek onder gehuwde en gescheiden personen in Nederland. *Tijdschrift Sociale Wetenschappen* 44(2): 1–15.

Kalmijn, M., et al. (2001b). Werk en echtscheiding: de interactie van economische en culturele invloeden. *Tijdschrift Sociale Wetenschappen* 44(2): 34–52.

Kalmijn, Mattijs, and Frank van Tubergen. 2006. Ethnic Intermarriage in the Netherlands. *European Journal of Population/Revue européenne de Démographie* 22(4): 371–397.

Kalmijn, Mattijs, Paul M. de Graaf, and Jacques P.G. Janssen. 2005. Intermarriage and the Risk of Divorce in the Netherlands: The Effects of Differences in Religion and in Nationality, 1974–94. *Population Studies* 59(1): 71–85.

Keshavjee, Mohamed. 2007. Alternative Dispute Resolution in a Diasporic Muslim Community in Britain. In *Law and Ethnic Plurality. Socio-Legal Perspectives*, ed. Prakash Shah, 145–175. Leiden-Boston: Martinus Nijhoff Publishers.

Khir, Bustami Mohamed. 2006. The Right of Women to No-Fault Divorce in Islam and Its Application by British Muslims. *Islam and Christian-Muslim Relations* 17(3): 295–306.

Liversage, Anika. 2013. Gendered Struggles over Residency Rights when Turkish Immigrant Marriages Break Up. *Onati Socio-Legal series* 3(6): 1070–1090.

Lünnemann, K.D., M.L.P. Loenen, and A.G. Veldman. 1999. *De onzichtbare standaard in het recht.* In *In- en uitsluiting van vrouwen, etnische minderheden en homoseksuelen in het familierecht, arbeidsrecht en strafrecht.* Deventer: Gouda Quint.

Luyckx, Kristel. 2000. *Liefst een gewoon huwelijk? Creatie en conflict in levensverhalen van jonge migrantenvrouwen.* Ed. A. De Munynck, M.C. Foblets, B. Hubeau, A. Martens and S. Parmentier, *Minderheden in de samenleving.* Leuven:Acco.

Madden-Derdich, Debra A., and Stacie A. Leonard. 2002. Shared Experiences, Unique Realities: Formerly Married Mothers' and Fathers' Perceptions of Parenting and Custody After Divorce. *Family Relations* 51: 37–45.

Mehdi, Rubya. 2003. Danish law and the practice of mahr among Muslim Pakistanis in Denmark. *International Journal of the Sociology of Law* 31: 115–129.

———. 2005. Facing the enigma: Talaq-e-tafweez a need of Muslim women in Nordic perspective. *International Journal of the Sociology of Law* 33: 133–147.

Merry, Sally Engle. 1986. Everyday Understandings of the Law in Working-Class America. *American Ethnologist* 13(2): 253–270.

———. 1990. *Getting Justice and Getting Even. Legal Consciousness among Working-Class Americans.* In *Language and Legal Discourse*, eds. William M. O'Barr and John M. Conley. Chicago- London: The University of Chicago Press.

———. 2003. Rights Talk and the Experience of Law: Implementing Women's Human Rights to Protection from Violence. *Human Rights Quartely* 25: 343–381.

Mir-Hosseini, Ziba. 2000. *Marriage on Trial. A Study of Islamic Family Law.* London-New York: I.B. Tauris.

Moors, Annelies. 2003. Introduction: Public Debates on Family Law Reform. Participants, Positions, and Styles of Argumentation in the 1990s. *Islamic Law and Society* 10(1): 1–11.

Nader, L. 1989. Orientalism, occidentalism and the control of women. *Cultural Dynamics* 2(3): 323–355.

Nielsen, Laura Beth. 2000. Situating Legal Consciousness: Experiences and Attitudes of Ordinary Citizens about Law and Street Harassment. *Law & Society Review* 34(4): 1055–1090.

Poortman, Anne-Rigt, and Tineke Fokkema. 2001. Economische gevolgen van echtscheiding voor mannen en vrouwen in Nederland, 1949–1998. *Tijdschrift Sociale Wetenschappen* 44(2): 68–90.

Razack, Sherene H. 2007. The 'Sharia Law debate' in Ontario: The Modernity/Premodernity Distinction in Legal Efforts to Protect Women from Culture. *Feminist Legal Studies* 15(1): 3–32.

Rhoades, Helen. 2002. The 'No Contact Mother': Reconstructions of Motherhood in the Era of the 'New Father'. *International Journal of Law, Policy and the Family* 16: 71–94.

Rosander, Eva Evers. "Getting a Divorce in Spain: A Moroccan Case of Legal Pluralism and Transnationalism." Nordisk Tidsskrift for Menneskerettigheter 26.4 (2008): 321–342.

Rozema, Hanneke. 2005. *Grenzeloze liefde.* Amsterdam: Bulaaq.

Ruiter, Marijke, Marijke Prins, and Josephine van den Bogaard. 1984. *Vrouwen in scheiding. Een onderzoek naar de situatie van gescheiden vrouwen in noord en midden Limburg.* Nijmegen: Wetenschapswinkel Nijmegen. Werkgroep gescheiden vrouwen.

Rutten, Susan. 1988. *Moslims in de Nederlandse rechtspraak.* Kampen: J.H. Kok.

———. 1999. Multicultureel familierecht. In *De onzichtbare standaard in het recht. In- en uitsluiting van vrouwen, etnische minderheden en homoseksuelen in het familierecht, arbeidsrecht en strafrecht,* eds. K.D. Lünnemann, M.L.P. Loenen, and A.G. Veldman. Deventer: Gouda Quint.

———. 2011. The Struggle of Embedding the Islamic Mahr in a Western Legal System. In *Embedding Mahr in the European Legal System,* eds. Rubya Mehdi and Jørgen S. Nielsen, 113–146. Copenhagen: DJØF Publishing.

Seron, Caroll, and Frank Munger. 1996. Law & Inequality: Race, Gender… and, of Course, Class. *Annual Review of Sociology* 22: 187–212.

Shah, Prakash. 2007. Rituals of Recognition: Ethnic Minority Marriages in British Legal Systems. In *Law and Ethnic Plurality. Socio-Legal Perspectives*, ed. Prakash Shah, 177–202. Leiden-Boston: Martinus Nijhoff Publishers.

Shields, Stephanie A. 2008. Gender: An Intersectionality Perspective. *Sex Roles* 59: 301–311.

Silbey, Susan S. 2005. After legal consciousness. *Annual Review of Law and Social Science* 1: 323–368.

Sonneveld, Nadia. 2012a. *Khul' Divorce in Egypt: Public Debates, Judicial Practices, and Everyday Life*. Cairo: The American University in Cairo Press.

Sonneveld, Nadia, and Monika Lindbekk. 2015. A Revolution in Muslim Family Law? Egypt's Pre- and Post Revolutionary Period (2011–2013) Compared. *New Middle Eastern Studies* 5.

Speelman, Gé. 1993. Mixed marriages. In *Muslims and Christians in Europe. Breaking New Ground. Essays in honour of Jan Slomp*, eds. Gé Speelman, Jan van Lin, and Dick Mulder. Kampen: Uitgeverij Kok.

———. 2001. *Keeping Faith. Muslim-Christian Couples and Interreligious Dialogue*. Meinema: Zoetermeer.

Sterckx, Leen. 2014. *Trouwen met een vreemdeling*. In *Afstand en nabijheid in de relaties van 'Turken' en 'Marokkanen' in een gemengd huwelijk*. Diemen: AMB.

Sterckx, Leen, and Carolien Bouw. 2005. *Liefde op maat. Partnerkeuze van Turkse en Marokkaanse jongeren*. Het Spinhuis: Amsterdam.

Strik, Tineke, Betty De Hart, and Ellen Nissen. 2013. *Family Reunification: a barrier or facilitator of integration? A comparative study*. Brussels: European Commission.

van der Werff, C., and B.J.W. Docter-Schamhardt. 1987. *Alimentatie na scheiding in 1982. Een landelijk dossieronderzoek*, Ed. WODC. 's-Gravenhage: Staatsuitgeverij.

van der Werff, C., E.M. Naborn, and B.J.W. Docter-Schamhardt. 1987. *Rechterlijke uitspraken over de regeling van het gezag en de omgang bij scheiding. Een landelijk dossieronderzoek*. 's-Gravenhage: SDU.

van der Zwaard, Joke. 2008. *Gelukzoekers. Vrouwelijke huwelijksmigranten in Nederland*. Amsterdam: Artemis & Co.

van Eijk, Esther. 2013. *Family Law in Syria. A Plurality of Laws, Norms, and Legal Practices*. Leiden: Proefschrift Universiteit.

van Huis, Mila, and Liesbeth Steenhof. 2003. Divorce risks for foreigners in the Netherlands. The second demographic transition in Europe, Spa, Belgium.

van Rossum, Wibo. 2007. Dutch Judges Deciding Multicultural Legal Cases. In *Explorations in Legal Cultures*, eds. F. Bruinsema and D. Nelken. Den Haag: Reed Business.

van Walsum, Sarah Katherine. 2008. *The family and the nation: Dutch family migration policies in the context of changing family norms*. Newcastle Upon Tyne: Cambridge Scholars Publishing.

van Wamelen, Charlotte Gezina Maria. 1987. *Ouderschap en ouderlijk gezag na scheiding*. Zwolle: W.E.J. Tjeenk Willink.

Verloo, Mieke. 2006. Multiple Inequalities, Intersectionality and the European Union. *European Journal of Women's Studies* 13(3): 211–228.

Voorhoeve, Maaike. 2009. The Interaction Between Codified Law and Divine Law: The Case of Divorce for Disobedience in Tunisia. *IBLA: Revue de l'Institut des Belles Lettres Arabes* 204: 267–286.

Walby, Joanne. 2010. Extended Holiday in Hurghada: Russian Migrant Women and '*Urfi* Marriage. *Surfacing* 3(1): 39–70.

Waldis, Barbara. 1998. *Trotz der Differenz: interkulturelle Kommunikation bei maghrebinisch-europäischen Paarbeziehungen in der Schweiz*. Freiburg: Universitätsverlag Freiburg Schweiz.

———. 2006. Introduction: Marriage in and Era of Globalisation. In *Migration and Marriage. Heterogamy and Homogamy in a Changing World*, eds. Barbara Waldis and Reginald Byron. Berlin: Lit Verlag.

Waldis, Barbara, and Reginald Byron, eds. 2006. *Migration and Marriage. Heterogamy and Homogamy in a Changing World, Freiburger Sozialanthropologische Studien*. Berlin: Lit Verlag.

Walzer, Susan, and Thomas P. Oles. 2003. Accounting for Divorce: Gender and Uncoupling Narratives. *Qualitative Sociology* 26(3): 331–349.

Weeda, Iteke. 1983a. *Van huwelijk tot echtscheiding. Een regenboog van ervaringen*. Mededelingen van de vakgroepen sociologie van de landbouwhogeschool: Wageningen.

———. 1983b. *Voor en na de echtscheiding*. Utrecht: Het Spectrum.

Wimmer, A. and N. Glick Schiller (2002). Methodological nationalism and beyond: nation-state building, migration and the social sciences. *Global Networks* 2(4): 301–334.

Williams, Charmaine C. 2004. Race (and Gender and Class) and Child Custody: Theorizing Intersections in Two Canadian Court Cases. *NWSA Journal* 16(2): 46–68.

Yilmaz, Ihsan. 2002. The challenge of post-modern legality and Muslim legal pluralism in England. *Journal of Ethnic and Migration Studies* 28(2): 343–354.

Zeidguy, Rabha. 2007. Analyse de la jurisprudence. In *Le code de la famille. Perceptions et pratique judiciaire*, eds. Malika Benradi, Houria Alami M'chichi, Abdellah Ounnir, Mohamed Mouaqit, Fatima Zohra Boukaïssi, and Rabha Zeidguy. Fes, Morocco: Friedrich Ebert Stiftung.

2

The Contexts of Transnational Divorce

To understand and explain the stories of spouses on handling law in marriage and divorce, it is necessary to look at the societal and historical contexts in which their marriages and divorces took place. I divide these contexts into the dimensions of *place*, *time*, and *distance*, arguing that these dimensions can, at least partly, explain the differences between the stories of spouses on handling law in marriage and divorce. This chapter will provide the information necessary for understanding these contexts. I will set out by discussing the aspect of *place*. The marriages and divorces in this study took place in three countries and in different regions within those countries. These places are distinguished by significant differences with regard to discourses on mixed or migration marriages and perceptions of the Other, but also in practical opportunities for transnational couples. Discourses and practical opportunities also change over *time*, retelling a history of Moroccan and Egyptian migration to the Netherlands and measures taken to limit marriage migration. Discourses on mixed and migration marriages shift over time, as do legal rules and regulations. As the transnational marriages and divorces in this research

---

Earlier versions of a few sections of this chapter have been published in Sportel (2013).

I. Sportel, *Divorce in Transnational Families*,
DOI 10.1007/978-3-319-34009-8_2

took place between the 1960s and 2012, time has had a different influence on different spouses.

Partly as a result of the first two contexts, place and time, the physical, social, and cultural *distance* between the spouses in a transnational marriage can vary, forming the third context in which spouses in transnational marriages handle law during marriage and divorce. This distance informs the main distinction between mixed and migration marriages. The legal context of marriage and divorce in all three countries will be described in the next chapter, including an overview of the history of family law with regard to marriage and divorce.

Place

The transnational marriages in this research took place in different countries and places, each with its own specific circumstances relevant for transnational marriages and divorces. Place, first of all, is important because of its practical dimension. For example, due to the migration flows from Morocco to the Netherlands, there is a certain migrant infrastructure and existing migrant networks available for Moroccan migrants in the Netherlands which are not present for Dutch migrants in Morocco and only partially for Dutch-Egyptian divorces. Secondly, each place also has its own discourses about transnational marriages. As we will see in subsequent chapters, the way people see their marriage has an influence on how they talk about the legal aspects of that marriage. Thirdly, the three countries in this research of course each have their own history, culture, social structures, and legal systems. These differences are not just present between the countries but also between places within these countries, for example, between the capital and more remote regions. A specific place relevant for this research is Egyptian beach resorts, where transnational marriages take place in a context different from those in the capital. Below, I will discuss the three countries and outline the national and local contexts of Dutch-Moroccan and Dutch-Egyptian migration, focusing on those local aspects that have been of specific importance for the transnational couples in this study.

Transnational marriages between the Netherlands and Egypt mostly consist of mixed marriages. These take place in two distinct places. First of all, there are so-called 'beach marriages', between couples who met in Egypt's tourist industry. Egypt is a major tourist destination for European tourists, some of whom stay after they have met an Egyptian partner. Some Dutch migrants and mixed couples have also found work or started businesses in the tourist industry. Egypt has a long history of European mass tourism, especially after the liberalisations by Sadat in the late 1960s and early 1970s (Gray 1998: p. 92–95). In 2010, the number of arrivals in Egypt was over 14 million.[1] At the same time, the rest of Egypt's economy declined, and the state failed in providing work for Egypt's young population, with many young men struggling to earn enough money to be able to meet the social requirements for marriage (Abdalla 2004: p. 30–39). The immense growth of the Egyptian tourist industry thus attracted young, unemployed males from all over Egypt to come and work in resort cities like Hurghada or Sharm al-Sheikh, outside their social environment and away from the control and support of their families. In his research on mixed relationships in Dahab, on the Red Sea Coast, Abdalla (2004) found how Egyptian men conduct *`urfi* marriages with foreign women as 'a survival strategy to overcome poverty and to legitimize sexual relationships' to protect themselves from intense policing and even harassment by the Egyptian police of unmarried mixed couples (Abdalla 2004: p. 31, 45–47). The Egyptian press describes such 'beach marriages' between Egyptian men and foreign women as forms of prostitution, degrading Egyptian society (see: Abaza 2001).

Similarly, among Europeans living in Egypt, the tourist marriages are infamous for what the Dutch Noor Stevens has called *Bezness*. In her book *Kus kus, Bezness* she tells the story of her marriage to an Egyptian husband.[2] The marriage started happily but ended with violence and exploitation. She now uses her experiences to help other 'victims' through her own organisation, *Bezness alert*, also aiming to raise awareness by

[1] World Tourism Organization UNWTO. This number declined after January 2011, when former president Mubarak was put out of office and the country went through a period of turmoil and violence. However, most of the fieldwork for this book was done just before the regime change.

[2] Stevens, Noor, and Tardio, Natasza (2011). Kus Kus Bezness. *Een Nederlandse vrouw gevangen in het web van een Egyptische liefdesfraudeur*. Amsterdam: De Boekerij.

appearing frequently in the Dutch and Belgian media. On her website, she describes the issue of *Bezness* as:

> [*Bezness*] means an impersonation of love in order to gain financially and/or to gain a residence permit/passport by way of emotional blackmail and manipulation. In the tourist areas of Bezznes-countries like Egypt, Tunesia, Turkey and the Caribbean this has become a true industry. There are enough women and men who underestimate the cultural difference, and fall for sweet talk (because they're adept liars). Swindle is universal, but the rights of foreigners are in a completely different legal system entirely obscure. [...] The illusion of 'real love' turns out to be 'one-sided love', but often too late. [...] There are many forms of *Bezness*, but one thing is certain: men/women working in the tourist industry are almost always part of that group '*Bezness*'. (http://www.Beznessalert.com/eng/what_is_Bezness.html, accessed on 23 November 2011)

During my fieldwork in Egypt, many referred to this practice in similar words.[3] Almost everyone I spoke to came up with stories about lonely middle-aged Western women having informal *`urfi* marriages with much younger Egyptian men, financial exploitation, and violence. These women were generally portrayed as the slightly stupid and sad victims of the cunning Egyptian men they loved. Western women, who could be considered more powerful with regard to financial means, mobility, race, and social class (Walby 2010: p. 43–44), become powerless victims because they fall in love, something they must be warned about. The Egyptian men, on the other hand, keep being disappointed when their foreign wives return to their countries of origin and leave them behind (Abdalla 2004: p. 40–45).

In this discourse, it is only the men for whom this is a 'false' marriage, as they apparently do not love their partners back. Thus, true love and material gain are framed as mutually exclusive, the first a proper and the second an improper reason for marriage. The Egyptian men are supposedly only interested in the marriage because of money, a visa or sometimes sex. Dutch women in relationships with Egyptian men are

---

[3] They did all not use the term Bezness, however. Noor Stevens' book had not yet been published when I did my Egyptian fieldwork.

therefore sometimes advised to deliberately take away these gains from the relationship, as a kind of test to see if his intentions are 'pure', that is, love. Moreover, the 'completely different legal system' in these countries is referred to as a further threat, obscuring the rights of foreigners, which adds to the 'othering' of these relations and the Egyptian legal system.

However, not all Dutch-Egyptian couples living in Egypt meet on a beach holiday. A second group of couples, living in big cities like Cairo, do not necessarily identify themselves with the 'beach marriages'. Some of these couples have met abroad, in the Netherlands or elsewhere, for example, during their studies. Some Dutch wives also came to Egypt for work or business and met their future husband as business associates or in the international nightlife of Cairo. The differences between these two places, Cairo and other Egyptian big cities and the resort towns and tourist areas also have a class dimension. The couples that met in the tourist industry, and especially those who have conducted informal '*urfi* marriages, are looked down upon by those living in Cairo. Informal marriages have often been described to me as a 'license to fuck' or a 'prostitute's contract' by Egyptians as well as Europeans living in Egypt and even by a lawyer who makes such contracts. In these marriages, the Egyptian husbands were generally poor, or at least less wealthy than their Dutch wives, and sometimes also younger, which invites allegations of *Bezness*. The Dutch-Egyptian couples living in Cairo, on the other hand, were more often Dutch women having married Egyptian husbands from wealthy, internationally oriented families and of the same age or slightly older than their wives.

Among Dutch-Moroccan couples, similar class distinctions seem to be made. Migration between the Netherlands and Morocco has, for a significant part, been from poorer, more peripheral regions of Morocco, with a mostly Berber-speaking population and with a long history of resistance to central power, especially the North-East Rif and the oases located south-east of the High Atlas mountain regions (de Haas 2007). In those regions, many families have connections to the Netherlands and other European countries. The children of the first generation of Moroccans residing abroad have, to some extent, concluded endogamous marriages among their own kin or to people from the same village or region, forming migrant networks. Due to the level of migration and return migration from specific regions in Morocco, certain services have developed, catering to these migrants, such as legal aid offices and schools offering Dutch language courses.

The difference between the main cities of Casablanca and Rabat, where French and Arabic are spoken, and the rural periphery is described by interviewees as large. One Moroccan interviewee from Casablanca described her experiences when first coming to the Netherlands and trying to find a job as a teacher of Arabic for Dutch-Moroccan school children:

> I don't get it. That attitude. I don't get it. Because I was dressed rather modernly. I had long hair and was I wearing it loose. Then the director [of the school she was applying to] said to me: 'well, those are Moroccans'. And he pointed out a number of Moroccans. I said: 'if those are Moroccans I'm not Moroccan'. Because I did not know such people in my own country. They are a type of people very different from those I'm used to living with. (Rabia, Moroccan woman divorced from Dutch-Moroccan husband, living in the Netherlands)

Similarly, a Dutch woman divorced from a Moroccan husband described her experiences with her Moroccan husband and in-laws:

> They're not traditional Moroccans. They never demanded that I should, for example, convert to Islam, or how we should live our lives. [...] I mean, they're people from the Capital, with a background very different from people from some village in the Rif. (Claudia, Dutch woman divorced from Moroccan husband, living in the Netherlands)

Similar to the Dutch-Egyptian couples living in Cairo, this interviewee describes her husband and family-in-law as highly educated and internationally oriented, and their life together as wealthy and full of international and expat contacts, distancing herself from the other, ordinary Moroccans in the rural Rif region. The difference thus seems to be more than just regional, but it also contains elements of social class.

Like Egypt, Morocco is a tourist destination, but on a smaller scale, and tourism makes a less important contribution to Morocco's economy. It is a fast-growing sector, with the number of tourist arrivals more than doubling between 2004 and 2015 from four to ten million.[4] The number of Dutch nationals living in Morocco is relatively small. The Dutch embassy estimates that around 600 Dutch nationals live in Morocco, including those with double nationality. It is a small and not very well organised group, missing the meeting points the Dutch community in Egypt has.

In the Dutch context, Moroccans form a much larger and more visible group of migrants than Egyptians.[5] While there is a well-established Moroccan immigrant community, and substantial amounts of information and social and legal aid are available on, for example, Moroccan family law in the Netherlands (see for a more elaborate discussion, Sportel 2011), Egyptian migrants seem to be a less-established group. Most Egyptian migrants are men, often married to Dutch or foreign women. The majority of the smaller number of Egyptian women migrated to the Netherlands for reasons of family reunification (Zuijdgeest 2005: p. 14–15).

An issue which has a prominent presence in Dutch discourses on transnational marriages is the issue of marriage as a way of exploitation or gain for one of the partners. Economic and social differences between the Netherlands, on the one hand, and Egypt and Morocco, on the other hand, can raise questions with regard to the intentions of the Moroccan or Egyptian spouse. In Dutch society, as well as policymaking, a 'romantic ideal of marriage' is dominant, where a 'real' marriage is solely based on love, without any other motives involved and between similar partners (de Hart 2003: p. 127–129). When other benefits, such as a residence permit, are involved in transnational Dutch-Moroccan or Dutch-Egyptian marriages, this makes these marriages easily suspect as being marriages of convenience.

---

[4] World Travel and Tourism Council 2015, p. 5.

[5] In early 2015, there were 380,755 persons of Moroccan descent living in the Netherlands. Of this group, 212,304 are so-called second-generation migrants, the majority of whom have two parents who were born abroad (CBS Statline, accessed in March 2016). In 2015, the Netherlands had a total population of 16,900,726 with 22,700 people of Egyptian origin living in the Netherlands in 2012. 12,776 were born in Egypt (first-generation migrants), 4783 have two parents who were born abroad and 5141 are children of one Egyptian parent and one Dutch parent (CBS Statline). Around two-thirds of Egyptians living in the Netherlands are Muslims, and one-third Coptic Christians. It is estimated that around 10 % of people living in Egypt are Christians (Zuijdgeest 2005: p. 15), meaning Coptic Christians are overrepresented in the Netherlands.

In the following chapters, I will account for the importance of place by referring to the place of living during the marriage for each interview. For couples aiming to live in the Netherlands during their marriage, migration laws and policies are often a major part of their experience with Dutch law and may prevent a couple from living together altogether. Also in the Netherlands, the recent negative discourse on immigration and Muslims, especially those of Moroccan origin, can colour the expectations of a couple and the reactions of their social environment. These discourses and policies have strongly shifted in the last 30 years, paralleling developments in Moroccan marriage migration to the Netherlands. This element of time will be the topic of the next paragraph.

Time and History

There is a wide diversity between the respondents in this research with regard to the moment of marriage or divorce. Some of the spouses first met in the 1960s or 1970s whereas others got married up to 2008. Some of these marriages have lasted for decades, others only a few months. Some respondents divorced in the 1980s; others had not yet finalised the divorce at the moment of the interview. The experiences of the interviewees with transnational marriage and divorce thus span roughly 50 years. During this time, several shifts have taken place in the social context of mixed and migration marriages and the legal context of migration measures and law, which, as will become clear in the next chapters, have had a major impact on the life of many spouses in Dutch-Moroccan and Dutch-Egyptian marriages. This impact took place on a practical level, such as migration procedures and limitations, but also on the level of societal discourses and response to transnational marriage and divorce. Unfortunately, I have found only limited sources for Moroccan and Egyptian public discourses and policies on mixed or migrant marriages and nothing specifically on Dutch migrants to Egypt and Morocco. This means that the information in this paragraph will have a strong focus on migration to the Netherlands.

The History of Marriage Migration to the Netherlands

Moroccan migration to the Netherlands started with a demand for foreign workers in the 1960s. Both Morocco and the Netherlands at first considered this a temporary arrangement, where the Netherlands would benefit from the extra labour, and returning guest workers' experience would strengthen Morocco's development (de Haas 2007: p. 12–13; Bonjour 2006). During the 1970s, a transition took place. In changing economic circumstances, restrictive measures were introduced to limit labour migration, while labour migrants already present could arrange more easily for their women and children to join them in the Netherlands (Bonjour 2006: p. 6–8). Meanwhile, Morocco was hit especially hard by the 1973 oil crisis and at the same time an increasing instable political climate and repression, making many migrants decide 'to stay on the safe, European, side of the Mediterranean' (de Haas 2007: p. 5–6). For the Dutch government, this meant an unforeseen shift from labour to family migration, and from adult men to women and children (Bonjour 2006: p. 6–8). Following this shift, male migrant partners, such as the foreign spouses of Dutch women or daughters from the first Moroccan labour migrants who married a spouse from Morocco, were seen as especially suspicious. Dutch policymakers feared marriages of convenience, by which they meant labour migration disguised as marriage migration. Up to 1979, women bringing a partner from abroad, therefore, had to deal with stricter regulations than men (de Hart 2003: p. 99–119; Hooghiemstra 2003: p. 3–5, 11–19; Bonjour 2006: p. 9).

The first wave of Egyptian migrants to the Netherlands differed from the Moroccan labour-oriented migration streams. Starting from the 1970s, after President Sadat made travel to Western countries easier, highly educated experts, students, and political refugees moved to Europe. Many of this first group of Egyptian migrants married Dutch or foreign women. A second wave of Egyptian immigrants arriving in the 1980s and 1990s consisted mostly of less educated young men looking for employment and wealth. Many found jobs in cafeterias selling Egyptian fast food and started businesses in this sector (Zuijdgeest 2005: p. 14–15).

From the 1980s, there was a shift in debates and policies on marriage migration. The continued presence of former labour migrants living in the Netherlands became accepted as a fact, and policy frames shifted from temporary migration to integration in Dutch society and equal rights. A new minorities approach was taken which, according to Bonjour,

> clearly bore the marks of the Dutch political tradition of pluralism. […] It was explicit and active government policy to grant ethnic minorities room for cultural expression as a group, while formal consultation procedures were set up so their representatives could be involved in the development of policy that concerned them. (Bonjour 2006: p. 10)

Following these shifts, all kinds of national and local organisations were formed to cater to the needs of the new minorities, including family law issues. Examples of these organisations are the MVVN (Moroccan Women's Association in the Netherlands, 1982) and the SSR (Association for the support of return migrants, 1989). Some of these organisations are still active in the field of transnational divorce and will be further discussed in Chapter 8. Some of the older transnational marriages in this research which took place in this period were clearly connected with what they called the 'minority field'. These interviewees were working as language teachers, teaching Dutch to migrants or Arabic to Dutch-Moroccan children, or as social workers specialising in minorities. No similar organisations were founded for Egyptian migrants in the Netherlands.

Concerns about the position of migrant women from Islamic countries (i.e. Morocco and Turkey) in the Netherlands prompted several legal manuals on the Turkish and Moroccan family law systems, aimed at social workers working in this field. No such handbooks were written for Dutch-Egyptian divorces. In 1993, a new official Dutch-Moroccan state-level commission, the *commission mixte*, was established, discussing the legal issues of Moroccan citizens living in the Netherlands and problems of interacting laws, especially with regard to the acknowledgement of Dutch-Moroccan divorces.[6]

[6] Based on commission documents, obtained from one of the former members.

This focus on cultural and social groups also had consequences for the perspectives on marriage migration. Whereas enabling the original labour migrants to live with their existing families in the Netherlands was considered to benefit their integration in Dutch society, the marriages of their children to spouses from Morocco or Turkey were seen as unwanted. This would bring in new generations of 'underprivileged' migrants. Thus, while family reunification restrictions were lessened during the 1980s for so-called 'first-generation migrants' with residence status and made similar to Dutch nationals, this did not happen for their children in transnational marriages who had to meet higher levels of income requirements before they could bring their partner to the Netherlands (Bonjour 2006: p. 11–12).

From the 1990s, the Dutch discourse of respect for multiculturalism and plurality started to lose ground, making room for a harsher, more populist discourse of assimilation and nationalism, fuelled by the attacks in the USA on 11 September 2001 and the murder of Dutch politician Pim Fortuyn. In this discourse, a backlash against multiculturalism, the politically correct approach of the old left-wing elite should make room for a no-nonsense, frank discussion of the problems of the ordinary people with Muslims living in the Netherlands, leaving behind old taboos like racism and focussing on issues like delinquency, poverty, and unemployment among migrant minorities (Prins and Saharso 2008, 2010: p. 74–77).

In this highly gendered discourse, gender equality and sexuality form a central demarcation line between white Dutch and Muslim migrants. Muslim women take centre stage in this discourse, being seen as victims of their culture and a group in particular need of emancipation (Prins and Saharso 2008: p. 368; Roggeband and Verloo 2007). Islamic family law acted as a strong marker of difference in these debates, with opponents generally using the Arabic term *shari`a*, which has strong connotations of extremism and violence. A number of NGOs and women's organisations started targeting Moroccan women living in the Netherlands, often with financial support from local or national governments. Several projects with regard to Moroccan family law were established, especially after the new Moroccan family law of 2004, aiming to educate women about their rights.

The new realism discourse has had a significant impact on Dutch marriage migration policies. In these policies, migration, and especially second-generation Moroccan migrants marrying transnationally to spouses from their parents' country of origin, is seen as threatening social cohesion in the Netherlands and hindering the integration of existing migrant groups (especially second-generation migrants) in Dutch society (Bonjour 2010: p. 302–306). From the beginning of the 1990s, a new wave of measures to limit marriage migration followed. Laws were also enacted with the aim of preventing marriages of convenience. From 1992, foreign documents have to be legalised in order to be usable in the Netherlands, a time-consuming and sometimes expensive procedure for transnational couples. From 1993 onwards, stricter income requirements have to be met before the foreign partner gets permission to settle in the Netherlands. These norms were further increased in 2004, until a 2010 decision from the Court of Justice of the European Union in 2010 (the *Chakroun* case) forced Dutch government to lower income requirements to the level of full-time minimum wage. In practice, this often meant that the Dutch partner needed to have near full-time employment, which can be a major obstacle, especially for women and minorities who tend to work fewer hours and have less well-paid employment in the Netherlands than white men. Moreover, this meant transnational couples in the Netherlands were no longer free to divide paid employment, household tasks, and care to their own preference.

In 2012, the Dutch government introduced further restraints on marriage and family migration. These included a prolonged dependent residency for the foreign spouse (from three to five years) and marriage or the equivalent of registered partnership as an official requirement for spousal migration. A new measure to limit marriage migration and promote integration/assimilation in Dutch society was the introduction of a language test; since 2006, migrants from certain countries, including Morocco and Egypt, have to take a language and knowledge of society test before being granted permission to come to the Netherlands (Bonjour 2010: p. 306). Apart from stimulating early integration, this test aims at keeping out immigrants with little interest in or motivation for integration (Wilkinson et al. 2008: p. 17).

In practice, this means a selection on class and level of education. In 2011, the language level of this test was increased to A1 and now includes a reading test (Strik et al. 2013: p. 15).

Thus, compared to the discourse of the early 1980s, as described by De Hart (2003: p. 99–119) and Hooghiemstra (2003: p. 3–5, 11–19), the discourse on Moroccan marriage migration has shifted. The fear of Moroccan men in marriages of convenience overflowing the labour market has lost its prominent position. Now it is the 'import bride' that is the main fear, an uneducated housewife from Morocco who is kept indoors by her husband, does not speak Dutch and cannot raise proper Dutch children, thus continuing a cycle of poverty, welfare dependence, and gender inequality for generations. Language tests, income, and age requirements should all work to prevent problematic, underprivileged migrants from coming to the Netherlands for their marriage.

These measures have had several effects on transnational marriages. First of all, it has become increasingly difficult to contract a transnational Dutch-Egyptian or Dutch-Moroccan marriage for those couples who aim to live in the Netherlands. The number of Dutch-Moroccan second-generation migrants who marry a partner from Morocco has declined, especially after the introduction of the new, stricter, immigration policies in 2004 and the introduction of the language test in 2006. Whereas in 2000 52 % of the second-generation Moroccan men and 56 % of Moroccan women marrying in the Netherlands had a so-called migration marriage with a partner from Morocco (Alders 2005: p. 47), in 2014 this was down to 7 % for men and 12 % for women. The number of marriages with native Dutch partners is more or less stable, around 12 % for men and 7 % for women. Most second-generation migrants of Moroccan descent (around 70 %) chose a marriage partner of Moroccan descent already living in the Netherlands. Interestingly, the number of migration marriages is still higher for Dutch-Moroccan women than for Dutch-Moroccan men, despite the income requirements.[7]

Second, strict migration rules might 'rush' transnational couples into marriage. Some couples who would have preferred to live together before marriage may choose to get married right away. Until 2004, there were

[7] *CBS statline*, accessed through www.cbs.nl in March 2016, percentages calculated by author.

stricter income requirements for couples living together than for married couples. Even when the income requirements were not a problem, some couples still thought getting married would help or even was necessary to get a residence permit for the foreign partner and got married even though they would have preferred to live together without being married (de Hart 2003: p. 163). Even couples who wanted to get married anyway, without living together, can choose to contract the marriage earlier than they would have done otherwise, because of the time-consuming procedure of getting permission for the foreign partner to live in the Netherlands. Below, I will go further into the differences between the categories of 'mixed' and 'migration marriages' when discussing the element of distance.

Distance: Mixedness as the Crossing of Borders

When marrying transnationally, state and other boundaries are crossed, implying an element of distance. Distance can have practical dimensions, such as the physical distance to one's family and social network after migration. But distance also has a social and cultural element. The social, physical, and cultural distances between the spouses are not equal in all situations, places, and times. Some of the transnational marriages in this research, those between a native Dutch partner and a Moroccan or Egyptian partner are seen, by the spouses and by society, as being mixed, while marriages between Dutch-Moroccans and Moroccans are generally not seen as such. According to Waldis, all marriages contain aspects of sameness and difference, and it is only those differences that are marked as significant which make a marriage mixed (Waldis 2006: p. 3). The main marker of difference between the two categories of marriages in this research is ethnicity, which also includes elements of religion and culture. Mixed marriages between a native Dutch and a native Egyptian or Moroccan partner—the largest group in this research—mostly involve a crossing of particularly strong ethnic boundaries, in which images of Orientalism and Occidentalism polarise 'Western' and 'Islamic' societies and culture. As we will see in Chaps. 4–8, this polarisation plays an important role in how people experienced their mixed marriage, how they explained their divorce, and their legal consciousness. In this paragraph, I will further introduce these two categories of mixed and migration marriages and the social images and discourses present in the three countries with regard to these marriages.

Mixed Marriages

In the Netherlands, there is a strong othering of especially Muslim men as being dangerous. Already in the 1990s, Kamminga (1993) found that Dutch and foreign men and women in mixed marriages are ascribed different positions and motives in the Dutch media. Especially marriages of Dutch women and (foreign) Muslim men are seen as problematic. In these marriages, representations of power relations between native and foreign and men and women collide (Kamminga 1993:p. 61). Hondius notes as well that fearful stories and negative representations in the Dutch media concern nearly exclusively Dutch women married to men from Muslim countries (Hondius 1999: p. 177).[8] Not surprisingly, many of the interviewed Dutch women reported that their friends and families were worried or disapproving of their choice of a Moroccan or Egyptian husband.[9]

In this context of fear of Muslim men, Islamic family law takes a special place. Islamic family law is presented as dangerous for women and as the direct opposite of Dutch law, which liberates women. Women from the Netherlands are warned about the dangers of marriages to Egyptian men, urging them to safeguard their legal rights as a precaution. On the website of the Dutch embassy in Egypt, for example, a detailed description of the documents needed to contract a marriage in Egypt and the procedures to obtain legalisation of these documents at the embassy is

[8] Altena describes how already in the nineteenth and early twentieth century, marriages between Dutch men and native women in Dutch colonies were acceptable while such inter-ethnic marriages of Dutch women were out of the question, as they were supposed to marry within their own group (Altena 2008: p. 123).

[9] I will return to the role of the social environment in Chapter 8.

accompanied by warning statements on the possibilities for an Egyptian husband to stop 'his wife and children from leaving Egypt by issuing a travel ban', the lengthy and complicated child custody cases, especially for non-Muslim and non-Egyptian mothers, and the differences in divorce options between men and women in Egypt. Moreover, Dutch citizens marrying in Egypt are urged to get 'professional legal advice before getting married', and to use a translator during the ceremony.[10] Similar warnings can be found on websites and internet forums for Dutch and other European nationalities living in Egypt.

In Morocco and especially Egypt, on the other hand, there is an othering of European women, and to some extent also of the Moroccan and Egyptian men married to them. Therrien (2012) describes how mixed marriages are often seen as threatening Moroccan social cohesion (Therrien 2012: p. 135). According to Behbehanian, from an Egyptian perspective, the gender inversions present in this situation are an important factor in making sexual relationships between Egyptian men and foreign women undesirable to the Egyptian state:

> These men not only come to represent sexual promiscuity to the state, but they also serve as bearers of a range of social ills perceived to be infiltrating the nation as a result of the tourism industry, including dishonesty, theft, drug use, imitations of 'Western' behavior and general moral decay. (Behbehanian 2000)

For Moroccan and Egyptian men living in Morocco or Egypt, a European wife is not always the obvious choice for a marriage partner. This might very well be an important reason for Moroccan or Egyptian men to marry their foreign spouse informally or secretly, without the presence or knowledge of their families. In Egypt informal '*urfi* marriages between Egyptians are often used in secret relationships, for example, when parents do not agree or in case of a second marriage (Abaza 2001). '*urfi* marriages will be further discussed in Chapter 4.

---

[10] Website Dutch embassy: http://egypt.nlembassy.org/shared/products-and-services/products-and-services/getting-married/getting-married.html?q=married&selectedLocalDoc=getting-married-in-egypt, accessed March 2016.

Migration Marriages

In so-called migration marriages, the children of the labour migrants who moved to the Netherlands from Morocco in the 1960s and 1970s chose spouses from Morocco. Though the partners have been raised in different countries, these marriages are not generally considered to be ethnically mixed. In the Netherlands, these marriages are often condemned as being a hindrance for integration and leading to an endless chain of new migrants. As migration marriages sometimes are arranged by the parents, and sometimes include spouses who are also family members, they are in Dutch public debates connected to a whole range of problematic issues. These issues are usually framed as the need to protect young migrant women from practices like forced marriages, abandonment in the country of origin, martial imprisonment, and even female genital mutilation.[11] Local and national governments as well as NGOs have started a range of campaigns, research projects, and legal measures to prevent these practices (Smit van Waesberghe et al. 2014).

The strong crossing of boundaries and othering experienced by some mixed couples was far less an issue in migration marriages in this research. Many partners in migration marriages marry spouses who feel 'close', from the family or the village, from the same religious background or other communities or regional identities they belong to in Morocco. This real or imagined closeness and their identity as Muslims may make Dutch-Moroccans less susceptible to the strong negative discourses on Islamic family law present in the Netherlands.[12] As one Dutch-Moroccan representative of a migrant welfare organisation said, 'Girls who have been born here [in the Netherlands] come into contact with two governments. We are married under two laws. In case of divorce, we therefore also need to arrange it under two laws' (Board member of Stichting Vrouw en Welzijn, 2 July 2009). She presented this statement as a simple fact, positioning the two legal systems at the same level, without the othering present in many stories about mixed marriages.

[11] *Kamerstukken* 2012–2013, 32 840, nr. 8 (amendment Arib-Hilkens).

[12] However, it must be noted that the Moroccan spouses from migration marriages are overrepresented in the research group, so my information on Dutch-Moroccan perspectives is limited to a few cases.

Conclusions

The three dimensions of context, time, place, and distance, I have introduced in this chapter have shaped the experiences of spouses in a transnational divorce in multiple ways and on multiple moments. They are important both because of practical dimensions, such as the availability of a transnational network of organisations providing legal aid between the Netherlands and Morocco (see Chapter 8) and the change of migration law over time which restricts the possibilities for transnational couples to live in the Netherlands (see Chapter 4). On the level of discourse, the frames available on mixed and transnational marriages inform how spouses speak about the end of their marriage, as well as some of the legal actions they took. In the following chapters, I will analyse the experiences of spouses and how their stories refer to and can be placed within these contexts.

References

Abaza, Mona. 2001. Perceptions of 'Urfi Marriage in the Egyptian Press. *Isim Newsletter* 7: 20–21.

Abdalla, Mustafa. 2004. *Beach Politics. Gender and Sexuality in Dahab. Cairo Papers in Social Science*. Cairo: The American University in Cairo Press.

Alders, Maarten. 2005. Prognose van gezinsvormende migratie van Turken en Marokkanen. *Bevolkingstrends* 2: 46–49.

Altena, Marga. 2008. The Lady and the Indian; Representing an Inter-ethnic Marriage in Dutch and Canadian News Media (1906–1928). *International Journal of Canadian Studies/Revue internationale d'études canadiennes* 38: 119–147.

Behbehanian, Laleh. 2000. Policing the Illicit Peripheries of Egypt's Tourism Industry. *Middle East Report* 30(216).

Bonjour, Saskia. 2006. Who's in and Who's Out? The Postwar Politics and Policies of Family Migration in the Netherlands. *ESSHC Conference, Amsterdam*, 22–25 March 2006.

———. 2010. Between Integration Provision and Selection Mechanism. Party Politics, Judicial Constraints, and the Making of French and Dutch Policies of Civic Integration Abroad. *European Journal of Migration and Law* 12(3): 299–318.

de Haas, Hein. 2007. Between courting and controlling: The Moroccan state and 'its' emigrants. *Centre on Migration, Policy and Society Working Papers. University of Oxford* (54).

de Hart, Betty. 2003. *Onbezonnen vrouwen. Gemengde relaties in het nationaliteitsrecht en het vreemdelingenrecht., Migratie- en Etnische studies.* Amsterdam: Aksant.

Gray, Matthew. 1998. Economic Reform, Privatization and Tourism in Egypt. *Middle Eastern Studies* 34(2): 91–112.

Hondius, Dienke. 1999. *Gemengde huwelijken, gemengde gevoelens. Aanvaarding en ontwijking van etnisch en religieus verschil sinds 1945.* Den Haag: Sdu uitgevers.

Hooghiemstra, Erna. 2003. *Trouwen over de grens. Achtergronden van partnerkeuze van Turken en Marokkanen in Nederland.* Den Haag: Sociaal en Cultureel Planbureau.

Kamminga, Marleen. 1993. *Grensoverschrijders.* In *De beeldvorming van bi-culturele relaties in Nederlandse dagbladen.* Amsterdam: Wetenschapswinkel Universiteit van Amsterdam.

Prins, Baukje, and Sawitri Saharso. 2008. In the Spotlight. A Blessing and a Curse for Immigrant Women in the Netherlands. *Ethnicities* 8(3): 365–384.

———. 2010. From toleration to repression: The Dutch backlash against multiculturalism. Vertovec, Steven and Susanne Wessendorf (Hg.), *The Multiculturalist Backlash. European discourses, policies and practices.* London: Routledge: 92–110.

Roggeband, Conny, and Mieke Verloo. 2007. Dutch Women are Liberated, Migrant Women are a Problem: The Evolution of Policy Frames on Gender and Migration in the Netherlands, 1995–2005. *Social Policy & Administration* 41(3): 271–288.

Smit van Waesberghe, Eliane, Iris Sportel, Lisanne Drost, Esther van Eijk, and Elja Diepenbrock. 2014. *Zo zijn we niet getrouwd. Een onderzoek naar omvang en aard van huwelijksdwang, achterlating en huwelijkse gevangenschap.* Utrecht: Verwey Jonker Instituut.

Sportel, Iris. 2011. Transnational Divorce in Dutch-Moroccan Families. The Semi-Autonomous Social Field of Legal Aid. *Recht der Werkelijkheid* 32(3): 37–51.

———. 2013. "Because it's an Islamic Marriage". Conditions at Divorce in Transnational Dutch-Moroccan and Dutch-Egyptian Marriages. *Onati Socio-Legal series* 3(6): 1091–1110.

Strik, Tineke, Betty De Hart, and Ellen Nissen. 2013. *Family Reunification: a barrier or facilitator of integration? A comparative study.* Brussels: European Commission.

Therrien, Catherine. 2012. Trajectories of Mixed Couples in Morocco: A Meaningful Discursive Space for Mixedness. *Papers: revista de sociologia* 97(1): 129–150.

Walby, Joanne. 2010. Extended Holiday in Hurghada: Russian Migrant Women and '*Urfi* Marriage. *Surfacing* 3(1): 39–70.

Waldis, Barbara. 2006. Introduction: Marriage in and Era of Globalisation. In *Migration and Marriage. Heterogamy and Homogamy in a Changing World*, eds. Barbara Waldis and Reginald Byron. Berlin: Lit Verlag.

Wilkinson, Clare, Matthijs Goedvolk, and Steven van Dieten. 2008. *Kortetermijnevaluatie Wet inburgering buitenland. Eindrapportage*. Den Haag: WODC, ministerie van justitie.

Zuijdgeest, Nicolien. 2005. Egyptenaren in Nederland. *Contrast: weekblad over de multiculturele samenleving* 12(13): 14–15.

3

Legal Aspects of Divorce

Although formal, state-enforced law is certainly not the only source of organised social order (Moore 2005), in this study I have chosen to use this quite narrow concept of the law. This approach makes it possible to study other social norms and fields separately and look at the interactions of these fields with the law. Moreover, transnational couples have connections with more than one legal system, creating a complicated (state) legal pluralism. I make a distinction between Moroccan, Egyptian, and Dutch law, as formal, state-enforced law and the broader notion of Islamic family law as a complex whole of—historical and contemporary—texts and traditions of interpretation and implementation divided in different schools of law.

Spouses in transnational marriages have connections to two family law systems, which can interact. The interactions of family law are regulated by private international law. Each country has its own private international law. The Moroccan and Egyptian family codes have similar and quite uniform international private law systems, which are both closely connected to nationality. In both countries, domestic family law applies to all cases in which one of the parties is of the nationality of that country or is a Muslim (for a more elaborate discussion, see Kulk

I. Sportel, *Divorce in Transnational Families*,
DOI 10.1007/978-3-319-34009-8_3

2013). This means that, for the couples in this study, according to Egypt and Morocco, Moroccan or Egyptian law is always applicable, even when the couple has been living abroad. Dutch private international law is more complicated and connected to all kinds of international treaties. Sometimes nationality is the main factor, but the applicable law can also be determined by the country of residence, depending on the legal issues at stake.

In this chapter, I will first of all outline developments in Egyptian, Moroccan, and Dutch family law. In the last 15 years, family law in all three countries has been a matter of much public debate and legal reform. I will describe these reforms and the developments that influenced the present family law. Secondly, I will outline different aspects of marriage and divorce regulations in Egypt, Morocco, and the Netherlands such as marriage contracts, financial rights and responsibilities during marriage and after divorce, arranging a divorce, and child custody and contact. Lastly, I will briefly pay attention to nationality and residence, which are highly relevant in transnational divorce cases, especially in the Netherlands. As the transnational marriages and divorces in this research have taken place in a time frame of almost 50 years, I will pay attention to old as well as current family laws.

Developments in Egyptian, Moroccan, and Dutch Family Law

In the last decades, all three countries have reformed their family law systems, and in all countries this was both the result and cause of heated public debates on gender and the family. In Morocco, the *Moudawana* was reformed in 1993 and, more radically, in 2004, when a new family code was introduced. In Egypt, a new procedural law was introduced in 2000, often called the *khulʿ*-law, because of the controversial new article giving women the right to divorce unilaterally by *khulʿ*.[1]

[1] This law is officially called law no. 1 of 2000 or *The law on Reorganization of Certain Terms and Procedures of Litigation in Personal Status Matters*. Besides the famous article on *khulʿ* (20), it contained other controversial clauses such as the recognition of informal (*ʿurfi*) and the later-removed article which would allow women to travel without the consent of their husband (Sonneveld 2009: p. 1).

Furthermore, new family courts were introduced in 2004, and in 2005 the age limit for *hadana*, child custody or daily care, was raised. In the Netherlands, reforms mostly concern the rights of parents and children after divorce. Since 1998, parents automatically share custody of their children after divorce and in March 2009, a new law was introduced stressing the importance of contact between both parents and their children after divorce, obliging parents to make a so-called 'parenting plan' at the moment of divorce. In 2012, a long-debated new law on marital property came into effect, which included some changes but maintained the general principle of communal property. Most recently, spousal maintenance has become the subject of similar gender-equality-based debates, and at the moment of writing (December 2015) new proposals for limiting the duration and rights to spousal maintenance were being discussed in parliament. These reforms were the result of social debates, reflecting views in society about the family. Apart from influencing legal reform, these local debates on gender, family, and family law may very well have influenced the legal consciousness of spouses in transnational families.

Law Reform in Egypt

In Egypt, Personal Status Law has been partly codified by Laws No. 25 of 1920 and No. 25 of 1929, during the rise of Egyptian nationalism and the struggle for independence from Great Britain (Berger 2005: p. 60; Berger and Sonneveld 2006: p. 21–22). All non-codified issues are regulated by referring to Hanafi *fiqh* (Kulk 2013). Since the 1970s, there has been much pressure, both nationally and internationally, to reform the Personal Status Law. Major reforms were made by Sadat in 1979, containing many provisions meant to improve the status of women, such as expanding the grounds for divorce to include polygamy as being injurious to women and giving women the right to work outside of the home.[2] However, judges refused to apply the reformed family law because they considered it a violation of *shari`a*, and it was declared unconstitutional

[2] This reformed law is often called Jihan's law, after Jihan Sadat, the wife of the president.

in 1985.[3] Later that year, a modified, watered-down version was accepted. Women now needed to prove that their husbands' polygamy caused them material harm; polygamy was in itself not enough to apply to the divorce ground of *darar* (harm), just like in the old law of 1929 (Sonneveld 2009: p. 32–34; Singerman 2005).

In 2000, a new procedural law was implemented, law No. 1 of 2000. It was meant to facilitate litigation in personal status cases such as divorce (Sonneveld 2009: p. 1). Although it was framed as a procedural law, it contained more than just procedural aspects (Singerman 2005: p. 175). In Article 20, women were given the right to *khulʿ*, unilateral divorce on the condition that they renounce their financial rights and pay back the dower (Sonneveld 2009: p. 2). This so-called *khulʿ*-law, was widely debated among different groups in Egyptian society. This debate was mostly dominated by religious discourse and claims of cultural authenticity. Women's groups and the government were often accused of westernisation, and of wanting to destroy the Muslim family. They countered this by using the language of Islam. According to Sonneveld, a kind of 'Muslim public sphere' was created, in which 'norms and values are legitimized only when expressed in the language of Islam' (Sonneveld 2009: p. 64–65).

Furthermore, between 2000 and 2004 new family courts were introduced. Egyptian mothers were enabled to pass their nationality to their children and the first female judges were installed (Sonneveld 2009: p. 52–56). In 2005, the age limit of *hadana*, child custody, was raised to 15 for both boys and girls, strengthening the position of mothers after divorce. Since the 2011 revolution, this and other family law reforms made under former president Mubarak are being reframed as part of the old regime, 'Suzanne's [the wife of the former president, Mubarak] laws'. A new fathers' rights movement has actively been campaigning for more visitation rights. Protesters claim recent amendments in family law are un-Islamic and the product of Western influences, referring to the classical *shariʿa* custody ages of seven and nine. Furthermore, fathers' rights activists claim fathers have to pay child maintenance, while revengeful mothers block access to their children. Protesters demand that visiting

[3] Although not for this reason but because of procedural aspects (Sonneveld 2009: p. 1).

hours are extended and that children can be taken home by their fathers. Demands were also made for the transfer of custody or even the imprisonment of mothers who do not comply with visitation arrangements. An Egyptian branch of British fathers' rights NGO *Fathers for Justice* has been established.[4] According to Lindbekk & Sonneveld, fathers' rights organisations such as *The Revolution of Men* and *The Network of Men Harmed by the Personal Status Laws* are promoting joint care by parents after divorce over a return to the former end of *hadana* at ages seven and nine. They relate this development of discourse to a sense of emasculation in an age where husbands can rarely meet the obligation to maintain their families (Sonneveld and Lindbekk 2015).

Morocco

In Morocco, the first family code, or *Moudawana*,[5] was introduced shortly after independence in 1956. After this codification, several attempts have been made to reform the law, but none of these ever made it to discussion in parliament. In 1992, King Hassan II decided to reform the family law, as part of a highly controlled political reform and democratisation project. The king declared that he did not want a political struggle over Islamic family law, and he used his role as *amir al-mu'minin* (commander of the faithful) to claim the authority to decide on the issue of family law (Buskens 2003: p. 78–80; Salime 2009). However, the reforms in 1993 were rather limited and mostly a symbolic gesture. According to Buskens, these reforms reflected the earlier reformist tendencies of the *Moudawana* of 1958; 'Most male prerogatives were preserved, out of respect for the venerable Maliki tradition and for traditional values and customs, in order to avoid social upheaval. Instead the government tried to protect weaker parties, women and children, against abuses of these privileges by men.' (Buskens 2003: p. 81). In March 1999, a new government presented a plan to improve the position of women in Moroccan society

[4] Divorced Fathers fight to see offspring, *The Egyptian Gazette*, 12 May 2011. Single fathers call for amending custody law, Safaa Abdoun, *Daily News Egypt* on 24 May 2011. Pamphlet of the Saving the Egyptian Family Movement retrieved from the tahrir documents website http://www.tahrir-documents.org/2011/06/save-egyptian-families/, accessed 8 May 2013.

[5] Also spelled *Mudawannah*.

and integrate them more fully into society and development, including provisions on issues such as education, reproductive health, economic development, and family law reform (Buskens 2003: p. 85).

After the death of Hassan II in 1999, and the succession of Mohammed VI, a known supporter of women's rights, the debate on family law reform increased in intensity and gained a new momentum (Buskens 2003: p. 94; Zoglin 2009; Sadiqi and Ennaji 2006: p. 105). Similar to the Egyptian case, claims of cultural authenticity and true Islam were important in this debate. Both parties claimed the right to *ijtihad*, or Islamic reasoning, in attaining legal reform (Buskens 2003: p. 102–103, p. 120). This debate spread to Moroccan communities abroad, including the Netherlands. In Moroccan mosques in the Netherlands, protest petitions against the reforms were circulated (Buskens 2003: p. 105). Dutch organisations, such as the 'Association of Moroccan Women in the Netherlands' (MVVN) and left-wing parties in parliament, supported the reform plan and tried but failed to mobilise support from the Dutch government.

After several appeals for his support, King Mohammed VI appointed a commission to draft a new family code, in which both men and women from various disciplines were represented. This reform was framed as being in line with human rights and with religion, by using the term *shari`a*, referring to his position as *amir al-mu`minin* (commander of the faithful) and by entrusting the commission with the task of *ijtihad* (Buskens 2003: p. 113). Eventually, the new *Moudawana* was accepted unanimously by all parties—under pressure from the King—and took effect in February 2004 (Jordens-Cotran 2007: p. 42–44).

The new law contained many reforms that improved the legal position of women both during marriage and after divorce. The most important reforms with regard to divorce were the introduction of two new divorce forms: *chiqaq*, or no-fault divorce, and divorce by mutual consent. However, the old divorce forms *talaq*, unilateral divorce by the husband, *khul`*, unilateral divorce in exchange for compensation from the wife and *tatliq*, fault-based divorce on specific grounds such as harm, non-maintenance or absence of the husband were not abandoned but only procedurally restricted.[6] Men can, for example, still use the old divorce

[6] *Talaq* is often translated as repudiation.

form of *talaq*, but the procedure became much more complicated, including requiring judicial permission and a need to prove that all financial obligations to the wife had been met (Jordens-Cotran 2007: p. 335, 360).

In Morocco, children seem to be far less central to social and legal debates about divorce than in Egypt. Although according to the preamble, the new Moroccan *Moudawana* of 2004 was 'based upon shared responsibility, affection, equality, equity, amicable social relations and proper upbringing of children' (translation: HREA 2004), both public debates as well as legal reform mostly focus on the rights of divorcing women and men, including issues such as access to divorce and maintenance. Although children are relevant in these discussions, for example, in discussions whether a mother can surrender her rights to child maintenance or even child custody in exchange for a divorce, they do not take central stage like in Egypt or the Netherlands.

The Netherlands

Similar to Morocco and Egypt, reforms in Dutch family law reflect changes in Dutch society since the 1960s. The current Dutch divorce laws originate from 1971, when fault-based grounds for divorce were replaced by a single, no-fault, ground.[7] Together with the introduction of the *Algemene Bijstandswet* (General Social Security Act), which gave women without paid employment the financial possibility to leave their husbands, these reforms caused a huge increase in the number of divorce cases (Wegelin 1990: p. 1). Other reforms include the equal treatment of children born inside and outside of marriage, the regulation of non-marital forms of cohabitation, and legal arrangements for the care and visitation of children after divorce (Vlaardingerbroek et al. 2011: p. 2–4). Dutch family law has been influenced by the European Convention on Human Rights (ECHR), and the jurisprudence of the European Court of Human Rights, especially Article 8 of the convention, the right to respect for family and private life.[8]

[7] This ground is *duurzame ontwrichting* or permanent breakdown of a marriage.

[8] Officially called Convention for the Protection of Human Rights and Fundamental Freedoms. Examples can be found in the work of Forder (2003, 2002).

Although there have been some reforms with regard to marital property, maintenance rights, and the division of pension benefits after divorce, most of the Dutch reforms since the 1970s were connected to the issue children and parenting. Since the 1970s, pressure groups of divorced fathers have been pushing for more rights to visitation after divorce. In 1998, the concept of custody of one parent after divorce was abolished and replaced by a construction where parental authority of both parents continued after divorce. In March 2009, a new law came into effect, called '*Wet bevordering voortgezet ouderschap en zorgvuldige scheiding*' (law [for the] promotion of continued parenthood and careful divorce). This law requires parents to agree on how they will deal with their children, in a so-called parenting plan, which needs to be presented to the court before a divorce request is processed. Moreover, after divorce, a child of which the parents share parental authority has 'a right to an equal treatment in care and upbringing by both parents' (BW 1:247:4). Furthermore, the 2009 divorce law states that: 'parental authority entails the right and the *obligation* of the parent to care for and raise his minor child' (BW1:247.1). In the preamble, however, it becomes clear that this parental obligation is limited to have *contact* with his or her child, not to take an equal share in the actual day-to-day care work. In all these laws and accompanying texts, strict gender-neutral wordings are used, emphasising the formal equality of both parents (cf Terlouw 2010: p. 11–13). At the same time, in legal practice, a wide range of new enforcement measures was developed for cases with problematic child contact, such as placing children into care or even criminal convictions of no-contact mothers.

Marriage as a Financial Contract: Legal Rights and Obligations of Marriage

Getting married has consequences for the financial position of spouses, for example, with regard to maintenance obligations between the spouses during, and to some extent after, the marriage. While the actual provisions differ between the three countries, all have some possibilities for marrying couples to deviate from them. Below, I will outline laws regarding marriage and divorce in Egypt, Morocco, and the Netherlands and then compare the consequences and possibilities for transnational families.[9]

Egypt

In Egypt, at the moment of marriage, a marriage contract is signed, in which it is possible to include different kinds of stipulations. The marriage can be dissolved if these conditions are not met, providing an easier divorce procedure. Although both men and women can include certain conditions in the marriage contract, most of these stipulations are included for the wife's benefit, as men can easily dissolve the marriage anyway. A couple can choose, for example, to include stipulations that enable the wife to work, travel, or finish her education.[10] Another possible provision is *isma*, giving the wife equal rights to divorce (revocable or not), without having to go to court (Welchman 2004: p. 71; Singerman 2005: p. 173). According to Welchman, 'The basic principle is that the stipulations may not make what is prohibited lawful nor what is lawful prohibited' (Welchman 2004: p. 71).[11] However, the aforementioned stipulations are controversial and only used by a small minority (Singerman 2005: p. 173). To make a marriage contract valid, a *mahr* needs to be included. The *mahr* consists of two parts, a prompt and a deferred dower. According to Jansen, the level of the deferred dower is often set with the risk of divorce in mind (Jansen 1997, 2005). The prompt dower is paid at the moment of marriage, while the deferred dower needs to be paid by the husband in case of divorce or death. According to Sonneveld, the *shabka*—an engagement gift often in the form of gold—is taking over

[9] In this chapter, I focus on those aspects of marriage that are relevant for divorce, such as stipulations in the marriage contract. For more information on how to arrange a Dutch-Egyptian or Dutch-Moroccan marriage and the paperwork required for issues such as the recognition of children see: (Kulk 2013).

[10] These last stipulations are controversial among many women's groups and activists because they believe women already have these rights (Singerman 2005: p. 173, Welchman 2004: p. 71). For discussions over the Egyptian marriage contract see also Hatem (2004), Shaham (1999), and Sonbol (2005).

[11] This means, for example, that the wife cannot stipulate that her husband will not divorce her, and that the husband cannot demand that his wife will not have children.

the place of the prompt *mahr*, which is often only a symbolic amount, and on which Egyptians believe taxes need to be paid (Sonneveld 2009: p. 111–117).[12]

In classical Islamic family law, a wife has a right to be maintained by her husband during the marriage, regardless of her own means (Welchman 2004: p. 33). In return for this right of maintenance, the wife must be obedient to her husband. If the wife is disobedient, *nashiza*, she loses her right to maintenance (Jordens-Cotran 2007: p. 693–695). Even though the content of obedience has been limited over time, maintenance in Egyptian family law is to some extent still linked to the wife's obedience, albeit not as completely as before. In legal practice, obedience means that the wife stays in the conjugal home. If she leaves the house without the permission of the husband, he can file a *ta`a* claim at the court demanding that his wife returns to the 'house of obedience', the matrimonial home or lose her right to maintenance (Welchman 2004: p.88). According to Cuno, for some time in Egypt it has been possible to have such obedience orders to return to the marital home enforced by the police, a legal innovation in a law from 1897. However, this never became common practice, and the involvement of the police in *ta`a* claims was curtailed in 1967 and abolished in 1979 (Cuno 2009: p. 11–18). A *ta`a* claim generally means that the marriage is over. Sonneveld describes *Ta`a*, *khulʿ*, and maintenance claims as parts of a complicated strategic exchange in the courts between the two partners which will often lead to divorce (Sonneveld 2009: p. 170–176). Husbands have no rights to maintenance from their wives, regardless of their wealth.

During the marriage, the property of the spouses remains separated. However, I have not been able to find the actual laws on this topic. It appears that this section of law has not actually been written down in the Egyptian code of personal status.[13] This means that, if a husband has paid employment, most property, including the marital home, will be his, whereas the wife owns her dower (both prompt and deferred), the

[12] For a further discussion on the meaning of gold and gifts at marriage in Algeria see: (Jansen 1997).

[13] Not all sections of Egyptian family law have actually been codified. When not codified, judges should resort to the teachings of the Hanafi school of law. See for a more elaborate discussion, Kulk (2013).

shabka, or engagement gifts and the household goods and other property she brought into the marriage.[14]

In Egypt, there are two main forms of divorce; judicial divorce and informal, out-of-court ways to divorce. These two forms are mostly divided by gender. Men can divorce their wives out of court by performing *talaq*, often translated as repudiation. This happens by pronouncing an oral formula, which needs to be registered afterwards. Since 2000, the legal effects of *talaq*, for example with regard to inheritance, take place only after registration of the *talaq* with the *ma`dhun*, or notary. The notary then has to inform the wife through a court usher (art. 5b).[15] Couples with a foreign spouse can only use the notary of the Ministry of Justice, in Cairo, for marriage and divorce (Kulk 2013: p. 32–33).[16] *Talaq* is revocable and can be revoked by the husband during the *`idda* or waiting period.[17] The consent of the wife is not necessary to revoke the divorce, just resuming spousal relations was considered enough. Since 2000, the husband does, however, need to inform his wife (Bernard-Maugiron and Dupret 2008: p. 60–62). The third *talaq* is final and irrevocable. If a couple has put a stipulation in their marriage contract that the wife has a similar right to divorce (*isma*), women can follow the same procedure as men performing *talaq*.[18]

When men divorce their wives, they must pay the deferred dower to their wife, maintenance during the *`idda* and a *mut`a* or compensation, equal to two years of maintenance, depending on the wife's fault leading to the divorce (art. 18b). After divorce, the entitlement to spousal maintenance stops after the *`idda* or waiting period. If the wife has *hadana* over children under 15, she may be entitled to child maintenance and compensation for child care. However, many men do not actually pay their maintenance obligations (Bernard-Maugiron and Dupret 2008: p. 72–73; Al-Sharmani 2008: p. 44–48). Al-Sharmani found that Egyptian court

---

[14] Or at least, those goods which have been written down in the *ayma*, which may include some possessions which have been brought into the marriage by the husband (Sonneveld 2012a).

[15] Law nr. 100 of 1985, amending law nr. 25 of 1929. However, not all men do so, leaving their wives in an insecure situation. See also Human Rights Watch (2004).

[16] Often called the *Shahr Iqari*, or land registry, after its other function.

[17] This period is 60 days for women who menstruate or 90 for those who count the *`idda* by month (Sonneveld 2009: p. 33). In pregnancy, this *`idda* lasts until the birth of the child.

[18] For a further discussion of stipulations in the marriage contract see, Chapter 7 and Sportel (2013).

cases on maintenance claims lasted for one to four years. Although temporary maintenance orders are possible during the procedure, only few women in Al-Sharmani's research had actually managed to get one. Moreover, all kinds of practical issues arose, for example, in proving the former husband's means and claiming the money if a maintenance order was eventually given by the court (Al-Sharmani 2008: p. 44–48).

Women who do not have an *isma* stipulation in their marriage contract can only obtain a divorce through the courts. Regarding judicial divorce, there are two options, fault-based divorce and no-fault divorce through *khul`*. Fault-based judicial divorce allows women to keep their financial rights, but they need to prove one of the grounds: injury or harm, non-payment of maintenance, certain physical or psychological conditions, or the absence of the husband for more than a year. In practice, however, it appears to have been difficult for women to prove injury in general, and psychological injury in particular, as a basis for divorce, and such claims often led to very long court procedures, sometimes even as long as five to seven years. Fault-based divorce also contains class-based differences, because women need to prove that this situation is injurious for women *like her*, meaning women from a similar cultural and social background (Welchman 2004: p. 39–40).

The other option for judicial divorce is a divorce by *khul`*. This no-fault option, introduced in 2000, entails the wife's renunciation of her financial rights after divorce and the return of the dower. No proof is needed, just the claim of the wife that she detests her life with her husband, and that she cannot continue her marital life for the fear that she will fail to abide by the limits of God. The judge must then appoint arbitrators to try to reconcile the spouses for a period of three months. Once issued, *khul`* is not open to appeal. According to Sonneveld (2009), around 50 % of women-initiated divorces are by way of *khul`*, even in cases where women could apply for a divorce on the basis of harm, because it is a faster and easier way (Sonneveld 2009: p. 128–129). According to al-Sharmani, all women in her research who filed for *khul`* also had grounds to file for a divorce based on harm (Al-Sharmani 2008: p. 8).

Although *khul`* should provide women with an easier way of divorce, Sonneveld has found that husbands, as well as judges, may use procedural obstacles such as the obligatory mediation by arbitrators and the ambiguity about the exact amounts needed to be paid back by the wife to slow down the litigation process (Sonneveld 2009: p. 140). Furthermore, in addition to the dower, other benefits received such as the *shabka* regularly need to be returned. Sonneveld has even found some indications that judges in *khulʿ* cases might actually be demanding that the wife 'returns' the property she herself brought into the marriage, recorded in the *ayma*, to her husband before awarding a *khulʿ* divorce (see: Sonneveld 2009: p. 118–119).

A last option is to conduct an agreement between the husband and the wife to end the divorce by *talaq* with *ibraʾ*, meaning that the husband will exercise his right to *talaq* while the wife will waive any financial rights from her husband (Welchman 2004: p. 68–69). As the husband has the right to *talaq* anyway, this means that there is a very unequal power position for the wife in determining the conditions. Before the introduction of *khulʿ*, some husbands used this option to obtain a 'cheap' divorce, without paying the deferred dower. A man could pressure or mistreat his wife until she would ask for a divorce, in some cases even letting his wife pay amounts of money in order to 'buy her freedom'. Since the introduction of *khulʿ*, women have a cheaper way of obtaining a divorce through the court, and they no longer need to resort to paying their husbands huge sums in order to get a divorce. Moreover, women can now use *khulʿ* as a strategy, for example, to get an *ibraʾ* divorce. Because it is embarrassing for men to be divorced by *khulʿ*, they will often comply. According to Sonneveld, the majority of *khulʿ* cases are aborted after a while. In many of these aborted cases, the court is effectively used as a strategy to obtain certain aims (Sonneveld 2009: p. 175–180).

As far as I have been able to find, the recognition of a Dutch divorce is not possible in Egypt. Whereas Egyptian men or Dutch men who have converted to Islam can perform *talaq* at the Egyptian embassy in the Netherlands, Dutch or Egyptian women who divorced in the Netherlands need to start a second divorce procedure at an Egyptian court, if their husband is unwilling to cooperate by performing *talaq*.[19] Some spouses from transnational marriages, especially women, have become stuck in an

[19] E-mail contact with the Egyptian Embassy in the Netherlands, July 2011.

in-between situation, where they were divorced in the Netherlands but still married in Egypt.

In Egypt, the law regarding child care after divorce is strongly and explicitly gendered. Regulations mostly weigh the gender of the caregiver and child over actual care during the marriage or capacity to care for the children after divorce. *Hadana*, often translated as custody, encompasses day-to-day care of the child. It was first codified in law nr. 25 of 1929, which has been amended by law 100 of 1985 and law nr. 4 of 2005. After divorce, mothers have the first right to *hadana* (Art. 20, law no. 100 of 1985, translation by El-Alami 1994: p. 127–129). There is a strong preference for a female custodian, preferably from the mother's family. If the mother cannot take *hadana* over her children, her mother is the first to take over. This is also the case when the mother remarries and thus loses her right to *hadana*. Only if there are no suitable female relatives at all, in either family, the father and other male relatives become eligible for *hadana*. In 2005, the right of mothers to *hadana* after divorce was extended to the age of 15, with a possible extension to 18 for boys and marriage for girls.[20]

Related to *hadana* is *wilaya*, or guardianship. This is the right of the father and entails, for example, the right to take decisions over the education (*wilaya al-ta` limiyya*) and property (*wilaya al-mal*) of the child. If the father is unfit or absent, *wilaya* would be awarded to a mirror list of male relatives (Kulk 2013: p. 153–154). *Wilaya* consists of multiple parts, including guardianship over the property of the child and guardianship over the person of a child and his or her religious upbringing. A father can take both roles; a mother can only have the guardianship over the property of the child. Since 2008, the person having *hadana* also has the educational guardianship over a child (Sonneveld and Lindbekk 2015).

Non-custodial parents are entitled to visit their children once a week, for at least three hours. If the parents cannot agree they can take their dispute to court. If custodial parents refuse to cooperate, judges can, ulti-

[20] This age used to be 10 for boys and 12 for girls, with a possible extension in the interest of the child to 15 for boys and marriage for girls. However, the custodian is not entitled to payment for custody during this extension (art. 20 law nr. 100 of 1985).

mately, change the custody of the child, provided these measures do not cause emotional damage to the child (art. 20, law no. 100 of 1985, translation by El-Alami 1994: p. 127–129).[21]

Morocco

In Morocco, marriage contracts are also signed at the moment of marriage. Like in Egypt, these conditions are mostly of an interpersonal nature, meant to improve the position of the wife. It is therefore the wife who has the right to petition for divorce on the ground of harm if one of the conditions is not met. Permissible stipulations are, for example, that the couple will not move abroad or live with in-laws or that the wife can keep her own business. Giving the wife a right to divorce equal to the husband, called *tamlik* in Morocco, is also possible. It is, however, not possible to deviate from the legal obligations of maintenance (Jordens-Cotran 2007: p. 142–152). However, like in Egypt, this possibility to include stipulations in the marriage contract seems to be rarely used. In research done in the early 1990s in Rabat, only 36 out of 1503 marriage contracts were found to include stipulations, mostly a stipulation that the wife had the right to work outside of the home (Bouman 1992). In the *Moudawana* of 2004, new possibilities have been introduced to include arrangements on the division of property in the marriage contract. At the moment of marriage, the *adoul*, or notary performing the marriage, needs to inform the couple that they have the right to attach an arrangement on the division of property in an appendix to the marriage contract (art. 49 new *Moudawana*). To make a marriage contract valid, a *mahr* needs to be included, although it is not obligatory to specify the amount paid (art. 27 New Moudawana, see also, Jordens-Cotran 2007: p. 126–135; Kulk 2013).

In Morocco, a wife is entitled to maintenance from her husband. Before 2004, in exchange, Moroccan wives were legally obliged to be obedient to their husbands, but the article on obedience has been left

[21] According to Abdel Hameed Galal, this was arranged in the 'decree of the Minister of Justice No.1087 for the year 2000 on places for seeing young Child' (Galal 2011: p. 4), see also Sonneveld and Lindbekk (2015).

out of the new family law. However, the wife can still lose her right to maintenance if she 'has been ordered to return to the conjugal home and has refused' (art. 195, translation: HREA 2004). This means that some connection between maintenance and obedience remains. Mir-Hosseini has described strategies in Moroccan courts before the reform of the *Moudawanah* in 2004 with regard to maintenance and obedience, which are similar to the Egyptian case. She observed that the court is often used as a kind of arena to negotiate the conditions of divorce. Most cases are withdrawn or abandoned before a ruling is issued because the desired result is already obtained (Mir-Hosseini 2000: p. 46–47).

In Morocco, marital property of the spouses remains separated at the moment of marriage: 'All possessions the wife brings with her to the marriage including furniture and accompanying items are her property [...]' (article 34 new Moudawwana. Translation: HREA 2004: p. 13). In this article, the separation of property is framed as a right of the wife, her personal property remaining her own. It is also possible to include another division in an addition to the marriage contract. If no such addition is made, it is still possible to divide property accumulated during the marriage based on the contributions of the spouses (art. 49 new Moudawana). According to Jordens-Cotran, this article has been introduced in the new *Moudawana* in 2004, coming from customary law in some parts of Morocco, to have both partners share in the increase of value of the marital property during the marriage (Jordens-Cotran 2007: p. 802–803). Engelcke sees this article, supported by both Islamist and women's rights groups, as a reflection of middle-class interests in the new law (Engelcke 2014).

In the 2004 reform process, new forms of divorce were introduced while older forms are still present, meaning that there is a large and complicated array of options. Before 2004, the possibilities for divorce were more or less similar to Egypt consisting of *talaq*; *khulʿ*—which is an out-of-court procedure in Morocco—and *tatliq*, fault-based judicial divorce on grounds such as non-payment of maintenance, long-term absence from the conjugal home or harm. As in Egypt, it is very difficult to prove harm, unless there is evidence of severe physical damage. In Mir-Hosseini's research (done in the 1980s), court-based divorce was an exception, most divorces occurred through *khulʿ* or *talaq*. Court cases can take years, and expensive specialist help in the form of lawyers is important in order to win a case. Moreover, the public discussion of a private conflict is in most cases a last resort. According to Mir-Hosseini, the lower classes are therefore overrepresented in the courts, where most of the cases are filed by women, because for them the financial interests at stake can be even more important than reputation (Mir-Hosseini 2000: p. 84–114).

Since 1993, *talaq* has been restricted. Before the *talaq* could be effective, the husband needed permission from a judge. The judge would determine the amount of *mut`a*, or compensation, that needed to be paid by the husband. The amount was not only based on the financial capacity of the husband and the needs of the wife but also on the motive for the *talaq*. This meant that an extra fault factor was introduced. This compensation needed to be deposited at the court or paid to the wife before the actual *talaq* could take place in front of two *`udul* (specialised notaries). However, an unsuspected effect of these measures to restrict *talaq* was the growth of the number of *khul`* cases. According to Jordens-Cotran, this could be explained by husbands mistreating their wives, pressuring them to sign a *khul`* divorce and giving up their financial rights (Jordens-Cotran 2007: p. 310–322).

Since 2004, the possibilities for *talaq* have been even further restricted. Men now only have 30 days to deposit all financial entitlements of their wife and children, or their request will be cancelled. Moreover, judges need to summon both spouses for a reconciliation attempt. If children are born from the marriage, two attempts must be made. If the husband is not present at this attempt, the procedure will be cancelled. However, this does not mean that the wife can stop the *talaq*. Also, even though husbands can still decide to take their wives back during the *`idda*, wives no longer need to submit to this, as they can easily start a *chiqaq* procedure (see below) (Jordens-Cotran 2007: p. 313, 333–334).

Apart from restricting *talaq*, two new forms of divorce have been introduced in 2004. The first is divorce by mutual consent, with or without conditions (article 114). The second new form of divorce is the *chiqaq* procedure, which can be started by the husband, the wife or both spouses together. In this procedure, the spouses in fact do not ask for divorce directly, but come to court to ask the judge to 'settle a dispute that risks to breakdown their marriage' (translation: HREA 2004: art 94). If the court does not succeed in reconciling the spouses, it will grant a divorce. Like in *talaq*, wives keep all their financial entitlements, and the *mut`a* is determined based on the fault each party has to the conflict. In theory, this could also mean that the wife pays *mut`a* to the husband. The judge cannot refuse the divorce. According to Jordens-Cotran, the introduction of the *chiqaq* procedure means that women and men in Morocco now have equal access to divorce. Furthermore, the two new forms of divorce, divorce by mutual consent and *chiqaq* divorce, in theory make *khul`* or *tatliq* divorce redundant (Jordens-Cotran 2007: p. 335, 360).

This theory seems to be confirmed in practice. According to LDDF numbers for 2006, two years after the introduction of *chiqaq*, there have been 26,023 applications for judicial divorce, 20,223 by women and no less than 5800 by men (Ligue Democratique des Droits des Femmes 2007: p. 3–4). One of the possible explanations for men using *chiqaq* procedures is that men did not need to deposit the financial entitlements of their wife and children at the court before the court would grant the divorce, unlike in case of *talaq*. Men could therefore use the *chiqaq* procedure as a 'cheap' way to divorce; they would get their divorce and then fail to pay. However, the Moroccan Ministry of Justice seems to have cut off this option by issuing a directive approving the Casablanca courts practice of insisting that husbands first deposit their wives' financial rights before granting both registration of *talaq* and judicial divorce.[22] Still, it could be plausible that *chiqaq* is becoming the 'standard' way to divorce for both men and women. Something similar has happened in Syria, where both men and women almost always divorce by way of *chiqaq*, even though other ways are possible (Carlisle 2007).

Before 2004, recognition of a foreign divorce was hardly possible in Morocco, except when Moroccan law had been applied by the foreign judge. Therefore, in the past, many transnational divorcees living in the Netherlands had to divorce twice if they wanted the divorce to be valid in both countries, once in the Netherlands and once in Morocco (in the case of *tatliq*) or at the consulate (in the case of *talaq* or *khul`*). According to Jordens-Cotran, some women started civil procedures in the Netherlands

[22] Results from unpublished research project by Jessica Carlisle, 2007–2008.

to force their husbands to comply with a *talaq* or *khul`* procedure at the Moroccan consulate. For Moroccan men, who can marry more than one wife, and who before 2003 had easy access to *talaq* in Morocco, this tended to be less of a problem. However, there have also been procedures initiated by Moroccan men who did not want to marry polygamously and who tried to force their wives to cooperate with a *khul`* divorce (Jordens-Cotran 2007: p. 437). Since 2004, it has become easier to get a foreign divorce recognised in Morocco, if certain conditions are met, such as an obligatory attempt by the court to reconcile the couple (Jordens-Cotran 2007: p. 435).

After divorce, the marital obligation of the husband to provide maintenance for the wife, including accommodation, remains intact during the *`idda*, the waiting period after a divorce and remains to be linked to obedience.[23] After this period has passed, the wife no longer has rights to maintenance from her former husband. Furthermore, a mother can be entitled to compensation for nursing and bringing up the children from their father, as she cannot support herself properly while taking care of the children (Jordens-Cotran 2007: p. 734). Apart from the right to maintenance, a divorced woman also has a right to a *mut`a*, or compensation for the divorce, and—if agreed on in the marriage contract—the deferred *mahr*. Although the *mut`a* is formally a kind of compensation for the damages done to the wife for being divorced by her husband, it is now also paid by husbands when women initiate a no-fault *chiqaq* procedure. According to Jordens-Cotran, this unlinking of the *mut`a* and fault, accompanied by developments in Moroccan legal practice would justify the qualification of the *mut`a* as a form of alimony or maintenance (Jordens-Cotran 2007: p. 737).

With regard to child care after divorce, mothers have the first right to *hadana*, or daily care and residence. After divorce, *hadana* is awarded 'first to the mother, then to the father, then to the maternal grandmother of the child' (article 171). During marriage, both parents have *hadana* over their children. *Hadana* used to end at age 15 for girls and age 12 for boys, after which the child could choose residence with one of the par-

[23] The *`idda* is meant to clarify the paternity of children. During this period, women cannot remarry. In principle, it will last three menstrual cycles or, if the woman is pregnant, until the child has been born, with a maximum of one year after the divorce.

ents or another relative (article 102 old *Moudawana*, 1993). Since 2004, mothers keep *hadana* of their children until the age of legal majority (18) for both boys and girls, but from the age of 15, the child can choose residence with either parent (article 166 new *Moudawana*). Since the introduction of the new *Moudawana*, the courts can also take the best interest of the child into consideration for custody or guardianship, introducing possibilities for litigation on the basis of different interpretations of the best interests of the child. Zoglin (2009) even considers the introduction of this concept in custody decisions to be one of the major innovations of this new family code (Zoglin 2009: p. 974). One often-debated provision has not been removed. If the mother remarries, she will lose *hadana* of children aged seven or older to their father, unless she also has *wilaya* over her children, or unless the transfer of *hadana* to the father is harmful for the child. The father has to claim *hadana* within one year after he has knowledge of the marriage (articles 174–176 new *Moudawana*).

Wilaya (translated by HREA as tutorship) is the right of the father, both during and after marriage. As article 236 states: 'By law, the father is the tutor of his children unless he is disqualified by judicial order. The mother may manage urgent affairs of her children in the event the father is prevented from doing so.' Legal tutorship entails the management of the child's affairs. This means that, generally speaking, only the father can make decisions on issues such as medical treatment or education. In Morocco, a father has a right to contact with the child, but 'the ward always spends the night at the custodian's house unless the judge decides otherwise' (art. 169 new Moudawana. Translation: HREA 2004). Fathers are second in line for *hadana* and mothers for *wilaya*. Remarriage has no effect on *wilaya*.

A father's duty to provide maintenance for his children continues after divorce. Legally, the mother is only obliged to provide for the children in case the father has no capacity to pay, or if she has renounced her rights to child maintenance in a *khulʿ* procedure.[24] The appropriate amounts of maintenance are determined by the court. Moreover, after divorce, a mother can be entitled to compensation from the father for nursing and

[24] However, since the new *Mudawwana* of 2004, women can easily choose another divorce form in which they do not need to renounce maintenance.

bringing up the children, as she cannot support herself properly while taking care of the children, which can be seen as a form of maintenance (Jordens-Cotran 2007: p. 734). In Morocco, the payment of maintenance for both spouses and children is an important matter. According to several Dutch-Moroccan and Moroccan lawyers I interviewed, in legal practice a father is not easily considered as having no capacity to maintain his children. Moreover, due to differences in standards of living between the Netherlands and Morocco, fathers living in the Netherlands, even those on Dutch social security, will certainly not be considered as not having any capacity to pay maintenance in a Moroccan court case. The non-payment of maintenance is actually a criminal offence, with sanctions of a fine or even up to 12 months of imprisonment (Jordens-Cotran 2007: p. 708–709, p. 721). As one Dutch-Moroccan lawyer said: 'In Morocco, not paying maintenance is *crime number one*', and taken very seriously.[25] In transnational cases where men live outside of Morocco, women who should have been receiving maintenance for their children can also turn to the court to have their children's father registered at customs. When entering or leaving Morocco, fathers will be detained until they have paid the arrears.

The Netherlands

In the Netherlands, a marriage certificate is the official document written to document the marriage at the civil registry. However, while couples receive a *trouwboekje* or marriage booklet, they do not automatically obtain a copy of the marriage certificate like in Morocco or Egypt. It is not possible to put any stipulations in the 'marriage contract' itself, but it is possible to sign a prenuptial contract in addition to the marriage regarding the division of property and financial resources during the marriage, called *huwelijkse voorwaarden* or conditions of marriage. These contracts need to be made and signed by a notary before the marriage, and it can be quite expensive in more complicated cases.[26] In 2009, in

[25] Interview, November 2011. English in original.

[26] Based on a basic comparison of notaries' websites, I estimate that the costs range from around 400–500 euro for the cheapest option up to 1000–1500 euro in more complicated cases. It is also

about one out of four marriages a prenuptial arrangement was made.[27] There are several kinds of prenuptial agreements possible. In 2009, almost 30 % of agreements were based on the principle of *koude uitsluiting*, or 'cold exclusion', meaning that the property of both spouses remains completely separated.[28] All other agreements have some kind of mix between community and private property, generally in the form of a *verrekenbeding*. This means that the property remains separated, but that the spouses equally share their income (Schols and Hoens 2012).

In the Netherlands, during marriage, both spouses owe each other '[…] faithfulness, aid and assistance. They are obliged to provide each other with the necessary [means of living]' (BW.01.81). Accompanied by the default system of communal property, this means that, legally, all assets and income are taken to be shared. Although this norm of spouses maintaining each other seems to be gender neutral, practices are highly gendered. According to CBS research based on the period 1990–1999, in 69 % of families, the husband provided over 60 % of the family income, in 23 % both spouses provided more or less equally and in only 8 % the wife provided more than 60 % of the income (Bouman 2004b: p. 21).

In the Netherlands, at the moment of marriage, all property and debts of both spouses become communal property, unless the couple agrees on writing *huwelijkse voorwaarden* or a prenuptial contract beforehand.[29] This is related to a view of marriage as an economic unit, in which both partners share profit and loss, regardless of who performs economic or household tasks. This view is based on a male-provider female homemaker model, meaning that the wife is compensated for her caring and household work by sharing in the income and property accumulated by the husband. However, the Dutch system of the communal property can

---

possible to make such a contract later, during the marriage, but that requires a more complicated and costly court procedure.

[27] These percentages include so-called *geregistreerd partnerschap*, the registered partnership, which is equal to marriage with regard to property.

[28] This seems to be a recent trend. Until 2003, the percentage was going down, with a low point of only 11 %, while in the past, the number of 'cold exclusion' arrangements was far larger, around 70 % in 1970. After 2003, the number of 'cold exclusions' went up sharply again. The researchers note that part of the difference may be related to a broadening of the definition of 'cold exclusion' (Schols and Hoens 2012).

[29] As arranged in art. 1:93–113 BW.

have severe consequences if, for example, during the marriage the business of one of the spouses becomes bankrupt. The debts of the business will then be recovered from the communal property, affecting both spouses. Together with large welfare differences between the spouses, one of the spouses owning a business is one of the main reasons for a prenuptial agreement (Mourik and Nuytinck 2006; Mourik and Burgerhart 2005).

Since 1971, no-fault divorce on the ground of *duurzame ontwrichting* or the permanent breakdown of a marriage is the only way to divorce in the Netherlands. Spouses can petition the court for divorce individually or make a joint application. Generally, a marriage is *duurzaam ontwricht* if one of the partners claims it to be so. Resistance to the divorce is therefore hardly ever successful; although spouses do have the right to appeal, it is, in practice, not possible to stop the divorce. During the divorce process, the assistance of a lawyer is obligatory. At the moment of research, there were several social services available to direct people to lawyers, and litigants with a low income could get government support for the costs of a lawyer.[30]

For transnational couples, a divorce can be a more complicated affair. In one and the same divorce, there can be differences between the law applicable to child custody, division of property, maintenance, and the divorce itself. Before 2012, there were two possible exceptions in which foreign family law can be applicable: first of all, in cases in which both partners have the same foreign nationality *and* if both parties explicitly choose so, and secondly, in cases in which both parties shared the same foreign nationality and did *not* choose for Dutch law. If the applicable law was disputed during the process, the judge decided based on the 'effective' (in case of dual nationality) or 'real' (in case of one nationality) nationality of the partners, looking, for example, at factors like the duration of residency, the command of the language, an application for Dutch citizenship or the wish to do so (Jordens-Cotran 2007: p. 409–415). Since January 2012, this has changed. Dutch law is now automatically applicable unless *both* spouses choose to apply foreign family law or if the other spouse does not object to the choice of law. In case of disagreement,

[30] Since 2009, a series of budget cuts has limited the possibilities for government-sponsored legal aid.

foreign family law will be applied if one of the spouses chooses so *and* if *both* partners have a 'real social connection' to the country of their shared foreign nationality (art. 10: 56 BW). This procedure is mostly relevant for Dutch-Moroccan migration marriages, in which the couple generally shares Moroccan nationality, due to the fact that it his nearly impossible to lose Moroccan nationality. Due to the significant differences between Dutch and Moroccan family law with regard to spousal maintenance, strategic choices can be possible, which privilege one partner over the other. The applicable law can thus become part of the conflict during the divorce process.

The implications of this situation are gendered, especially before 2004 (see also Van Den Eeckhout 2003). Dutch judges are generally reluctant to grant men the right to *talaq* in a Dutch court. Because this kind of divorce is only possible for men, it is not considered to be in accordance with the principles of equal treatment of men and women.[31] However, judges seem to have no problems with issuing a *tatliq* divorce, for example based on the non-payment of maintenance, also a highly gendered ground because only men need to pay maintenance (Jordens-Cotran 2007: p. 420–424). In practice, this meant that Moroccan women in the Netherlands had more options to divorce than Moroccan men. Under certain conditions, women could choose between Moroccan and Dutch family law whereas, according to Jordens-Cotran, no Dutch judge has ever granted a Moroccan man a divorce based on Moroccan family law (Jordens-Cotran 2007: p. 428). In one case, the application for divorce by a Moroccan man was actually refused, because Moroccan law was applicable but the Dutch judge could not accept a *talaq*. A divorce by *talaq* in Morocco would also not be acknowledged, meaning that this man simply could not legally divorce in the Netherlands. Eventually the Supreme Court of the Netherlands decided that the Dutch judge should have applied Dutch law to the divorce if a divorce based on Moroccan law was not possible, instead of simply refusing the divorce (see also Jordens-Cotran 2007: p. 428).[32] However, this has changed with the introduction

---

[31] The form of the *talaq* (which takes place by the declaration of the husband, even if a judge is involved) is another, more formal, reason for its non-recognition.

[32] Hoge Raad (HR), 9 December 2001, ECLI:NL:PHR:2001:AD4011.

of the *chiqaq* divorce, which is roughly similar to the Dutch ground of *duurzame ontwrichting*, and therefore does not contradict Dutch public policy.[33] For Egyptian men in the Netherlands, similar problems can still occur, as in Egypt *talaq* is the only way men can divorce.

Another option for transnational couples is the recognition of foreign (Egyptian or Moroccan) divorces in the Netherlands. *Tatliq* divorces are generally accepted without any problems, but in case of out-of-court divorces such as *khul`* or *talaq*, certain conditions have to be met.[34] Again, these have to do with issues of equal treatment of men and women. The most important condition is proof of the consent of the wife.[35] This can be proven either by the fact that the wife is the one to register the divorce or, if a man wants to register the divorce, by a declaration of approval by the wife or, for example, the fact that she has married again. Again, this means that it is far easier for Moroccan and Egyptian women than Moroccan and Egyptian men to have a foreign divorce recognised, whether it is through *tatliq*, *talaq*, or *khul`*. In practice, this can be of great importance for Moroccan or Egyptian men who want to become Dutch by naturalisation, as their application will be rejected if they are 'polygamous' because the *talaq* of an earlier wife is not recognised (Jordens-Cotran 2007: p. 465–467; see also Van Den Eeckhout 2003).[36]

I argue that these gendered limitations to the application or recognition of Islamic family law in the Netherlands need to be seen in the light of the general discourse in the Netherlands that Islamic family law is bad for women and therefore incompatible with Dutch public policy, as has been described in Chapter 2. This effort to 'protect' women from Islamic countries from gender inequality in Islamic family law actually produces gender inequality in another way, making it more difficult for men than

[33] For an example in which the husband successfully applied for a divorce on the ground of *chiqaq*: Rechtbank Alkmaar, 26 January 2006, ECLI:NL:RBALK:2006:AV0789.

[34] BW10:57. Before 2012, this was arranged in article 3 Wet conflictenrecht inzake ontbinding huwelijk en scheiding van tafel en bed (3 WCE).

[35] This was, for example, the case when the marriage of an Egyptian man, married to a Dutch woman, was annulled after ten years because the husband could not prove sufficiently that his ex-wife, whom he divorced in the late 1980s, had agreed or resigned to the divorce: HR 21 December 2007, ECLI:NL:HR:2007:BB8076.

[36] See for more information on recognition of Moroccan divorces in the Netherlands, Kruiniger (2015).

for women to obtain a divorce in the Netherlands. Moreover, it is not always true that the application of foreign law based on Islamic law is disadvantageous for women. In some disputes on financial matters, for example, women ask for Moroccan family law to be applied because it brings them more financial rewards.

After divorce, this obligation of both spouses to maintain each other and their children continues, based on the *lotsverbondenheid* or solidarity created by the marriage. The amount of maintenance that needs to be paid is based on both the need of the one partner and the capacity to pay of the other partner. It can be determined by the court or arranged by the partners themselves if they prefer. The obligation to pay spousal maintenance lasts 12 years or, if the marriage lasted less than five years and no children were born, as long as the marriage lasted.[37] The amount is corrected for inflation each year and can be altered if needs or ability to pay changes. The obligation of maintenance ends if the receiving partner remarries or cohabits with a new partner. Even though the Dutch system of no-fault divorce makes fault-based moral claims irrelevant, there are some moral claims possible in maintenance cases. As maintenance is based on the continuing solidarity of the spouses after marriage, this solidarity can, in rare cases, be breached, for example, when the spouse receiving maintenance abuses or mistreats the paying ex-partner.[38]

Because, legally, maintenance of children takes priority over maintenance between spouses, spousal maintenance is less common than child maintenance (Vlaardingerbroek et al. 2011: p. 166, 187). In 2007, only in one out of five divorces the husband needed to pay spousal maintenance to the wife, whereas in less than 1 % of the divorces in 2007, the wife paid maintenance to her former husband (Sprangers and Steenbrink 2008: p. 17). Moreover, as the amount of spousal maintenance awarded is in half of the cases less than 600 euro per month, many divorced women who have no or only a limited income of their own need to apply for

---

[37] This period of 12 years has become the subject of much public debate. Since 2012, a new bill has been pending in parliament, limiting the maintenance period to a maximum of five years, based on 'important changes in the relationships between men and women'. *Kamerstukken II* 2011/12, 33 311, nr. 3, p. 1–2.

[38] See for an example in which the wife took the children abroad without the consent of the maintenance-paying father, Hof Leeuwarden, 26 May 2011, ECLI:NL:GHARN:2011:BQ7255.

social security or find a job. The maintenance they receive for themselves or their children will then be deducted from any social security payments, thus often making no difference in their financial situation. According to Bouman, the financial effects of divorce are generally different for men and women. The financial situation of men generally improves, especially if the children stay with the mother, whereas the financial situation of women generally deteriorates after divorce, even when taking into account that men generally need to pay (child) maintenance (Bouman 2004a, b, Verstappen 2011).

After a divorce, the communal property needs to be divided between the spouses. If no prenuptial agreement has been made, all property, including debts, should be shared equally. If prenuptial agreements have been made, there may still be a need to divide property, based on the type of agreement. The spouses are free to divide the property between them as they wish, or they can, in cases of conflict, ask a judge to decide about the division (Mourik and Nuytinck 2006; Mourik and Burgerhart 2005; Vlaardingerbroek et al. 2011). In transnational divorces, a Dutch judge needs to decide whether Dutch or Moroccan/Egyptian law is applicable to the division of property. This has been arranged in the *Hague Convention on the Law Applicable to Matrimonial Property Regimes*, article 4, and can be a rather complicated affair, even for lawyers and judges. Main factors taken into account are the shared nationality of the spouses (if any) and the first communal country of residence after the marriage (if any).[39] As nationality and country of residence are not always stable or clear in transnational marriages, this can lead to legally complicated situations, where part of the property accumulated in the marriage is divided according to Dutch law and another part following Moroccan or Egyptian law. However, if a couple has made an explicit choice in a prenuptial arrangement or marriage contract regarding the legal system they want to be applicable to the property this choice takes precedence (Jordens-Cotran 2007: p.801–806).

In the Netherlands, both the prompt and the deferred *mahr* from Moroccan and Egyptian marriage contracts can cause problems at the

[39] Morocco, the Netherlands, and Egypt are all on the list of *nationaliteitslanden*, article 4, lid 2 sub a, Haags Huwelijksvermogensverdrag 1978. See alsoJordens-Cotran (2007: p.808).

moment of divorce. Sometimes the deferred *mahr* is interpreted as a form of maintenance after divorce (Rutten 2011). If the wife has her own property or source of income, the judge may therefore decide not to grant the deferred *mahr* to her because she is not in need of financial assistance or because the *mahr* agreed upon overburdens the husband's capacity to pay.[40] The prompt *mahr*, and other marriage gifts such as the *shabka*, which are paid at the moment of marriage, can cause other legal problems during a divorce in the Netherlands. If Dutch law is applicable, and the spouses have not arranged *huwelijkse voorwaarden*, all property will be considered community property and will need to be divided after divorce. This can mean that the wife needs to return half of the gifts she received at marriage to her husband, even though these gifts are socially considered to be her private property.[41]

Generally, after divorce, children live with one of their parents, mostly the mother, with the father paying his share of the child maintenance to the mother. The right to maintenance for children is determined by two factors, the need of the child and the financial capacity of both parents (art. 1.397 BW). The need of the children is also partly determined by the financial circumstances of the parents during the marriage, the general principle being that the child should keep the same standard of living as it was used to during the marriage. In legal practice, a quite detailed and complicated system has been developed by judges to calculate the appropriate amounts of child maintenance taking these factors into account, the so-called *tremanormen* (for an elaborate discussion see: Dijksterhuis 2008).[42] However, parents are not obliged to have a judge calculate the appropriate amount; they are free to negotiate among themselves (see also Jonker 2011). For transnational marriages, the children's country of

---

[40] See for an example with a Dutch-Egyptian couple: Hof 's-Gravenhage, 17 December 2008, *ECLI:NL:HR:2009:BG4822*. See for an Iraqi-Dutch case in which the *mahr* was awarded as maintenance, but without looking at need or means Rechtbank Utrecht, 30 January 2009, ECLI:NL:RBUTR:2008:BC2923.

[41] See for two Dutch-Turkish examples in which the bridal gift consisted of jewellery, Hof 's-Gravenhage, 15 November 2006, ECLI:NL:GHSGR:2006:AZ2935and Hof 's-Gravenhage, 19 April 2006, ECLI:NL:GHSGR:2006:AY5780. Remarkably, in both cases, the disputed jewellery was missing and both wives accused the husbands of stealing it during the divorce process.

[42] The system has been formalised to such an extent that there are apps available to calculate the amount of maintenance.

habitual residence is decisive in determining the applicable law on child maintenance, which means a Dutch judge would apply Moroccan law or Egyptian law when the children are resident in Morocco or Egypt, respectively (Jordens-Cotran 2007: p. 749–752). If maintenance is not paid as determined by the court, the receiving partner (e.g. the mother) can call on the LBIO, the *Landelijk Bureau Inning Onderhoudsbijdragen*. This Dutch agency will help claim arrears in child maintenance payments and, since 2009, also in spousal maintenance payments. The LBIO has quite far-reaching possibilities to recover the arrears, even abroad.

Nationality and Residence

The nationality of a country does not only represent a certain bond with a country or its citizens, but also entails certain rights and obligations such as the right to access and residence or to hold property and the obligation to do military service (de Hart 2012: p. 18–22). Nationality can be also highly relevant in (transnational) divorce as an important factor in determining the applicable family law. The Netherlands, Egypt, and Morocco all have a nationality system based on *ius sanguinis*, meaning that nationality is passed on to children by their parents, even when they live abroad.[43]

Because of the aforementioned practical implications, it can be very useful for partners in a transnational marriage to acquire the nationality of the country they live in. In Morocco, a Dutch woman married to a Moroccan man can easily acquire Moroccan nationality if she has lived for at least five (before 2007, two) years in Morocco, together with her husband. Dutch men married to Moroccan women cannot obtain Moroccan nationality through their marriage.[44] In the Netherlands, for-

[43] This happens on the condition that there is a legal relationship between the parents and the child. If there is no marriage between the parents, a Moroccan or Egyptian father generally cannot pass on his nationality. A Dutch unmarried father needs to acknowledge his child, preferably before birth (see for an elaborate discussion, Kulk 2013).

[44] They can, however, follow the 'normal' naturalisation procedure, not based on the marriage. Requirements include five years of residence, knowledge of Arabic and proof of being able to keep oneself (Kulk 2013: p. 140–141).

eigners married to a Dutch national can acquire Dutch nationality after three years of marriage, but they will need to pass a citizenship test (see: van Oers 2013). The foreign wife of an Egyptian national can request Egyptian nationality, but the marriage needs to last for another two years after the application; only after those two years, Egyptian nationality will be granted. Foreign husbands of Egyptian wives cannot obtain Egyptian nationality through their marriage (Kulk 2013: p. 137–138).[45]

Acquiring new nationalities can also have consequences for the 'old' nationalities. In principle, Dutch nationals lose their nationality if they acquire another. Because of the practical, emotional, and even financial consequence of losing one's primary nationality, this could be an obstacle in acquiring a new one. Since 2003, people acquiring the nationality of their (foreign) spouse are exempted from this rule. On the other hand, foreigners married to a Dutch national are exempted from the requirement to renounce their own nationality when acquiring Dutch nationality (de Hart 2012: p. 57).

Having the nationality of the country of residence automatically enables the foreign partner to remain there after divorce. However, if the foreign partner did not acquire the nationality, for whatever reason, residence can become an issue after divorce. For Moroccan and Egyptian spouses, Dutch residency can give access to a society with a higher level of prosperity and the social security provisions of a welfare state. On a more personal level, it can be difficult to leave a country where one has lived for a prolonged period of time and involuntary return migration can pose financial as well as social difficulties. The presence of children living with the ex-husband or wife can be another important reason for prolonged residence. In the Netherlands, until 2012, spouses in transnational marriages could obtain an independent residence permit after three years of marriage to a Dutch national.[46] Until that time, the residence permit is dependent on the marriage, which means the foreign partner must leave the country in case of divorce. Exceptions can sometimes be made in

[45] Requirements for normal naturalisation include ten years of continuous residence in Egypt, knowledge of Arabic, and being able to keep oneself. See for a more detailed discussion of requirements, Kulk (2013: p. 138)

[46] This term has been changed to five years in 2012. However, all interviews in this study were conducted before this reform.

case of special circumstances, such as domestic violence, or the care or contact with Dutch children from the marriage or of the foreign children with a Dutch parent. According to de Hart, this link between marriage or child contact and residence changes the Dutch partner into a kind of gatekeeper, a powerful but ambiguous position. This position can also have negative consequences, such as creating insecurity as to whether the former spouse will be able to stay in the Netherlands after divorce to take part in child care (de Hart 2002: p. 101–103). In Egypt, foreign divorcees of Egyptian men can also get temporary residence permits when children are under their custody.[47]

Migration law and nationality law thus restrict the possibilities for transnational couples to choose their country of residence. At the moment of divorce, dependent residency can mean that the foreign spouses may need to leave the country as well as the marriage. Dutch spouses in transnational marriage have easier mobility and access to Morocco or Egypt than Egyptians and Moroccans to the Netherlands. Interactions between legal systems also influence the relative power positions of spouses and sometimes provide spouses with possibilities for strategic action, using so-called forum shopping. The question remains how and why the spouses in this research, divorced from transnational Dutch-Moroccan and Dutch-Egyptian marriages, actually used the different family law systems in their divorce.

Conclusions

This chapter discussed the legal context in which transnational divorces take place. In all three countries, family law is and has been the subject of fierce social and political debate and conflict. As a result, family laws have changed over time, which means that the transnational couples in this research have divorced in different legal contexts.

Although the Dutch, Egyptian, and Moroccan legal systems at first sight seem very different, especially with regard to gender, all three fam-

[47] http://www.moiegypt.gov.eg/English/Departments+Sites/Immegration/ForignersServices/EkametAlAganeb/residence5/ accessed November 2011.

ily law systems can be seen as based on similar underlying notions of a gendered division of labour between the spouses, in which the husband (mainly) provides the means of living and the wife (mainly) provides care work. However, the three family law systems have each used different mechanisms to arrange for the upkeep of the partner doing the care work during marriage and after divorce. In Morocco and Egypt, the financial position of women and mothers is protected by separating the marital property, a prompt and deferred *mahr* and an obligation for the husband to provide for the family, regardless of the wife's means. The Dutch legal system found a solution in a system of communal property and prolonged spousal maintenance after divorce. With regard to children, Dutch laws use strictly gender-neutral wording and make the child welfare discourse central, thus creating formal equality, while Morocco and Egypt have explicitly gendered laws. However, in all three countries, actual practice means that it is mostly mothers who provide day-to-day care, while fathers have limited contact arrangements and have the power to take, or participate in, major decisions. A focus on formal gender equality, instead of substantive equality, overlooks this important similarity between the three countries. Thus, the legal systems of all three countries are based on a similar image of the family, but the Netherlands, on the one hand, and Morocco and Egypt, on the other hand, have chosen different or even contradictory solutions to protect wives and mothers from the financial consequences of divorce.

Specific for transnational couples is the interaction of family law systems through private international law and the influence of nationality and migration law. First of all, the interaction of legal systems means that the legal status of a transnational marriage or divorce is not automatically the same in both countries. If spouses in a transnational marriage aim for recognition of their marriage or divorce in two legal systems, knowledgeable and sometimes expensive action is required, implying that elements of social class are relevant. The interactions of legal systems have different consequences for spouses, based on gender and nationality. As the example of the recognition of *talaq* divorces demonstrates, it can be more difficult for men to get their Egyptian or Moroccan divorce registered in the Netherlands then for women, in some cases even making it impossible for Egyptian or Moroccan men (before 2004) to divorce in the Netherlands at all. The recognition of Dutch divorces in Egypt or Morocco, especially before 2004, is more of an issue for Moroccan or Egyptian women, especially if they aim to remarry.

Migration law and nationality law restrict the possibilities for transnational couples to choose their country of residence. At the moment of divorce, dependent residency can mean that the foreign spouses may need to leave the country as well as the marriage. Dutch spouses in transnational marriage have easier mobility and access to Morocco or Egypt than Egyptians and Moroccans to the Netherlands. Interactions between legal systems also influence the relative power positions of spouses and sometimes provide spouses with possibilities for strategic action, using so-called forum shopping.

References

Al-Sharmani, Mulki. 2008. Recent Reforms in Personal Status Laws and Women's Empowerment. In *Family Courts in Egypt*. Cairo: The American University in Cairo Social Research Center.

Berger, Maurits S 2005. *Sharia and Public Policy in Egyptian Family Law*. Amsterdam: UvA.

Berger, Maurits S., and Nadia Sonneveld. 2006. Sharia en nationaal recht in Egypte. In *Sharia en nationaal recht in twaalf moslimslanden*, eds. J.M. Otto, A.J. Dekker, and L.J. van Soest-Zuurberg, 19–40. Amsterdam: Amsterdam University Press.

Bernard-Maugiron, Nathalie, and Baudouin Dupret. 2008. Breaking up the Family: Divorce in Egyptian Law and Practice. *Journal of Women of the Middle East and the Islamic World* 6: 52–74.

Bouman, Louis. 1992. *Huwelijksvoorwaarden in het islamitisch huwelijksrecht van Marokko*. In *Van de doctrine tot de praktijk*. Leiden: Doctoraalscriptie Arabische taal- en letterkunde.

Bouman, Anne Marthe. 2004a. Financiële gevolgen van echtscheiding op de lange termijn. *Bevolkingstrends* 4: 85–89.

———. 2004b. Financiële gevolgen van echtscheiding voor man en vrouw. *Bevolkingstrends* 2: 19–23.

Buskens, Léon. 2003. Recent Debates on Family Law Reform in Morocco: Islamic Law as Politics in an Emerging Public Sphere. *Islamic Law and Society* 10(1): 70–131.

Carlisle, Jessica. 2007. Mother Love: A Forced Divorce in Damascus. *Anthropology of the Middle East* 2(1): 92–105.

Cuno, Kenneth M. 2009. Disobedient Wives and Neglectful Husbands. Marital relations and the first Phase of Family Law Reform in Egypt. In *Family, Gender, and Law in a Globalizing Middle East and South Asia*. Syracuse, New York: Syracuse University Press.

de Hart, Betty. 2002. Slachtoffers of 'gatekeepers': zwarte, migranten-en vluchtelingenvrouwen en Nederlandse vrouwen met een buitenlandse partner in het familierecht. In *Bundel VN-Vrouwenverdrag*, ed. R. Holtmaat, 95–106. Den Haag: E-Quality.

———. 2012. *Een tweede paspoort: Dubbele nationaliteit in de Verenigde Staten, Duitsland en Nederland*. Amsterdam: Amsterdam University Press.

Dijksterhuis, Bregje Monique. 2008. *Rechters normeren de alimentatiehoogte : een empirisch onderzoek naar rechterlijke samenwerking in de Werkgroep Alimentatienormen (1975–2007)*. Amsterdam: Leiden University Press.

El-Alami, Dawoud S. 1994. Law no. 100 of 1985. Amending Certain Provisions of Egypt's Personal Status Laws. *Islamic Law and Society* 1: 116–136.

Engelcke, Dörthe. 2014. Processes of Family Law Reform: Legal and Societal Change and Continuity in Morocco and Jordan. PhD thesis: University of Oxford

Forder, C.J. 2002. Het mensenrechtelijke hart van het familierecht: overzicht van de ontwikkelingen 1995–2002 (Deel 1). *NJCM bulletin* 27(8): 992–1011.

Forder, C.J 2003. Titel: Het mensenrechtelijke hart van het familierecht: overzicht van de ontwikkelingen 1995–2002 (Deel II). *NJCM bulletin* 28(1): 19–36.

Galal, Abdel Hameed. 2011. Child Custody in Egypt. *Lex arabiae. Legal News of the Gulf* 15(3): 2–5.

Hatem, Mervat F. 2004. The Nineteenth Century Discursive Roots of the Continuing Debate on the Social-Sexual Contract in Today's Egypt. *Hawwa* 2(1): 64–88.

HREA. 2004. *The Moroccan Family Code (Moudawana) of February 5, 2004. An unofficial translation of the original Arabic text.*

Human Rights Watch. 2004. Divorced from Justice: Women's Unequal Access to Divorce in Egypt. *Human Rights Watch* 16: 8.

Jansen, Willy. 1997. Gouden huwelijksgaven. Symbolen van liefde en strijd. In *Het geschenk. Over de verschillende betekenissen van geven*, ed. Aafke Komter, 207–221. Amsterdam: Amsterdam University press.

———. 2005. Divorce and Custody: Contemporary Pratices. In *Encyclopedia of Women & Islamic Cultures*, ed. Suad Joseph, 98–100. Leiden: Brill.

Jonker, Merel. 2011. Nieuwe wegen in het kinderalimentatierecht. In *Actuele ontwikkelingen in het familierecht. Vijfde UCERF symposium*, eds. Katharina Boele-Woelki, Brigitte Chin-A-Fat, Merel Jonker, Leo Hendriks, Pieter Boeles, Machteld Vonk, and Ted de Boer. Nijmegen: Ars Aequi Libri.

Jordens-Cotran, Leila. 2007. *Nieuw Marokkaans Familierecht en Nederlands IPR*. Den Haag: SDU Uitgevers.

Kruiniger, Pauline. 2015. *Islamic Divorces in Europe: Bridging the Gap between European and Islamic Legal Orders*. Den Haag: Eleven International Publishing.

Kulk, Friso. 2013. *Laverend langs grenzen. Transnationale gezinnen en Nederlands en islamitisch familie- en nationaliteitsrecht*. Nijmegen: Wolf Legal Publishers.

Ligue Democratique des Droits des Femmes. 2007. *Rapport Annuel 2006*: Centre D'Informations et D'Observation des Femmes Marocaines.

Mir-Hosseini, Ziba. 2000. *Marriage on Trial. A Study of Islamic Family Law*. London-New York: I.B. Tauris.

Moore, Sally Falk. 2005. *Law and Anthropology. A Reader*. In *Blackwell Anthologies in Social and Cultural Anthropology*, ed. Parker Shipton. Oxford: Blackwell Publishing.

Rutten, Susan. 2011. The Struggle of Embedding the Islamic Mahr in a Western Legal System. In *Embedding Mahr in the European Legal System*, eds. Rubya Mehdi and Jørgen S. Nielsen, 113–146. Copenhagen: DJØF Publishing.

Sadiqi, F., and M. Ennaji. 2006. The Feminization of Public Space: Women's Activism, the Family Law, and Social Change in Morocco. *Journal of Middle East Women's Studies* 2(2): 86–114.

Salime, Zakia. 2009. Revisiting the Debate on Family Law in Morocco. Context, Actors and Discourses. In *Family, Gender, and Law in a Globalizing Middle East and South Asia*, eds. Kenneth M. Cuno and Manisha Desai. Syracuse, New York: Syracuse University Press.

Schols, F.W.J.M., and F.M.H. Hoens. 2012. CNR-Huwelijksvoorwaardenonderzoek, deel 1: algemeen en koude voorwaarden. De ontwikkeling in de praktijk der huwelijks- en partnerschapsvoorwaarden in de periode 2004–2009. Resultaten van een voortgezet onderzoek. *Weekblad voor privaatrecht, notariaat en registratie* 143: 943–953.

Shaham, Ron. 1999. State, Feminists and Islamists: The Debate over Stipulations in Marriage Contracts in Egypt. *Bulletin of the School of Oriental and African Studies, University of London* 62(3):462–483. doi: http://www.jstor.org/stable/3107575.

Singerman, Diane. 2005. Rewriting divorce in Egypt: Reclaiming Islam, legal activism, and coalition politics. In *Remaking Muslim politics*, ed. Hefner R.W., 161–188. Princeton: Princeton University Press.

Sonbol, Amira El-Azhary. 2005. History of Marriage Contracts in Egypt. *Hawwa: Journal of the Women of the Middle East and the Islamic World* 3(2): 159–196.

Sonneveld, Nadia. 2009. *Khulʿ Divorce in Egypt. Public Debates, Judicial Practices, and Everyday Life*. Proefschrift: UvA.

———. 2012a. *Khulʿ Divorce in Egypt: Public Debates, Judicial Practices, and Everyday Life*. Cairo: The American University in Cairo Press.

Sonneveld, Nadia, and Monika Lindbekk. 2015. A Revolution in Muslim Family Law? Egypt's Pre- and Post Revolutionary Period (2011–2013) Compared. *New Middle Eastern Studies* 5.

Sportel, Iris. 2013. "Because it's an Islamic Marriage". Conditions at Divorce in Transnational Dutch-Moroccan and Dutch-Egyptian Marriages. *Onati Socio-Legal series* 3(6): 1091–1110.

Sprangers, Arno, and Nic Steenbrink. 2008. Bijna 33 duizend echtscheidingszaken afgehandeld in 2007. *Bevolkingstrends* 3: 14–18.

Terlouw, A.B. 2010. *Gelijkheid en diversiteit in de multiculturele samenleving.* Den Haag: SDU.

Van Den Eeckhout, Veerle. 2003. "Gelijkheid" in het internationaal privaatrecht. Een kritiek op de gangbare structurering van het debat. *Nemesis* (5/6):177–189.

van Mourik, M.J.A., and W. Burgerhart. 2005. De ontwikkeling in de praktijk der huwelijks- en partnerschaps-voorwaarden in de periode 1997–2003. *Weekblad voor privaatrecht, notariaat en registratie* 136(6648): 1027–1043.

van Mourik, M.J.A., and A.J.M. Nuytinck. 2006. *Personen- en familierecht, huwelijksvermogensrecht en erfrecht*. Deventer: Kluwer.

van Oers, Ricky. 2013. *Deserving Citizenship. Citizenship Tests in Germany, the Netherlands and the United Kingdom*. Nijmegen: Radboud University.

Verstappen, L.C.A. 2011. Koude uitsluiting en de scheefgroei van inkomens en vermogens na scheiding. *Justitiële verkenningen* 37(6): 68–84.

Vlaardingerbroek, P., K. Blankman, A. Heida, A.P. van der Linden, and E.C.C. Punselie. 2011. *Het hedendaagse personen- en familierecht*. Deventer: Kluwer.

Wegelin, Margreet. 1990. *Moeders en vaders, scheiden en delen. Constructies van gelijkheid in de verdeling van het ouderschap na echtscheiding*. Amsterdam: UvA.

Welchman, Lynn, ed. 2004. *Women's rights & Islamic Family Law. Perspectives on Reform*. London-New York: Zed Books.

Zoglin, Katie. 2009. Morocco's Family Code: Improving Equality for Women. *Human Rights Quartely* 31: 964–984.

4

The Transnational Divorce Process

In this chapter, I analyse how the interviewees look back on the transnational divorce process. How did spouses arrange their divorces, and how does this relate to law in the different legal systems? I demonstrate how the differences in context between mixed and migration marriages, as introduced in Chapter 2, informed some of the choices respondents made when arranging their marriage and divorce as well as the stories interviewees tell about getting divorced. In analysing these choices, I will pay specific attention to the images and perceptions of the legal systems of the countries in the stories of the interviewees, using the concept of legal consciousness.

Below, I will first of all go into the issue of marriage. Many decisions which inform the divorce process have already been taken at the moment of marriage. Secondly, the reasons given for divorce will be analysed, focusing on the transnational aspects of the stories of the spouses in which they explain the end of their marriage. Thirdly, a discussion follows of the divorce procedure and the choices spouses made in arranging their divorce. Lastly, I will go into the issue of legal consciousness, discussing the

---

A few sections of this chapter have also been published in Sportel (2013).

I. Sportel, *Divorce in Transnational Families*,
DOI 10.1007/978-3-319-34009-8_4

images and perceptions of law and the different legal systems in the stories of the interviewees and how these informed some of the choices spouses made. I will add to existing literature on legal consciousness by exploring the legal consciousness of spouses who get into context with multiple legal systems and by analysing the impact of legal consciousness on legal action.

A Transnational Marriage

> R: How I met my husband? He is from my family. […] The first year, when we came here, in Morocco, permanently, my father said: we will just stay here, in Morocco. And then it was like: my younger sisters were allowed to go to school. But I was 17 years old. How could you [do such a thing] to a 17 year-old? I could hardly speak Moroccan. So I was not allowed to go to school. Dutch was of no use, because nobody speaks Dutch. And English, in those days there was no English education or anything. So the only option for me was to get married. Engaged. So when he asked for my hand, my father said: 'well, it's such a good guy. He's a good husband for you. He does not smoke. He has no bad [habits]. So, he will be a good husband for you, you should take him.' And you saw what my father is like. I can't say no to him. […]
>
> But I said to my mother: how can I spend my life with him? He is my opposite. He's not my type. 'No', she told me. 'No, you'll manage. He's very kind, and he's this, and he's that.' And at some point I thought: what would I do here, in Morocco. I don't have an education. I cannot go back to the Netherlands. I'm just stuck at home. Well, then I gave up. I told them: do as you like. Then they began to arrange for the marriage. After a year-and-a-half. First we had the engagement party. Then the wedding. Well, and then my catastrophe began. (Samira, Dutch-Moroccan woman divorced from Moroccan husband, living in Morocco)

> R: I was a cultural worker in [Dutch city]. And there I taught foreigners. He was one of them. And that's how we met.
>
> I: So he was already living in the Netherlands?
>
> R: Yes, he was already living in the Netherlands. He already came to the Netherlands when he was 18. So, well, he wanted to learn some more Dutch. Afterwards I learned they came for the girls [laughs]. Well, that's how we met. And I thought he was interesting, and fascinating, and I had always wanted to visit Egypt. So I thought, I will learn about the

culture, because I'm also interested in anthropology, in other cultures.[1] So I thought, well, that's interesting. Not that I was really in love with him, but he was a handsome man. He is a handsome man. He has intelligent eyes. Yes, a handsome man. From Egypt. Moreover, I was already 27. I thought it was time to commit myself. I had already had a few relationships. They always failed, and, well, then you start to come across as desperate. So well, in fact, those were the reasons. (Margriet, Dutch woman divorced from Egyptian husband, living in the Netherlands).

These two quotes, on the one hand, demonstrate the diversity in the transnational marriage and divorce stories in this study, while, on the other hand, they show some striking similarities. Both women had been unhappy in their marriage and, as will be discussed in the next chapter, both had experienced violence in their relationship. Looking back on the beginning of their marriage, being asked how they met their former spouse, they both tried to explain their 'bad decision' of choosing a marriage partner they did not love, from being desperate, although for different reasons. However, there is a notable difference between the two stories. Whereas Samira married a good husband 'from the family', Margriet chose a handsome, exciting man from another culture her parents initially did not approve of. Whereas Samira explained that she gave in to her parents to marry the obvious partner, Margriet explained her choice for a more unusual husband. These two stories represent a recurring pattern in this study. On the one hand, in 'migration marriages', spouses marry someone from the same ethnic group, sometimes even belonging to the same extended family or village, but raised in another country, whereas in so-called mixed marriages, the marriage does not only cross state boundaries but also ethnic or religious barriers.[2] As I will further demonstrate below, this social and cultural distance between

[1] We had just discussed my background as an anthropologist.

[2] Of the 26 interviews in this study, 17 were with spouses from a mixed marriage. All but one of the 11 Dutch-Egyptian divorces were mixed couples, whereas 7 of the 15 Dutch-Moroccan divorced were mixed, the others being migration marriages. Most mixed couples consisted of a Dutch woman and a Moroccan or Egyptian husband. In two cases, the husband was the Dutch partner of an Egyptian or Moroccan wife. Most migration marriages consisted of a husband who had grown up in the Netherlands and a wife who had grown up in Morocco or Egypt. In three cases out of eight the wife was the Dutch partner.

the partners as well as other context factors, such as negative discourses surrounding mixed and migration marriages, have an impact on how spouses frame and experience their marriage and the reasons for divorce.

Moreover, they also inform some of the decisions spouses have taken with regard to the arranging of the legal marriage and divorce. In the interviews, Dutch women divorced from both Egyptian and Moroccan men regularly referred to certain legal precautions they had taken, or felt they should have taken, at the moment of marriage:

> I: Did you have any special conditions in the contract?
> R: Yes. I included certain conditions with regard to divorce, second wife. I need to think: to be free to work, free to travel; and I included a stipulation that, in case I die, part of my money would be for my children. I have two sons in the Netherlands. Otherwise, everything would go to my husband's family, because it is an Islamic marriage.
> I: ok
> R: So I sorted out everything well beforehand, gained more in-depth knowledge of the law. I indeed bought a readable book in the Netherlands to see what all the rules are like, for men and women. There have been certain reforms that women get more rights if they marry. (Inge, Dutch woman divorced from Moroccan husband, no common residence during the marriage)

Framing her marriage and Moroccan family law as 'Islamic', Inge felt a need to inform and protect herself from its gendered effects. She started reading about Moroccan family law.[3] The text on inheritance in the Moroccan family law consists of a long and complicated enumeration of all kinds of family members, from which Inge easily could have gotten the impression that her husband's family would inherit everything. However, from a legal perspective, the stipulation about inheritance does not make sense. As Inge was a Christian, her husband, a Muslim, could not inherit anything from her. And even if she would have converted to Islam, he would only have inherited a small part of her property, the rest would have been inherited by *her* children and *her* other family members. In either

[3] The informant did not remember what book it was exactly. I expect it might have been the Dutch translation of the Moudawana by Berger (2004).

case, the Moroccan family-in-law would not inherit from her. Moreover, as they were planning to live in the Netherlands, and as Inge's property was located there, Dutch inheritance law would have been applicable. In the Netherlands, her husband would inherit all property upon her death. Her children could claim their shares only after his decease, if any of the property was left by then. Thus, to make sure her children would inherit, Inge should not have included stipulations in her Moroccan marriage contract, but in a Dutch will.[4] As she considered her marriage an Islamic one and Islamic family law as problematic, she only informed herself about Moroccan family law, completely missing these aspects of Dutch law. Crossing the marked boundary between Muslims and non-Muslims, as well as between the Netherlands and Morocco, negative discourses on Islamic family law seemed to have had an effect on her legal consciousness and, subsequently, on the way she arranged her marriage.

A second interviewee also carefully considered the legal aspects of her marriage, in reaction to the fearful stories circulating among the Dutch community in Egypt, as described in Chapter 2. But instead of informing herself on Egyptian family law, Monique, a Dutch woman living in Egypt, intended to marry in the Netherlands:

> We never considered getting married in Egypt. I would not have done that. Because then you lose all your rights. I know what it is like with an Egyptian. And all those stories you hear. And the money. I did not even know Noor [Stevens, from NGO *Bezness alert*] back then. I know that if you have a government marriage, or get married at the embassy, you're stuck there anyway. And if you've got children you could never get them out of Egypt. It was clear to me. If we get married, we get married in the Netherlands. He also had a [European] passport, so that wasn't a problem. When he left me on [date] I was busy arranging all his paperwork for the immigration. (Monique, Dutch woman separated from Egyptian partner)

In this story, Islam is less prominent than in the previous one. Instead of Islamic family law, Monique saw harm in an Egyptian marriage. She feared losing all her 'rights' and being stuck in Egypt the moment she

[4] For a more elaborate discussion of this case see: (Sportel 2013). For more information about Moroccan and Dutch inheritance law see Kulk (2013) and Rutten (1997).

would get married there. Other Dutch women referred to similar fears of losing rights upon marriage in a foreign family law system, of becoming a person without any agency. These fears award an enormous, though unspecified, power to Egyptian family law. Monique aimed to avoid being subject to this power by concluding her marriage in the Netherlands.[5]

These two cases are clear examples of how negative and frightening images of Moroccan/Egyptian or, in some cases, Islamic, family law prompted some of the respondents in mixed marriages, especially those concluded more recently, to take certain precautions at the moment of marriage. However, although most respondents from mixed marriages referred to these negative discourses on Islamic family law, only a few actually took legal action, for example by including conditions in the marriage contract.[6] This puts into question the connection between legal consciousness and legal actions. I will return to this point below.

The crossing of boundaries and othering experienced by some mixed couples was far less an issue in migration marriages than in mixed marriages. As illustrated by the story at the beginning of this chapter, many partners in migration marriages marry spouses who feel 'close', from the family or the village, from the same religious background or other communities or regional identities they belong to. Naima, a Dutch-Moroccan woman, explained how her parents were the 'typical migrant family'. When asked how she met her husband, Naima starts telling the story of her migration to the Netherlands, framing her parents as typical migrants who had troubles raising their children in a Dutch society. This introduction serves as an explanation of the choice of her parents to force her to marry at a very young age, a controversial issue taking a prominent place in the Dutch discourses surrounding migration marriages. After having described how, during a summer holiday at age 17, men came to ask for her hand the interviewee relates how she got married:

[5] From a legal perspective, it is hard to say whether this would be an effective strategy. For example, regardless of where the marriage takes place, in both the Netherlands and Egypt, permission of the other parent is necessary to leave the country. Furthermore, being more prosperous than her husband-to-be, Monique might actually be better off financially in the Egyptian system of separate marital property and no spousal maintenance obligations for women (see Chapter 7).

[6] I will discuss the different types of conditions in the marriage contract, and how they were used, in Chapter 7.

> [My parents thought] like, get married as soon as possible, before she'll cause some kind of scandal. [laughs]. […] At that moment I also saw marriage as an escape. I'm really honest about that. My parents married me off, in the sense that they confronted me with a choice. During a holiday they said: you're getting married, but you can choose yourself with whom among the people who have come to ask. They gave me that much. But you really have to get married. And I, *deep down* [English in original], of course I just felt that there is no one here who I know will understand me or whom I would actually want to marry. But let's do it, because this roundabout way is an easier way to demand my freedom. It would be easier to say something to my husband than to my parents. […] A boy came. I knew him, he lived in our neighbourhood [in Morocco]. I did not feel anything, the only thing he had was just that he had a sense of humour. I could laugh with him. He was a friend of my uncle. That was all I shared with him. But well, in those circumstances… Then matters were all settled quickly. Within about two days. [laughs]. And then I went to sign. And the beauty of it all was, I'll really never forget it, at the moment I was signing I thought: what are you getting yourself into? What are you doing? (Naima, Dutch-Moroccan woman divorced from Moroccan husband, living in the Netherlands)

Naima married someone who felt close, from the same neighbourhood, even though she had not been actually living in that neighbourhood for over a decade. In her story, she explains events from the position of her parents, how it was a logical choice in their situation, even granting her the choice of picking her own future husband from among those who came to ask for her hand. Moreover, she also claims agency. Even though she was married off as a minor, she clearly shows what she aimed to gain from the marriage and how she signed the contract herself.

Informal Marriages

Some respondents in this study, all from Dutch-Egyptian mixed marriages, concluded an informal *`urfi* marriage. The *`urfi* marriage is a private marriage contract, which is not registered by the Egyptian authorities.[7]

[7] See for a more elaborate discussion of types of informal marriages in the Middle East and the Netherlands, Moors (2013).

Therefore, it is not valid under Dutch law, and can thus not be recognised in the Netherlands. In Egypt, *`urfi* marriages between Egyptians are often used in secret relationships, for example, when parents do not agree or in case of a second marriage (Abaza 2001), or in 'semi-secret' second marriages between men, who already have a first wife, and divorced or widowed women (Sonneveld 2012b). In relationships between foreign women and Egyptian men, however, *`urfi* contracts have a more public function. These marriages can be religiously valid, but, more importantly, they protect the couple from police interference and enable them to share a hotel room or rent an apartment together. The presence of *`urfi* marriages in Egyptian tourist resorts can be explained from what Behbehanian (2000) calls 'intense and aggressive police activity'. *`Urfi* marriages are used as a safety measure to be able to publicly show a mixed relationship without being harassed or arrested, but without all the obligations connected to an official marriage:

> When it started it was great fun. Because he was a tour guide, and worked with [employer]. So we tried to see each other in Luxor, or Aswan, Hurghada or Sharm al-Sheikh. The only problem was, if you want to be together in a room, you need to be married. If you are a non-Egyptian couple, it's no problem. But in our case we had to. So we were married *`urfi* pretty soon. [...] We got married *`urfi* in a hotel lobby. I was wearing a black dress. I still have it. [...] Now I've got an exciting contract, an *`urfi-contract*, but he wrote it down himself. Two friends were witnesses, and we signed and that's it. (Janneke, Dutch woman divorced from Egyptian husband, living in Egypt).

In Janneke's story, the marriage was an accidental, minor occurrence, a practical matter to be able to share a hotel room. She did not seem to be very much occupied with the actual contract, finding the entire happening 'exciting'. But this did not mean the moment of getting married had no meaning to her, she had even kept the dress although the marriage took place almost 20 years before and the couple had been divorced for several years. Later, after the couple had formalised their marriage, they kept the original *`urfi* marriage date. Without the context of the policing of non-married mixed couples, Janneke would probably not have married so soon after the start of her relationship. In cases like this, the `*urfi-contract* is used as a first step to a 'real', formal marriage, leaving open the possibility to break off the relationship and destroy the contract or to take steps to formalise the marriage by registering it with the Ministry of Justice in Cairo.[8]

Interestingly, I found that in Hurghada, a semi-legal form of marriage seems to be developing between the formal, state-recognised, and the informal `*urfi* marriage. Here a 'home-made' `*urfi* contract is not sufficient for hotel owners, landlords, or local authorities to permit a couple to be together publicly. Couples need an `*urfi* contract signed and stamped by a lawyer. A market has thus evolved for lawyers offering these services to transnational couples. They can provide standard bilingual contracts.[9] This procedure gives an official tone to a marriage form that is otherwise characterised by a lack of substantive involvement of authorities. In his study of Dahab, another resort town, Abdalla also describes lawyers overseeing `*urfi* contracts (Abdalla 2004: p. 8–9). Still, an `*urfi* marriage contract stamped by a lawyer is not valid in the Netherlands.

The End of the Marriage: Reasons for Separation

Many of the interviews in this study were painful narratives of conflict, crisis, or abandonment, eventually leading to the end of the marriage and the separation of the transnational couple. Some of these stories had distinct transnational elements. For example, conflicts arose over country of residence or marriages ended because the migration process of the foreign partner failed, which meant some couples divorced before having ever lived together. Other reasons for divorce were similar to those in 'regular', non-transnational marriages, such as one of the spouses meeting a new partner or the couple growing apart. However, in the context of transnational divorce, some spouses framed such 'normal' conflicts in

[8] Especially for couples residing in the Sinai or Upper Egypt, the distance and costs involved in travelling to Cairo and taking time to do all the necessary paperwork (Kulk 2013) might involve a considerable investment of time and effort.

[9] A Hurghada-based lawyer I interviewed charged 50 euro for this service, but I have heard reports of others charging more.

terms of religion, ethnicity, or culture. An especially strong frame, which changes the entire perspective on the marriage, is the frame of false love or '*Bezness*', closely connected to the context of '*urfi* marriages. Below, I will discuss three main reasons for divorce related to the transnational context: conflicts over country of residence, framing marital conflicts as cultural and the frame of false love.

One of the main characteristics of transnational marriages is that one of the spouses has migrated. In about one third of the cases in this study, this migration had already happened before the start of the relationship. In the other cases, one of the spouses had to leave his or her country to set up a communal household. Sometimes this lead to conflicts regarding the country of residence:

> R: Well, in the end, he wanted to go to the Netherlands. And I did not want to go to the Netherlands anymore. So that's also one of the reasons we divorced. And now he lives in the Netherlands, and I live in Egypt. [laughs] (Conny, Dutch woman divorced from Egyptian husband)

In other cases, spouses did agree on the country of residence, but did not succeed in establishing a communal residence in the Netherlands. When migrating to the Netherlands, procedures to gain legal residence can be long and complicated. Not all marriages in this study survived this process.

When looking back on their marriage and divorce, most of the informants try to explain what happened during their marriage and why it ended, telling or retelling the story of their marriage and divorce. In many of these stories, cultural differences were a recurring theme. While some spouses from migration marriages also referred to cultural differences, for example, between different regions of Morocco, stories about cultural difference were far more prominent for mixed couples. Speelman (1993) discerns several context levels on which differences can be placed, ranging from personal aspects such as character and education, to more general aspects such as culture or religion (See also, Breger and Hill 1998). One interviewee, after discussing a wide range of conflicts on matters which she interpreted to be culture related—from child-rearing to dealing with medical problems and her husband's bad temper—summarised their conflicts as follows:

R: So there is always, always, some fuss. I really had the feeling I have been fighting some strange culture for five years. But you cannot win, because it's just ingrained (Ingrid, Dutch woman divorced from Moroccan husband, living in the Netherlands)

In this first quote, the husband's culture is a strange and negative one, something the interviewee had to fight against. His culture was standing between them, a barrier Ingrid could not overcome, as it was a part of him, over which he nor she apparently had any agency or control. Janneke, also a Dutch woman, described conflicts over cultural differences in another way:

R: Then it became clear what our main problem was. Look, when he met me I wore short skirts and shorts. That was all right with him. I knew he was religious. He did not drink [alcohol]. But, I mean, I never saw him pray, and he was friendly with people. Just at a distance. But just a nice guy. But when I was his wife, it began to creep in, like, well, rather no shorts anymore. No short skirts. No wearing trousers anymore. I had a long-sleeved shirt. I didn't care for those veils at all. But in the end. I said that, well, if we would go to certain areas, out of respect, and in order not to be hassled, I would be willing to button on a headscarf. Well, I couldn't get out of that one. So I walked around wearing a headscarf, covered up. I wasn't allowed to do anything. I wasn't allowed to drink [alcohol], I wasn't allowed to dance, I wasn't allowed to smoke, I wasn't allowed to swim. I wasn't allowed anything. And it wasn't evil intent. He just wanted a Muslim wife. But of course I wasn't one. In that regard I was very naive. And I think I might not have loved myself enough. And women are tremendous pleasers. That I thus actually went along much too far. Until the moment I didn't recognise myself anymore. I was terribly unhappy. So all I did was stuff myself. I really weighed 20 kilos more than I do now. I said: this just doesn't work for me. It was just two different cultures you know? If you have the same faith, the same sense of humour, and the same interests. Then a relationship can work. With us it was all different. And the first two fences can be leapt. But at the third you just go down mercilessly. It just doesn't work. We really tried, but it didn't work. (Janneke, Dutch woman divorced from Egyptian husband, living in the Netherlands).

Janneke also explains her divorce as a result of cultural differences, but from the perspective of her own unhappiness while trying to meet her husband's expectations. Whereas Ingrid uses the metaphor of a fight, a confrontation between cultures, Janneke's story does not portray the two former spouses as adversaries. It centres on the failure of both Janneke and her former husband to jointly overcome their many differences caused by culture and maintain their relationship. In this process, she describes losing herself, both in a mental as well as a physical way. Her husband did not force her to change out of malice, but according to Janneke, he had certain expectations that she could not meet, as she fundamentally is not what he wanted or needed: a real Muslim wife. In this story, Janneke presents her former husband and herself thus solely as representatives of their respective cultures and gender positions, which leaves little room for the discussion of personal traits or conflicts. Even though the tone of this story is different from Ingrid's story of a cultural fight, in fact, both share the very static view of culture as being fundamental and insurmountable, downplaying individual personalities and agency.

In one story of mixed marriage, cultural differences were almost completely absent.

> R: Well, right, I really think that she just is disturbed, and that she is troubled by a narcissistic disorder. That's what I [realised] later, after just reading things and such, and trying to understand what's going on. What I thought of myself. I'm not a psychiatrist. But well, in my view, the picture fits well, as an explanation. (René, Dutch man divorced from Egyptian wife, living in the Netherlands).

Like the other respondents, René is looking for an explanation for his former wife's behaviour, which in his eyes caused the breakdown of their marriage. But instead of placing their differences on a cultural level, he considered his former wife's behaviour a personal characteristic, finding explanations in the symptoms of a psychiatric condition. This is remarkable because of the marked cultural boundaries that are crossed in a mixed marriage, in which cultural difference is often seen as one of the main characteristics. In the Netherlands, Dutch and 'Islamic' culture are framed as almost directly opposite, a context inviting explanations of cultural difference. There are two possible explanations for this absence of cultural explanations in René's story of his divorce. First of all, many of the negative discourses on mixed marriages and cultural difference are highly gendered, seeing especially Dutch women with Muslim husbands as a problem, as detailed in Chapter 2. As a Dutch man with an Egyptian wife, René has a different position, which might contribute to his lack of interpreting conflicts as cultural. Secondly, in this specific Dutch-Egyptian case, elements of social class also played an important role. René's wife came from a wealthy upper-class family, while he came from a lower-middle-class family, but he had become a wealthy businessman. Highly educated and mobile professionals, they both had experience with working and living abroad. This also meant that the negative frame of *Bezness* marriages, containing references to financial gain or visa, did not apply.

These quotes show how respondents make use of the frames of cultural or personal differences to explain their marriage ending. However, informants frequently used more than one frame, shifting during the interview between explaining their partner's behaviour as a consequence of him or her being part of a group or culture and as an individual with a certain personality. In one interview, for example, Margriet, a Dutch woman, discusses the behaviour of her Egyptian husband. Because of his business, he was often absent, leaving her alone with the children in the Netherlands. On these business trips, he frequently slept with other women. In the interview, Margriet refers several times to the fact that 'Egyptians are allowed to have more than one wife' when discussing her former husband's extramarital affairs. But she also speaks at length about her former husband's behaviour without referring to culture at all, for example: 'All those years, I was really manipulated and indoctrinated in my marriage. Kept under his thumb. I lost myself.' (Margriet, Dutch woman divorced from Egyptian husband, living in the Netherlands). Similar to Janneke's story, as discussed above, Margriet refers to losing herself in the marriage, but not due to a foreign culture, but due to the controlling and manipulative personality of her specific, individual husband.

Bezness

A particularly strong frame used by some interviewees to explain their divorce is that of 'false' love, of marriage as a way of exploitation or gain for one of the partners. This issue, relevant for both migration marriages as well as mixed marriages, includes but is not limited to what NGO

Bezness alert calls *Bezness*. The Dutch or Dutch-Moroccan partners in these marriages are seen as attractive partners because of their financial or residence status, not because they are loved as a person. One Dutch-Moroccan interviewee, Naima, describes herself as a 'ticket to Europe', already when she was still in high school. From the beginning of her (arranged) marriage, she knew that her Dutch residency was an important incentive for her former husband to marry her. She did not go through with the immigration process and soon lost contact with her Moroccan husband. However, years later, when Naima announced she wanted a divorce her husband refused:

> R: Because at the moment I told him: 'I want to divorce from you', he didn't want to. First he claimed that he supposedly loved me, you know, and that I should try. Blah-blah. [...] I knew damn well that for him [love] didn't have to do anything with it. Later he kind-of admitted it to me. Because he said: then you'll have to pay me 30,000 euro. 30,000 *gulden* it was back then; it was in *guldens*.[10] And for that he would have wanted to divorce me. [...] because he told me: 'Listen. Bring me to the Netherlands and I will divorce you.' I really told him like, and I meant it with every nerve in my body: 'that's the last thing I would want to do. I absolutely won't do it. Even if I never could come to Morocco, I really wouldn't do that'. (Naima, Dutch-Moroccan woman divorced from Moroccan husband, living in the Netherlands)

According to Naima, her husband tried to put a claim to her based on a frame of love, while afterwards he demanded money to compensate for the loss of his opportunity to migrate to the Netherlands. He was using his relative power position under the old Moroccan *Moudawana*, in which it was far easier for men than for women to initiate a divorce. She refused to pay the price he asked, deciding to resolve the divorce herself. However, Naima did not love her husband, and she knew he did not love her when she married him. This makes her story different from the deception that characterises the *Bezness* stories.

[10] Approximately 13,600 euro. The 2002 currency change confused the stories of several interviewees.

The '*Bezness*-stories' in mixed marriages take a slightly different angle. Looking back on their marriage, some women felt they had been deceived by their former husbands. They say they now realise that his intentions were not a 'real', love-based marriage, but financial gain or a residence status, while they themselves did start the marriage with the proper reasons:

> [...] Actually, apart from losing my money, I escaped unscathed. And the real main reason I divorced, [although] he never dared say it to my face, is that I had the idea it was actually about the visa to get to the Netherlands after all. At the moment the visa wasn't awarded, then he subsided into a kind of lethargy. As if his world collapsed. (Inge, Dutch woman divorced from Moroccan husband, no common residence during the marriage)

Inge reinterprets her experiences almost exclusively by using the frame of false love to explain her former husband's behaviour and give meaning to her experience of loss. She blames her husband for not being honest with her, not telling her to her face that it was all about the visa after all, as only this could explain his behaviour in her eyes. In her story is an element of discovery, only after the visa procedure fails, his 'true intentions' become clear.

In another example, Anna, a Dutch woman who came to Egypt to work in the tourist industry had been living together with her Egyptian husband for some time when she noticed that some of her possessions were disappearing. Only later she found out that her husband had been stealing from her to cover his pressing debts and alcohol abuse. Eventually, she came home one day to find that her husband had disappeared, taking her jewellery and other precious possessions with him. This was the moment of discovery which changed her view on the marriage.

> He always said like: 'I don't understand how those other men can do such a thing. I'm not like that, I'm honest through and through. I have never wronged someone.' In the beginning I fell for it with my eyes open. [...]. Well, now I think: 'how could I have been so blind, why didn't I see that'. Well, especially because he tried so hard for such a long period of time. To build something together. (Anna, Dutch woman divorcing from Egyptian husband, living in Egypt).

In this quote, Anna refers to her—and her husband's—familiarity with the frame of false love. Looking back on her marriage, the husband turned out to be 'one of those men' after all. Anna did not see this, until the final, changing incident. Outside of a transnational context, her story might have been interpreted as one of addiction and abuse or mental illness. This couple had been living together in Egypt for a year and a half, and she had good contacts with his family, whom she continued seeing even after he disappeared.

The explanatory frame of false love or *Bezness* is a very strong frame, excluding all other reasons for divorce. In hindsight, it changes the entire memory of the marriage. It focuses solely on the behaviour of the Moroccan or Egyptian spouse. By deceiving and lying, they abused the real love of their wives in order to gain financially or secure residence status benefits from the marriage. They share a moment of discovery, which changes the perception and meaning of the entire marriage. In retrospect, these wives now, finally, see what has really been going on and that their husbands did not really love them. As such, the frame is only accessible for and used by Dutch, or Dutch-Moroccan partners. I also collected stories from Moroccan or Egyptian spouses from migration marriages who had faced violence and financial exploitation at the end of their marriage to a Dutch or Dutch-Moroccan partner. They, however, blamed their former wife and husband individually, and did not reframe their marriage in a discourse of false love.

This also changes the relationship from a marriage between equals into a perpetrator–victim relationship. This positioning as a victim disconnects the wife from the agency she could normally derive from her relative power position as being the wealthier, more mobile spouse. 'Blinded by love' she could not see that her husband was really 'one of those men' after all. This reframing of their marriage also enables them to relate to other European or Dutch victims of swindle in Egypt. For example, at *Bezness alert* meetings or on the website, stories were also heard from Dutch *couples* who had been swindled while doing business investments in Egypt or buying property.

Use of the *Bezness* frame also had consequences for how spouses arranged and experienced their divorce procedure. For example, three women who saw themselves as *Bezness* victims had not just turned to the family courts. As no-fault divorce provides little space for discussing or correcting the wrongs of the marriage in the divorce procedure, these women also tried to report their husbands' behaviour as a crime, hoping to instigate criminal procedures to have their former husband punished, or they started civil procedures to get 'their money back'. Below, I will discuss the divorce procedure and the steps interviewees have taken to divorce in one or both countries.

The Divorce Procedure

Divorce is not a single incident. The end of a marriage, separation, and formal divorce do not necessarily take place at the same time, or in the same order. Some couples decided to end their marriage, file for divorce, and then arrange the separation of their communal household and finances. In other cases, it took some time to start the formal divorce procedure after the relationship ended. Respondents waited because they hoped their spouse would return, or they still doubted whether they should return to their marriage themselves, postponing the divorce as a kind of final step. Other reasons mentioned were to wait until the children were grown, or that they only just had come around to arranging the formal divorce. In two cases, postponing the divorce had a distinct transnational dimension. In both of these cases, the former spouse was living in another country, and arranging the formal divorce was postponed for years. One of these interviewees, a Dutch woman, did not start a divorce because she did not like the idea of Dutch child services, which she considered to be inadequate, becoming involved in her family:

> I: Would child protection be brought in automatically?
> R: Yes. At the moment of divorce. Especially with a foreigner who is not present it is obligatory to have everything right.
> (Karin, Dutch woman divorced from Egyptian husband, living in Egypt).

But even when the children were adults, and after she had moved first to another European country and then to Egypt, she still did not arrange the divorce right away:

R: In the Netherlands I went to a lawyer. And he said he could not do it. He could take [the case], but back then it was a very tough case. Because she would have to hire a representative in Egypt.[11] Of course, that's what you get in an international case. And that would soon mount up. So she advised me to do it in Egypt. Then I moved to [another European country], so I thought, I could do it there. Of course, that wasn't possible, because they had nothing to do with it. And then I did it [arranged the divorce] in Egypt.

I: Did you have a certain reason to apply in the Netherlands first?

R: Because back then, I was still living in the Netherlands. So it was the logical thing to do. But for the rest, no, not really. So when it didn't work out I thought, never mind. (Karin, Dutch woman divorced from Egyptian husband, living in Egypt).

From this quote, it becomes clear, again, that arranging the legal divorce had little priority for Karin. After her first attempt in the Netherlands turned out to be too expensive, significant amounts of time went by before each next attempt was made. She talks about the divorce more as a bothersome chore than as a something major and important to her everyday life. Moreover, in the interview she does not mention any effects, positive or negative, of maintaining the legal marriage long after her husband had left her and their children.

In another case, the interviewee only found out later that they had been divorced by their husbands while she still considered herself to be married, and lived as such. Samira had not been involved in the formal divorce procedure at all:

R: I don't know why I have been so stupid. Right, one day he came to me and said: 'Samira, you should help me. Can you help me? We are going to do this and that, and my brother is in danger, and my mother too, and the entire house. It all depends on you. You can help us.' […] Then I went with him. He brought me to an office. There I got a white sheet of paper, and I signed it. Well, a few days later he came to pick me up again and said […]: 'you should come with me again'. I put my signature

[11] The interviewee changes between 'he' and 'she' while speaking about her Dutch lawyer. It is unclear to me whether there were two lawyers, or whether there is another explanation.

again. At another office. Well, and a few months later I got a phone call from his family in Nador. And what do you think I heard?

[Family member:] 'Samira, what did we hear? What happened?'
I said: 'what's going on?'
They said: 'Your husband has a wedding'
[I said] 'Oh. You can't be serious?'
They said: 'Yes, we are invited. It's next week. Next week, really, next week your husband has a wedding'. And, well, it turned out to be true. (Samira, Dutch-Moroccan woman divorced from Moroccan husband)

After her husband's wedding, Samira was thrown out into the street with her daughter by her husband and her mother-in-law. This made her start to reinterpret recent events, including the signing of papers a few months earlier. She started to do some research and found out she had unknowingly signed her own divorce papers, agreeing to the divorce, and renouncing all her financial rights, while she thought she was helping her family with financial troubles. She was raised in the Netherlands and cannot read Arabic. Furthermore, she claims to have been signing blank papers at the first office. Later she found out her husband had brought another woman to the court to gain permission for the divorce, pretending to be Samira, and using Samira's identity card. She tried to confront the lawyer who had handled the court case, as well as finding sponsored legal aid to undo the signing of the papers in which she agreed to renounce spousal maintenance during the *`idda* and the *mut`a*, but it was too late to be able to change anything. By arranging the entire divorce behind her back and using deception, her former husband had effectively excluded Samira from the divorce procedure, profiting from his superior knowledge of the Moroccan legal system and (written) language.

Generally, the first step in the legal procedure is to find a lawyer. For part of the respondents, especially in the Netherlands, this is also where their involvement ends. Their lawyer is the only point of contact between them and the legal system. They submit all the necessary paperwork but they never see a court or a judge, everything is handled by their lawyer. Even when at some point in the procedure they had to appear in court, most respondents left choices in the procedure to their lawyer who was also their main source of legal information. Some were not even aware of the kind of divorce they had applied for. Only in three cases, respondents took the lead in their divorce procedures themselves, having reasons for requesting specific procedures and divorce forms. Leila, a Moroccan woman, for example, requested a fault-based divorce in her Moroccan divorce procedure on the grounds of absence and non-maintenance, when she could more easily have asked for a no-fault *chiqaq* divorce with the same effects. However, she felt wronged by her Dutch-Moroccan husband who kept her waiting for four years, failing to provide residence in the Netherlands and thus preventing them from starting their married life together.

In the Netherlands, couples can also share a lawyer, which can save time and costs. In this study, only two out of 14 couples divorcing in the Netherlands used this option, which is much lower than the Dutch average of 60 % communal divorce requests (Wobma and de Graaf 2009: p. 18). Interviewed lawyers specialising in transnational divorce confirm this picture. There are several factors which might explain this difference, such as the relative high proportion of high-conflict divorces and the fact that several spouses were living in different countries during the divorce process.

In Egypt, men can simply register a divorce, without need for a court procedure or lawyer.[12] Therefore, mixed couples also do not need a lawyer to divorce if they divorce at the initiative of the husband or if both agree. They can go to an office at the Ministry of Justice—where marriages are also contracted—bring two witnesses and divorce on the spot. Two out of three respondents who were formally divorced in Egypt used this option. The other had to start a court case, as her husband—represented by his family due to illness—refused to cooperate in the divorce.

When choosing a lawyer to start the divorce procedure, a decision is also made about where—in which country—the procedure will take place, as most lawyers only work in one country. If one of the spouses has already started a legal procedure in one country, there are generally less options for the other partner to choose where the divorce should take place. Interestingly, and contrary to my expectations before starting this

[12] As for marriage, mixed couples can only register their divorce at a specific office at the Ministry of Justice.

study, there seems to be little evidence of so-called forum shopping, in the sense that spouses strategically choose where to arrange their divorce case, influencing which law will be applied to their case, and choosing the location which would benefit their specific situation most. Almost all respondents who initiated their divorce chose a lawyer in the country they lived in at that moment. The two respondents who chose a lawyer in the country of residence of their former spouses happened to be the same two who had waited for a very long time before starting the divorce procedure. The Dutch-Moroccan Naima did so because she did not register her marriage in the Netherlands, and thus had no reason to divorce there. She wanted a Moroccan divorce in order to be able to visit her family with her child. Karin, a Dutch woman, did visit a Dutch lawyer once. There she found out that it would be a very expensive affair, as she did not qualify for government-sponsored legal aid, and she decided to wait until she would be able to travel to Egypt to arrange her divorce over there, which she did only after having moved to Egypt herself. Even though forum shopping could in some cases have influenced the results with regard to, for example, financial issues such as maintenance, none of the respondents in this study made use of this tactic. Moreover, only in a few Dutch divorce cases the possibility of applying Moroccan or Egyptian family law was an issue. I will return to this in Chapter 5 on child care after divorce and Chapter 6 on financial aspects of divorce.

In only a few cases, spouses used the court to solve conflicts resulting from their divorce. In these cases, the divorce case was intertwined with court cases over maintenance, the division of property or child custody and sometimes also the residence of the children. Some interlocutors, especially Egyptian and Moroccan men living in the Netherlands, felt that their minority background influenced the outcome of their case. Farid, a Moroccan man, for example, was involved in a long and bitter series of court cases involving domestic violence, divorce, the right to contact with his child and, subsequently, as he had a dependent residence permit, his rights to residence in the Netherlands, which was based on his visitation arrangements with his son. According to Farid, his being Moroccan influenced the judge's decision: 'sometimes judges go deep, sometimes not. When he [a judge] reads at the top of the file "Morocco? Clear out!"' (Farid, Moroccan man divorced from Dutch wife, living in

Morocco). Latif, an Egyptian man who had considered a court case on child custody after his relationship with a Dutch woman, had the same impression:

> R: The Netherlands is a mothers' country. All rights over children are for mothers. I'm just a foreigner, it's her [ex-wife] own country. I checked the internet, the *Dwaze Vaders* website.[13] If a Dutch man has no rights, I certainly don't. (Latif, Egyptian man separated from Dutch partner, living in the Netherlands).

In this quote, Latif refers to his position in two intersecting discourses of inequality. First of all, he feels that, in the Netherlands, he would have few rights as a man and father, referring to a fathers' rights discourse. Secondly, he has the impression that, as an Egyptian father, he would have even less chance of winning a court case over his children than a Dutch father would. Informed by his legal consciousness of Dutch law, he did not consider a (Dutch) court to be able to help with his child custody issues. However, he did not present himself as powerless in the rest of the interview. Instead of going to court, he used extra-legal ways to increase his power position when negotiating with his ex-wife over their children, and they reached an agreement which he considered favourable.

The Second Divorce: Divorcing in Two Countries?

Thus, when choosing a lawyer and starting a divorce procedure in one of the two countries, almost all initiating spouses chose to arrange their divorce in the country they were living in. However, this divorce is not automatically known in the other country. Spouses who had registered their marriage in both countries can be divorced in one country but remain legally married in the other, a so-called limping marriage. If one wants to make sure the marital status is the same in both legal systems, the first divorce needs to be either recognised in the second country,

[13] *Dwaze vaders* or 'foolish fathers', a Dutch fathers' rights NGO established in the 1980s. The name possibly refers to the mothers of the Plaza de Mayo; this organisation is called the *dwaze moeders* or 'foolish mothers' in Dutch.

or sometimes a full second divorce procedure is needed, as has been discussed in Chapter 3. The issue of getting a marriage and subsequent divorce recognised in both countries is much debated, both by NGOs and other organisations as well as in legal literature (e.g. Kruiniger 2008, 2015; Jordens-Cotran 2007; Rutten 1988, 1999, Kruiniger 2015). However, all of these studies take a legal approach towards the subject, considering limping legal statuses to be a problem, without going into the actual reasons people may have to (not) register their marriage or divorce.

In this study, only about half of the participants had registered their marriage in the other country after it took place, and even less had registered their divorce.[14] However, not all of them considered this to be a problem. Participants had different reasons for registering or not registering their marriage or divorce in the other country. Sometimes these were legal reasons, for example, informal *`urfi* marriages cannot be registered in the Netherlands. The most important reasons to register a marriage had to do with (return) migration plans, for example:

> Because I had the idea that we would probably live in the Netherlands. That's why I registered it in the Netherlands. But the marriage is just valid, right, the Egyptian marriage is valid. It's actually not necessary. (Conny, Dutch woman divorced from Egyptian husband, living in Egypt)

In most cases, the couple married in Morocco or Egypt and then, if they planned to migrate, started the immigration procedure to the Netherlands. The registration of the marriage then took place as one of the steps in that procedure. None of the three couples that married in the Netherlands—all of them mixed marriages—had their marriage recognised in Morocco or Egypt. Similarly, interviewees that married in Egypt or Morocco and who did not intend to live in the Netherlands generally chose not to register their marriage there:

[14] For Dutch *residents* it is obligatory to register a foreign marriage, with the exception of Egyptian `urfi marriages which are not valid in the Netherlands. Although there is only a small chance of discovery, if someone fails to do so, the consequences, for example, with regard to the paternity of children, can be severe. For the legal complexities of this issue see: Kulk (2013). However, for Dutch citizens living abroad registering a marriage or divorce in the Netherlands is optional.

I: Did you legalise the marriage in the Netherlands?
R: No. You know, it wasn't an option to live in the Netherlands. I'm not interested in the passport for living in the Netherlands at all [laughs]. No, for us it was no option at all. Moreover, I was glad I did not do so. Because with the divorce. I mean, then you have to go to the Netherlands, and this, and that. [...] And I was thinking like: why should I? I'm married *here* [in Egypt] am I not? (Janneke, Dutch woman divorced from Egyptian husband, living in Egypt)

To a question about registration of her Egyptian marriage in the Netherlands, Janneke automatically responds that she would not want to live there, implying that this would be the only reason for her to register a marriage. This absence of interest of this and other interviewees to register their marriage abroad if they did not aim to live there is remarkable compared to research done by Kulk (2013) on transnational couples with children, who describes how his respondents had both legal as well as practical reasons for registering the marriage in the second country.

If a couple did not—voluntarily—register their marriage in the other country, generally this also meant there was no need for the recognition of the subsequent divorce. But even of the respondents who registered their marriage in both countries, only a minority had already arranged for the recognition of their divorce at the moment of the interview, although some intended to do so in the future. Again, decisions to arrange for the recognition of the divorce were taken based on their ongoing connection to the other country.

I: When you got divorced, did you ever consider arranging the divorce in Egypt?
R: No... No no. Could be that over there I'm still his wife. Could very well be. But I never return to Egypt so... (Sofia, Egyptian woman divorced from Egyptian husband, living in the Netherlands)

Due to her husband's refusal to finance a plane ticket to Egypt, Sofia never managed to visit Egypt during the marriage. After the divorce, she was living on social security and could no longer afford to go. At the time of the interview, she was already in her 70s, and due to health problems she was no longer able to travel. Although Sofia was born and raised in Egypt, she claims never to have had Egyptian nationality.[15] After her move to the Netherlands, she thus no longer had any formal connections to the Egyptian state; and she had never felt the need to register her divorce.

Like with marriage, in the absence of—plans for—return migration or remarrying a new spouse from the other country, many respondents from both migration or mixed marriages simply did not see the need to arrange for the recognition of their divorce. Rabia, a Moroccan woman explained why she did not see the relevance of getting her divorce acknowledged in Morocco:

> R: Because I could arrange my situation here. Because here is my life and home. So afterwards I didn't really do anything. Back then some women told that they actually had problems with customs when entering Morocco etcetera. But I was here [in the Netherlands]. Because of the debts, I could not go back for six years. […] Actually I did not really need the acknowledgement. I will not marry again. Not with six children, certainly not. That's impossible. My life was over actually. That's why I didn't take those steps. Well, I've got my divorce here, and I take it [the divorce papers] with me every time. But, knowing him, he didn't do anything about me. Because he knows he is wrong. That he should have paid [child] maintenance to me. Expensive. In the eyes of the judge I'm divorced from him. So, that's why I didn't take steps in Morocco. Because I did not have the time to go there all the time. I didn't have the money to go there all the time. I didn't have the money to send to the lawyer all the time. I used the money to do something for my children. (Rabia, Moroccan woman divorced from Dutch-Moroccan husband, living in the Netherlands)

Although Rabia had heard the rumours about the consequences of not having a Dutch divorce recognised in Morocco, she chose to avoid the

[15] As has been explained in the introduction, I have categorised the interviewees on the basis of the country where they had been born, in addition to categorising so-called second-generation migrants as, for example, 'Dutch-Moroccan'. Sofia's family was originally from Europe but had already been living in Egypt for several generations before she was born. Therefore, I have qualified her as Egyptian, even though she would not necessarily agree with this category.

hassle and costs of going through the recognition procedure. Moreover, she invokes a moral discourse here. Both the former husband and the judge would consider him to be in the wrong, for leaving his children without paying maintenance. She trusts that the court would take the right action. For this respondent remarriage would be the only reason to arrange for recognition, but this was something she considered impossible. Her argumentation also contains elements of belonging, the Netherlands being the place where she lives.

A minority of participants, all Dutch women, did believe that their still-existing marriage in the other country could have certain consequences for them:

> I intentionally did not visit Morocco, on the advice of my [Moroccan-Dutch] friend. She told me I could be arrested at the border. If he started those [proceedings]. Then they arrest you the moment they enter you into their computer. After which you can go to prison. Because I was still married in Morocco but divorced in the Netherlands. Also, a few months ago, she [the friend] scanned and emailed the official divorce papers for me. So he can, in Morocco [register the divorce]. If he did so, I don't know. But he retrieved the divorce papers from me. I did not ask him: are you going to marry again, or are you registering it? Because that wasn't even important to me. So I can't visit Morocco again. That's out of the question at the moment. But if I would want to go to Morocco, I could ask my friend to check whether the divorce has indeed been registered. (Inge, Dutch woman divorced from Moroccan husband, no communal residence)
>
> It is important that the Egyptian divorce is taken care of. Otherwise he could even re-register our marriage in the Netherlands, and then I could start over again.[16] He has a Dutch passport. [...] He could also use shari`a to arrange an entry ban for all Islamic countries, including Indonesia. (Manon, Dutch woman divorced from Egyptian husband, living in the Netherlands)

These women were afraid that the ongoing marriage in Morocco or Egypt would give their former husband power to mobilise the state against them. For Manon, these fears were a reason to intend arranging her

[16] This is not legally possible.

Egyptian divorce in the near future, whereas Inge now avoided Morocco, although she did migrate to another Muslim-majority country.[17] Their perception of their (former) husbands' power under Islamic family law is probably inspired by negative discourses on Islamic family law, which grant enormous but vague powers, but in a gendered way, positioning men as powerful and women as powerless in these legal systems. However, both women could get into trouble visiting Egypt or Morocco after remarriage or having a new partner, which would make them bigamists or adulterers.

The procedure to arrange the recognition of the divorce in the other country is often represented as complicated and expensive. This provided a barrier for many respondents who did not have a pressing reason, such as migration, to do so, as can also be seen in the stories quoted above. In Dutch-Moroccan cases, legal aid in this process has developed into a market with small businesses specialising in arranging recognition of Dutch divorces in Morocco, as will be further discussed in Chapter 8 (see also Sportel 2011). It was mostly the foreign partner who had arranged for the recognition of the divorce in the other country, especially if they had returned to live there after the divorce. This echoes what Kulk (2013) has written about the legal division of tasks in transnational marriages, each spouse being responsible for the legal paperwork of his or her 'own' country. A lack of contact after a divorce meant that in some cases the respondents I interviewed did not know whether their former spouse had actually succeeded in arranging for the recognition of their divorce. In this study, only two respondents, one Dutch woman and one Moroccan man, had already arranged for the recognition of their divorce themselves, both in their own country of origin, even though more planned to do so. Both succeeded more or less with ease, having sufficient cultural and social capital to arrange all the necessary paperwork. For example, Farid, a Moroccan man who had been deported from the Netherlands after his divorce from a Dutch woman, had his Dutch divorce recognised by a Moroccan court. His brother, a lawyer, arranged this for him.

[17] Legally, Moroccan men do not have the right to limit their wife's movement, nor is it possible for an Egyptian man to prohibit his (former) wife from entering all other Muslim-majority states. As will be discussed in Chapter 7, husbands can file claims at Moroccan or Egyptian courts to have their wives return to the marital home. However, the only possible sanction is the loss of maintenance rights. Also, it is no crime to divorce in another country.

Above I have described how spouses from transnational marriages have arranged their marriage, the reasons for ending their marriage and the steps taken in the divorce procedures. Decisions made and stories told were sometimes informed by certain images and notions about the legal systems. Below, I will further discuss these images, using the concept of legal consciousness and how they impacted the choices spouses have made in the transnational divorce process.

Legal Consciousness

In the preceding paragraphs, I have outlined some of the choices transnational couples have to make during the divorce, such as how, when, and where to arrange the divorce. In this section, I will explore the relation between images of law, or legal consciousness, and choices during the divorce process. I will argue that legal consciousness can be related to both earlier experiences with the law as well as negative discourses on Islamic family law and mixed marriages.

First of all, legal consciousness is not static but develops and changes in contacts with the legal system (Hernández 2010, Merry 1986). Some respondents described how being in a transnational marriage and subsequent divorce changed their perception of the legal system. In her story, Eva, a Dutch woman, tells of how she gained legal knowledge and understanding during the Dutch divorce process:

> R: It's weird. I didn't know all that. You get divorced, and the date of the divorce is November three, or something. While we were standing there [at the court] in October. But you're not divorced until the day that it has been entered in the books [civil registry], you know. [...] I would notice like, oh, that's the way it works. In that sense we both had the idea that this was a new part of the voyage of discovery [...]. (Eva, Dutch woman divorced from Moroccan husband, living in the Netherlands)

Eva describes the divorce process as part of a 'voyage of discovery' which had already begun at the moment of their mixed marriage. Gradually she learned to handle the Dutch legal system and, especially, those parts specific for transnational couples. In this process, she also lost some of her trust in the law:

> R: I was a bit in that scene, where you notice that the law in the Netherlands isn't as law abiding as you would want to rely on. And it's exactly the same in Morocco, where we also have received fines for things we did not do, with the aim of extracting money from me. But I think many Dutch think that in the Netherlands you'll always be treated well. And I saw from working with *allochtonen* a lot that this isn't always the case. (Eva)

Through her own experience, as well as those of others in her network connected to migrants in the Netherlands, Eva's trust in the legal systems of both Morocco and the Netherlands was lessened. Especially Dutch law lost some of its lustre as to ensuring that 'you always get treated well' in the Netherlands. De Hart, in her study of mixed relationships and migration law in the Netherlands, also describes how, through their confrontation with migration law, the Dutch partners in mixed relationships had an 'unexpected meeting' with the Dutch state (de Hart 2003: p. 2–3).

Negative experiences in earlier court cases, before the divorce, had made some respondents turn away disappointed from the legal system altogether. One Moroccan man, for example, told a negative and suspicious story about the Dutch legal system. At the moment of the interview, he was involved in prolonged court cases against the Dutch state for residence and social security after being expelled from the Netherlands:

> I want to live like everybody else. I already feel Dutch. I don't need any papers for that, it's in my head. In the Netherlands I have no rights, no human rights, nothing. (Amar, Moroccan man abandoned by Dutch wife, living in Morocco)

In his story, Amar had somehow lost his residence in the Netherlands. When he was expelled from the Netherlands, his Dutch wife followed him to Morocco. Once living there, three children were born, and it turned out that they could not get child benefits or Dutch passports, despite their mother being Dutch.[18] One by one, Amar had lost all rights he felt he and his children were entitled to.[19] He felt wronged by the Dutch state and legal system and was distrustful of Dutch courts. These experiences informed his negative and distrusting legal consciousness of the Dutch legal system.

In these and similar stories of respondents, multiple and unrelated court cases and other legal experiences sometimes became one coherent story about Dutch, Egyptian, or Moroccan law, linking residence/migration law, social security law, and family law. During their experiences and procedures, they had lost their trust in what Merry, in her research on the legal consciousness of working-class Americans has called 'the ideology of formal justice', in which individuals see themselves as having a 'broad set of legal rights, loosely defined, which shade into moral rights', and which are taken seriously by the state (Merry 1986: p. 257). Merry describes how people discover through their experience with the courts that this ideology is not always correct, and that the daily practice of the court is far messier. 'Justice' is not automatic but depends on the circumstances and characteristics of the parties in the conflict. What Merry calls 'situational justice' is an acquired, and often more realistic, perspective. In situational justice, the outcome of a court case also depends on who you are, for example, being part of a mixed marriage with a migrant (Merry 1986: p. 258–259).

However, as I will further demonstrate below, it is not just court experience that influences people's legal consciousness, but a whole range of everyday life experiences with (foreign) institutions and, especially, Dutch migration procedures. Through their experiences in a transnational marriage and divorce, their 'voyage of discovery', their legal consciousness has changed, and they have lost some of their sense of 'legal entitlement' (Hernández 2010). This is contrary to the process which Hernández describes for disadvantaged women in a poor US neighbourhood, who start from having very little trust in the law and, after contacts with the legal system and sponsored legal aid, gradually developed a more positive

[18] From his story, I cannot understand why the children would not have Dutch nationality since birth, as they have a Dutch mother.

[19] Amar did not really understand why he was expelled from the Netherlands. I have not been able to establish what happened exactly and why he lost his residence.

image of the law and a sense of legal entitlement (Hernández 2010). The interviewees in this research project, most of whom came from a far more privileged background, often lost rather than gained trust in the legal system through experience.

This shift in legal consciousness does not necessarily take place for both legal systems, nor does it work for all respondents in the same way. One Dutch woman, Karin, whose story has already been partly discussed above, had far more trust in the Egyptian legal system than in the Dutch system. Throughout the interview, she illustrated her point of view with stories about the differences between the two countries ranging from telephone lines and electricity bills to her fears that Dutch social workers would take away her children after divorce, or at least monitor her closely for being a single mother divorced from a foreign father. In her story, the Netherlands was characterised by bureaucracy and complicated procedures; whereas in Egypt, services offered were better, more reliable, and procedures more efficient (Karin, Dutch woman divorced from Egyptian husband, living in Egypt).

Nora, a Moroccan woman divorced from a Moroccan man and living in Morocco at the time of the interview, also used opposite perspectives for the two legal systems she came into contact with. After losing custody over her child in a Moroccan divorce case—in which she suspected her former husband to have won through bribes and corruption—she hoped that the case would be settled in the Netherlands. Her mother, who was present during the interview, was severely disappointed in the Moroccan legal system: 'There is no law in our country, just money. (…) In Europe, law is law, not in Morocco, even though we have Islam.' This mother and daughter had lost the trust implied in the ideology of formal justice for Morocco, but not for the Netherlands.[20]

In other interviews, the differences in legal consciousness of the legal systems in the two countries were subtler. For example, Monique, the Dutch woman who refused to get married in Egypt because of her fear of losing all her rights in the Egyptian legal system, started a criminal court case to force her former fiancée to return the money he owed her.

---

[20] I have not spoken to this interviewee since the interview in Morocco. However, indirectly I have heard that, after several years and multiple procedures, this woman indeed was able to return to the Netherlands and regain custody over her child.

I: What do you expect that this whole court case will bring?
R: I hope everything. I don't know. [...] Well I think, we have so much proof. [...] I mean, here [in the Netherlands] the case would have been abundantly clear. But then, Egypt is Egypt. He always said, I've got contacts in [city]. I say: that doesn't mean a thing, with regard to this I've got more contacts than he does.
(Monique, Dutch woman separated from Egyptian partner, living in Egypt)

When describing her motivations for not getting married in Egypt, as quoted earlier in this chapter, Monique described Egyptian law as something to be feared and avoided, as it leaves European women without any rights. However, in this quote, this negative discourse is remarkably absent. Instead, she shows signs of a situational legal consciousness, in which proof and presentation of facts is important and justice is not automatic. Although her trust in the outcome of the case would have been greater in a Dutch court than in an Egyptian court, she still trusts in winning the case. Although she does refer to Egyptian courts being open to corruption, she also hints at a certain competence in handling those aspects too, having more local contacts than her former fiancée.

In the interviews, stories of distrust were thus regularly connected to negative experiences and stories about corruption of lawyers and courts, chaotic bureaucracy, discrimination, and messy procedures. This demonstrates how legal consciousness is not only informed by experience with the courts in the field of family law but also by other experiences with the 'people of the law' and the legal system.

Moreover, powerful negative discourses about Islamic law also played a role. As has been described earlier in this chapter, women feared that their former husbands had immense power under Islamic law to harm them. However, these negative discourses on Islamic family law were much more present in the stories about marriage contracts than in the stories about divorce. While these aspects of their legal consciousness clearly informed some of the choices interviewees have made when getting married, including where to get married, it never actually determined or even influenced their choices on where, in which legal system, to arrange the divorce. I will return to the influence of legal consciousness on decisions in the divorce procedure in subsequent chapters about child care after divorce and the financial aspects of divorce.

Conclusions

In this chapter, I have analysed the divorce narratives of spouses from transnational marriages, starting at the moment of marriage. In accounting for the end of their marriage, some spouses used explanatory frames of cultural difference, while others blamed their former partners more individually. For mixed marriages, the frame of *Bezness* is exceptionally strong, causing the entire marriage to be reinterpreted in hindsight and the partners to be recasted as perpetrator and victim. Especially this frame had an impact on the divorce procedure, as women who felt themselves to be victims of *Bezness* did not only start a divorce procedure, but they also (tried to) involve the police, hoping to mobilise the authorities to punish their former husband as a perpetrator.

During the transnational marriage and divorce process, couples are faced with many choices and decisions. Some couples in this study made a lot of effort to arrange the legal aspects of their marriage, making marital agreements in a communal language or seeking advice from specialised lawyers in their divorce procedure. However, most made such decisions as they went along, getting married in a hotel lobby to be able to share a room, or randomly choosing a local lawyer to handle their divorce. The law played little part in their choices as they navigated (Kulk 2013) between practical and financial concerns. Most couples only registered their marriage in the other country when it was necessary for the migration procedure and some only started a formal divorce procedure when there was a practical, immediate cause to do so. The presence of transnational ties was the most important factor in these decisions. In the absence of ongoing relationships with the other country, respondents simply had no cause to go through the trouble of a second divorce. Specific laws in one of the two legal systems were never actually mentioned as a reason for choices in the divorce procedure. Knowledge, images, and perceptions of the law—legal consciousness—thus were often not as relevant for the choice of legal system as might be expected. However, legal consciousness was important in the stories they told and, as we will see in later chapters, for some of the decisions taken in arranging child care and financial matters after divorce.

Especially in the stories of Dutch interviewees married more recently to an Egyptian or Moroccan husband, Moroccan or Egyptian law is presented as both very powerful and completely gendered and ethnicity-based, providing Egyptian or Moroccan men with certain, unspecified rights while taking away rights from Dutch women. Dutch law is either remarkably absent in these fearful stories or presented as a safe refuge, which does not encourage further investigation of the actual law in the Netherlands. These stories share a perception of the law as being all-powerful and consistently enforced by the state similar to the ideology of formal justice, as described by Merry, which is promoted by the state and the legal systems themselves.

During their transnational marriage, respondents came into contact with corruption, bureaucracy, discrimination, and Dutch migration law. These sometimes seemingly unrelated contacts with the legal systems could be presented as one coherent story about law and the legal system, both in their 'own' as well as in the country of their former spouse, though not necessarily in the same way. In these stories, the law loses some of its lustre as being an all-powerful—either positive or negative—power, its power gaining more personal dimensions, and touching some more than others. Thus, in a transnational context, legal consciousness can be different for each legal system spouses come into contact with. In the next three chapters, on power relations, issues relating to children and the financial aspects of divorce, I will return to these issues.

References

Abaza, Mona. 2001. Perceptions of 'Urfi Marriage in the Egyptian Press. *Isim Newsletter* 7: 20–21.

Abdalla, Mustafa. 2004. *Beach Politics. Gender and Sexuality in Dahab. Cairo Papers in Social Science.* Cairo: The American University in Cairo Press.

Behbehanian, Laleh. 2000. Policing the Illicit Peripheries of Egypt's Tourism Industry. *Middle East Report* 30(216).

Berger, Maurits S 2004. *Mudawwana. Marokkaanse familiewet.* Nijmcgen: Ars Aequi Libri.

Breger, Rosemary, and Rosanna Hill, eds. 1998. *Cross-Cultural Marriage. Identity and Choice. Cross-Cultural Perspectives on Women,* ed. University of Oxford The Centre for Cross-Cultural Research on Women Oxford: Berg.

de Hart, Betty. 2003. *Onbezonnen vrouwen. Gemengde relaties in het nationaliteitsrecht en het vreemdelingenrecht., Migratie- en Etnische studies.* Amsterdam: Aksant.

Hernández, Diana. 2010. "I'm Gonna Call My Lawyer:" Shifting Legal Consciousness at the Intersection of Inequality. *Studies in Law, Politics, and Society* 51: 95–121.

Jordens-Cotran, Leila. 2007. *Nieuw Marokkaans Familierecht en Nederlands IPR.* Den Haag: SDU Uitgevers.

Kruiniger, Pauline. 2008. *Marokkaanse verstotingsvormen in de Nederlandse rechtspraktijk.* In *Een juridische beschouwing over de Marokkaanse khul` en talaq in het kader van erkenning in Nederland.* Tilburg: Celsus juridische uitgeverij.

———. 2015. *Islamic Divorces in Europe: Bridging the Gap between European and Islamic Legal Orders.* Den Haag: Eleven International Publishing.

Kulk, Friso. 2013. *Laverend langs grenzen. Transnationale gezinnen en Nederlands en islamitisch familie- en nationaliteitsrecht.* Nijmegen: Wolf Legal Publishers.

Merry, Sally Engle. 1986. Everyday Understandings of the Law in Working-Class America. *American Ethnologist* 13(2): 253–270.

Moors, Annelies. 2013. Unregistered Islamic marriages: Anxieties about sexuality and Islam. In *The Application of Sharia in the West,* ed. Maurits Berger, 141–164. Leiden: Leiden University Press.

Rutten, Susan. 1988. *Moslims in de Nederlandse rechtspraak.* Kampen: J.H. Kok.

———. 1997. *Erven naar Marokkaans recht : aspecten van Nederlands internationaal privaatrecht bij de toepasselijkheid van Marokkaans erfrecht.* Antwerpen: Intersentia.

———. 1999. Multicultureel familierecht. In *De onzichtbare standaard in het recht. In- en uitsluiting van vrouwen, etnische minderheden en homoseksuelen in het familierecht, arbeidsrecht en strafrecht,* eds. K.D. Lünnemann, M.L.P. Loenen, and A.G. Veldman. Deventer: Gouda Quint.

Sonneveld, Nadia. 2012b. Rethinking the Difference between Formal and Informal Marriages in Egypt. In *Family Law in Islam. Divorce, Marriage and*

Women in the Muslim World, ed. Maaike Voorhoeve, 77–110. London-New York: I.B. Tauris.

Speelman, Gé. 1993. Mixed marriages. In *Muslims and Christians in Europe. Breaking New Ground. Essays in honour of Jan Slomp*, eds. Gé Speelman, Jan van Lin, and Dick Mulder. Kampen: Uitgeverij Kok.

Sportel, Iris. 2011. Transnational Divorce in Dutch-Moroccan Families. The Semi-Autonomous Social Field of Legal Aid. *Recht der Werkelijkheid* 32(3): 37–51.

———. 2013. "Because it's an Islamic Marriage". Conditions at Divorce in Transnational Dutch-Moroccan and Dutch-Egyptian Marriages. *Onati Socio-Legal series* 3(6): 1091–1110.

Wobma, Elma, and Arie de Graaf. 2009. Scheiden en weer samenwonen. *Bevolkingstrends* 4: 14–21.

5

Marital Power and the Law

In marriage, like in all social relations, power comes into play. Looking back on their marriage, some of the interviewees described their marriage as being unequal, oppressive, or even violent. Although transnational marriage can be connected to a range of intersecting power-related issues, such as the division of labour during the marriage, access to divorce and dependent residence status, little is known about the power relations in transnational marriages or their impact on divorce. In this chapter, I will provide a theoretical framework and focus on two power-related issues: the division of labour in marriage and domestic violence. As we will see, these two issues are of great importance for power relations in transnational marriages, as well as prominent in the marital power literature. I will return to issues of power relating to, for example, child care or finances in subsequent chapters.

This chapter is divided into three parts. First, I will outline the theoretical framework on marital power relations which will be used in this and subsequent chapters. Second, I will discuss resource theory and the division of labour within marriage. Third, I will discuss domestic violence, a recurring power-related theme in many of the interviews, and its consequences in the divorce procedure.

I. Sportel, *Divorce in Transnational Families*,
DOI 10.1007/978-3-319-34009-8_5

Theoretical Framework: Marital Power

In this chapter, I will build on the concept of marital power as developed by Komter (1989, 1985). Komter studied marital power in Dutch marriages and defines power as 'the ability to affect consciously or unconsciously the emotions, attitudes, cognitions, or behaviour of someone else' (Komter 1989: p. 192). She makes a division between *manifest power*, *latent power*, and *invisible power* in marriage. These are based on the three dimensions of power distinguished by Lukes (1978). Manifest power, the first dimension of power, 'surfaces in visible outcomes such as attempts at change, conflicts, and strategies' (Komter 1989: p. 192). Most research on marital power focuses on this first and most obvious dimension of power, mostly by describing differences in power over decision-making. However, according to McDonald (1980), attention must not just go to the outcome of power, but also describe '(1) who controls the definition of the family situation which determines the possible range of relevant decisions; (2) who actually decides which decisions are to be confronted and which are not; and (3) in the case of delegated authority, who decides which individual will implement the final decision' (McDonald 1980: p. 844–845). These power processes can be seen as the second dimension of power. According to Komter, 'Latent power can be at stake when no changes or no conflicts are reported. It can be identified when the needs and wishes of the more powerful person are anticipated, or when the reasons for not desiring or attempting change or refraining from conflict produce resignation in anticipation of a negative reaction or fear of jeopardizing the marital relationship' (Komter 1989: p. 192).

The last dimension of power is described by Komter as invisible or hidden power. 'Invisible power was defined as the result of social or psychological mechanisms that do not necessarily surface in overt behaviour, or in latent grievances, but that may be manifest in systematic gender differences in mutual and self-esteem, differences in perceptions of, and legitimations concerning, everyday reality. The effects of invisible power generally escape awareness of the people involved' (Komter 1989: p. 192). In her study, Komter found several invisible power mechanisms that helped maintain the status quo. First of all, characteristics attached to men are culturally valued over characteristics attached to women, which gave them more bargaining power. Secondly, there was a perceptual bias. Husbands systematically overestimated their own contributions to the household work and underestimated that of their wives, meaning they can dismiss a request for help by their wives as unjustified. Lastly, husbands and wives apparently seemed to agree on the reasons for the current situation being natural, necessary, and unchangeable. However, reasons such as 'she enjoys it [doing the housework] more than he does' turned out to be untrue when measured by Komter (1989 p. 207–210).

All of the three dimensions of power as described by Komter are highly relevant for understanding the power relations in transnational marriages, including invisible power. Although this last dimension of marital power cannot be directly found in the present study, in which only one of the spouses is interviewed, it is important to keep the existence of these structural dimensions of power in mind when reading this book.

Resource Theory

> She stayed at home, with the children. I was the man; I took care of the money. (Latif, Egyptian man separated from Dutch wife)[1]

In all three countries, domestic labour and care tasks have traditionally been seen as the wife's responsibility, while the husband was responsible for generating income. However, it must be noted that in Europe and the USA, and possibly Egypt and Morocco as well, this situation is historically more of an ideology than actual practice; income levels being so that most households could not survive on just one salary meant that women (and in many cases children) had to work as well (Helmers 2002: p. 24–25; Gentry et al. 2003: p.3). Based upon this gendered model of the division of labour in the family, Blood and Wolfe (1960) devised their much-followed resource theory. In this theory, marriage is an exchange relationship or contract; resources brought into the marriage by both partners are exchanged. Men, as breadwinners, trade economic resources for the

[1] The interviewee uses the Dutch word 'man', a word which means both adult male and husband.

domestic labour and care provided by wives (Vogler 1998: p. 688–689; Tichenor 2005: p. 191). However, this exchange model has been criticised. First of all, it is not an equal exchange, but a gendered one, in which the spouses have different power positions based on their gender role. Moreover, resource theory does not pay attention to the wider context in society, such as gender differences in payment (Vogler 1998: p. 689). As Komter also noted, there is an 'implicit hierarchy in worth, whereby every individual man benefits from the cultural valuation of men over women [...]' (Komter 1989: 208).

That the exchange of resources in the family is a gendered one is especially clear when looking at the situation of female breadwinners. As will be further discussed below, migration in general and especially migration law can impact the marital division of labour, leading to a relatively high percentage of female breadwinners in this study. Most interviewees that had a marriage in which the wife was the main or sole breadwinner described this not as a deliberate choice, but as a failure of the husband to provide. This was a frequent source of conflict and frustration as both husbands and wives expected otherwise.

Studies in non-migrant, Western contexts show that a change in gender roles regarding paid employment does not necessarily change the division of house work. Bartowski, in his article on marital division of labour in American Evangelical families, notes that husbands who cannot fulfil the male-provider role outside of the household are all the more likely to act according to the male-provider ideal inside the house, that is, by non-participation in household work. Similarly, wives who worked full-time jobs invested in their roles as homemaker as well. Using a 'both/and gender strategy' enabled them to retain the homemaker label, which is closely connected to femininity in the conservative Protestant circles they live in (Bartowski 1999: p. 43, 58). Similar patterns have been described by Luyckx (2000) in her research on migration marriages of second generation Turkish migrants living in Belgium, and Buitelaar (2000) for couples of Moroccan descent in the Netherlands. Luyckx even describes some husbands taking more responsibility for household tasks after they found a job (Luyckx 2000: p. 51–53).

However, only a few studies analyse what such gender role inversions mean in terms of marital power relations between spouses, and none of these studies connect these issues to law or migration. Tichenor (2005) found that women earning more and working in higher-status jobs than their husbands do not necessarily gain power in their marriages. Their money does not grant them power in the same way as it does the husband-breadwinners in more 'conventional' marriages. She explains this by referring to Lukes' third dimension of hidden power. She argues that '[...] gender ideology at the institutional level, specifically conventional conceptualisations of masculinity and femininity, shapes the interactions and gender identity constructions of spouses in ways that subvert the cultural link between money and power *for women* and reproduces men's dominance within marriage' (Tichenor 2005: p. 192).

According to Pyke (1994), the meanings given to resources, such as an income or household work, brought into the marriage by one of the partners are crucial in determining the impact of these resources on marital power. In some situations, women's paid employment can even be seen as a burden her husband has to bear for her instead of an asset to the family income. Moreover, women can sometimes try to compensate for their partner's lack of social status or power outside the house by transferring all marital power to their husband (Pyke 1994: p. 80–81). Speelman noted a similar development in marriages between Dutch women and Egyptian men living in the Netherlands (Speelman 2001: p. 168). What then, does this mean for the division of labour and marital power relations in transnational families, and to what extent can these be connected to migration and law?

Marital Power and Division of Labour in Transnational Marriages

While there are many more issues in marriages on which couples can disagree, most research on marital power centres on the division of labour in the marriage. Although my focus on the topic of the division of labour in this chapter reproduces this existing bias in the marital power literature, the division of labour is of specific interest in the study of transnational marriages and divorces. The migration process as well as migration law regulations can have an effect on the gendered division of labour, providing new insights into the connection between the division of labour and marital power relations. Moreover, the marital division of labour can be of great importance in the divorce process because choices made during the marriage influence the possibilities of each partner to make a living and/or care for children after divorce.

There were significant differences between the interviews in this study with regard to the arrangements of income and care responsibilities during the marriage. Of the twenty-six interviews, in only four cases both spouses provided more or less equally. In eight cases, the wife was the main or sole provider, and in ten cases it was the husband. In four cases, the couple had never actually lived together in the same country and thus never formed a communal household.

In those families where the husband was the main or sole provider, this was mostly related to the couple having children and not to migration. Most of these couples followed the 'standard' Dutch pattern of fathers working full-time and mothers working part-time or not at all after children are born.[2] Two Dutch women, for example, both already had been successfully employed in Egypt when they met their respective husbands, and both stopped working when they had their first child. Two Moroccan women, one Dutch-Moroccan woman and one Egyptian woman had never had paid employment at all and were living at the home of their parents before their marriage. Only in one case, for Malika, a Moroccan woman, working fewer hours was explicitly related to her migration. In Morocco, she had been working full-time and caring for her daughter as a single mother when she married a Dutch man and moved to the Netherlands. Because her diplomas were not recognised there she could only find badly paid freelance employment. This caused conflicts in the relationship with her husband, who expected she would participate equally in providing for their family and would take financial responsibility for her own daughter.

In eight cases, the wife had a bigger share in providing for the family. In six of these families, there were children. Amar, a Moroccan man,

[2] Korvorst and Traag (2010). In 2009, 57 % of couples had two employed partners. However, only in 20 % of these couples, both partners worked full-time, and in over 80 % it was the husband who had a highest income. (CBS, see: http://www.cbs.nl/nl-NL/menu/themas/inkomen-bestedingen/publicaties/artikelen/archief/ 2011/2011-3291-wm.htm, accessed on 22 July 2013).

married to a Dutch wife living in Morocco explained how he and his wife decided that she would work and he would stay at home:

> She was working at [employer], a Dutch company. Our situation was also Dutch. I wasn't a strict Moroccan husband. [I asked her]: 'do you want to work or comfortably stay at home?' What do you think, she was young, had an education, she wanted to work. [... details about wife's education]. I did not work, it was not allowed because of the procedure.[3] I was also using heavy medication. I did everything at home. She wasn't able to do much; she did not even know how to cook. (Amar, Moroccan man, married to Dutch wife, living in Morocco)

During their marriage, Amar stayed at home and took care of their three children. This Moroccan man did not consider himself to be a typical Moroccan husband and described their inversed care arrangement as 'Dutch'. However, he still presents himself as the one deciding, *offering* his wife a choice instead of determining it for her as a 'strict Moroccan man' would do. Moreover, men being principal caregivers is an exception in the Netherlands as well (Korvorst and Traag 2010). During his stay in the Netherlands, this man had worked in child care and geriatric care. In the Netherlands, these sectors are also generally considered women's employment.[4] The fact that his wife eventually deserted him and their children to return to the Netherlands, as described in Chapter 6, also points to an inversion of the male breadwinner female caregiver pattern. As the couple resided in Morocco, the husband's care work was not legally compensated by maintenance after divorce or communal property. I will return to this below.

In contrast, in the other interviews, a female breadwinner was not framed as a deliberate choice but as a failure of the husband to provide. This was regularly a source of conflict and frustration as both husbands and wives expected otherwise. Anna, a Dutch woman, for example, had already moved to Egypt and had employment there when she married

---

[3] I suspect the interviewee refers to the social security procedures for illness he started after being expelled from the Netherlands.

[4] With 4.9 % of employees in geriatric care being male and 3.4 % in child care in 2006 (van der Velde et al. 2009: p. 8-13).

her husband. When he lost his job, she unexpectedly became the sole provider:

> And I had my work at [employer] and well, a lot of things happened, but he did not get anything done. He was home all day, but he did not do anything. So there were some tensions, because he expected from me that, when I came home, I would also cook for him, while he was hanging out on the couch all day, watching telly. So that's when the contradictions began. And then I also said, like, if you don't have a job, and you're at home all day, I really expect that, if I come home, at least you've done something about [the house]. And keep the house clean as long as you don't have a job. And he was less than pleased of course. (Anna, Dutch woman divorced from Egyptian husband, living in Egypt. No children)

As can be seen from this quote, it was not a deliberate choice to become the main breadwinner in their marriage, and Anna considered it to be a temporary arrangement. Although she was prepared to cover the costs of living on her own, she did expect of him to do the housekeeping in return. However, her husband did not comply, and, looking back, Anna interprets this as a first sign of the events taking place afterwards, when she discovered her husband had left her while stealing her personal belongings, placing her story in a *Bezness* frame.

In a second example, Rabia, a Moroccan woman divorced from a Dutch-Moroccan husband was the main breadwinner and the main caregiver in their marriage with six children, even though she was the one who had migrated in their marriage:

> I: Your children, if you were working, who took care of them?
> R: The day-care centre.
> I: They went to a day-care centre, so your husband did not take care of them?
> R: No, he thought that was something for women. He was a man. He took the car and took us to school. Then I stayed there all day, of course, and he had the entire day for himself. Or he went back to sleep until noon. And then he went into town and went somewhere. I don't know. And then, at three thirty, he came to pick us up. [...] Then I had extra duties, fetching the children from day-care, after a very long working day I did

> that, and then go home and cook, bathe the children, and so on. Just duties, and in the evenings, at eight, I'm pleased to sit at all, with the children. And the next morning it starts all over again. (Rabia, Moroccan woman divorced from Dutch-Moroccan husband)

In these examples, earning most or all of the household income did not give these women the power to demand their husbands doing the household work in exchange. Even in Amar's story, he claims a position of power, granting his wife a choice, an opportunity to work, while he did everything at home. Not in exchange, but because he could not work anyway, and because he was better at it. As described above, migration might possibly lead to reinforcement or inversion of gendered patterns of division of household labour. Though this seems to hold true in some of the cases described above, actual practice is far more complicated. For example, when the foreign partner had already been working in the country of residence before the marriage, the effects of migration were less visible. In those marriages, the differences in income and working hours between the partners were related to children being born, following a gendered pattern of care, or even to sheer coincidence, such as a job being lost.

A specific power-related issue of marriages in which only one spouse has an income is the ability of the other partner to spend money. In all but one case in which it was the husband who was the sole provider, he also took financial decisions, which sometimes caused conflicts between the partners, for example:

> R: I had to ask everything. Everything. And if he thought: no, you do not need that, then the [answer] was no. [...] When his father died, he went [to Egypt]. When my mother died, I did not have money.
> I: So you did not return when your mother died?
> R: No. I did not have the money to think about it.
> I: But he could have given you the money?
> R: Yes. Certainly.
> I: But he did not do so?
> R: Yes. [he said:] I have to work, and who will take care of the children, and the food, and... (Sofia, Egyptian woman divorced from Egyptian husband, living in the Netherlands).

As she had no money of her own, it was up to her husband to grant Sofia the means to travel. As he preferred her to stay and take care of the children, she never managed to return to Egypt after the family migrated to the Netherlands, and never saw her parents again.

Although the inability to spend money independently was a recurring theme in stories of the interviewed housewives, illustrating the tensions of being in a dependent position financially, the earnings of women did not automatically bring them similar power of control over family financial resources, or even autonomy. To Rabia, being responsible for both the housekeeping, taking care of six children, and providing the family income was a great burden and no voluntarily choice or strategy:

> I felt myself becoming smaller and smaller, so to say. The open and free person I was, was completely gone. The entire environment got smaller and darker to me. So well, I did not pay any attention to myself. I was a well-dressed girl. I wore mini-skirts. I also wore those nice boots. But afterwards, it was my hair in a bun and work and the children [sighs]. I did not have time to talk and to cry. And for days on end, days on end, he was free and I was wrecked. Completely wiped out. As worn out as I was, I really couldn't go on. That's why I asked for help. That's how deep it was. After all those years, it was finished. The day he left, I was also pleased. It was better, for the children and for me. I really was released. (Rabia, Moroccan woman divorced from Dutch-Moroccan husband, living in the Netherlands)

The departure of her husband was a relief from what Rabia felt to be an unequal and unfair relationship. However, even though she had been providing during their marriage, her former husband had been managing the finances, giving her no control over her earnings or even knowledge over their financial situation. When he eventually left her, he left behind a lot of debts and she had no idea how to handle administrative matters in the Netherlands.

Thus, the connection between power relations and the division of labour is less clear than it seems in classical resource theory. On the one hand, several women, in different settings, complained about how their former husband tightly controlled the money he earned, behaviour which sometimes continued after divorce. On the other hand, some women who were the main provider in their relationship still lacked control over spending. Moreover, their providing as a resource was most of the time not sufficient to 'trade' for domestic labour and care. This illustrates how the meaning of resources is strongly gendered. As we have seen, some of the interviewed women experienced how their former husbands used their greater access to money as a means of power and control, while other women failed to exercise similar differences in wealth to have power over their husbands. In the interviews, another important means of exercising direct power over a spouse was regularly mentioned as domestic violence. I will further discuss this below.

Marital Power and Domestic Violence

When I started this research project, I intended to exclude cases of domestic violence. I did not want to write a story of 'extreme cases' but of 'ordinary divorces', the distinction being based on my presumption that domestic violence was rare and exceptional. My choice for 'ordinary divorces' was both informed by an unwillingness to reproduce a dominant discourse of Muslim men as being violent as well as by my own unease with the subject.[5] However, when I started doing the fieldwork, references to domestic violence kept coming up in the interviews. Still, it was not until I did a systematic analysis of the interviews with divorced spouses for references to domestic violence that I gained a grasp of the profound presence of the issue in my research material. Out of 26 interviews, no less than 11 interviewed spouses, 10 women, and 1 man, described how they had been the victim of some form of psychological or physical violence: all women by their former husbands, the man by his former family-in-law who beat him up after his wife left him. In addition, three men mentioned being falsely accused of violence towards their former wife or their children in the divorce process. This also is a remarkable number considering I only interviewed five

[5] This meant that, for example, when initially approaching NGOs or lawyers for potential respondents in the first phase of my fieldwork I also asked them not to include cases of domestic violence. However, after the first four interviews all contained at least some reference to domestic violence, I changed my approach and no longer mentioned domestic violence as an issue to exclude when looking for research participants.

men. In short, the issue of domestic violence claimed a place for itself in this study.

In all three countries, research has been done on the prevalence of domestic violence in the general population. However, the results of these studies are not easily comparable, due to methodological differences. In Morocco and Egypt, for example, only violence used by husbands against wives was researched. Moreover, different forms of violence were studied; in Morocco this also included the withdrawal of financial support. Therefore, I will limit the discussion here to physical violence, which was studied in all three countries, although there was no specific study of transnational marriages. According to research by Anaruz, an organisation of *centres d'écoute* (legal aid centres) in Morocco, 30.4 % of women reported have been subjected to physical violence by their spouse.[6] Moroccans living in the Netherlands, conversely, seem to report far less domestic violence, with 6 % of men and 16 % of women having ever been the victim of physical violence (not limited to spousal violence). However, the response amongst Dutch-Moroccans was low, and these figures are therefore not very reliable (van Dijk and Oppenhuis 2002: p. 21–24).[7] In statistics from the 1980s, 21 % of Dutch women had been the victim of one-sided violence by a (current or former) male partner, and 6 % had been involved in communal violence. Another analysis found 16 % of women and 7 % of men had been the victim of physical or sexual violence by their partner, with little differences between majority and minority groups (See for an overview of data: Verwijs and Lünnemann 2012). In Egypt, 34 % of women reported having ever been beaten by their *current husband* (Diop-Sidibé et al. 2006: p. 1265).

With almost half of the women in this study reporting incidents of domestic violence, mostly without having been asked questions about the topic, this is higher than can be expected on the basis of these national statistics. How can this be explained? Are transnational

[6] Unfortunately I have not been able to access the full report, but a summary can be found on the Women Living Under Muslim Law website http://www.wluml.org/fr/node/6113, accessed 13 May 2013.

[7] There were more reasons to suspect underreporting, for example, that no Dutch-Moroccans over 50 reported any domestic violence (van Dijk and Oppenhuis 2002: p. 9, p. 21-24).

marriages more prone to violence than national marriages? It must be noted that this study of transnational couples is small and not a random sample. Its results cannot be generalised to all transnational Dutch-Moroccan and Dutch-Egyptian marriages. Secondly, as discussed in the methodology section of the introduction, I have the impression that special cases are somewhat overly present in my research sample. This might be explained by having found many respondents through NGOs and professionals who may tend to remember cases that are somehow extraordinary, for example, those including issues of involuntary abandonment in the country of origin, parental child abduction, or severe violence.

Nevertheless, it could also be argued that transnational marriages could be more prone to domestic violence. There is an ongoing debate in the literature on domestic violence, already starting with the terms used, such as gender-based violence or intimate partner violence. In this debate on domestic violence, the role of gender is central. Intimate partner violence is either described as gender-based, with mostly male perpetrators and female victims, connected to gender relations in society or described as simply an escalation of everyday conflicts in relationships, in which women are just as likely to commit violence as men (Johnson and Leone 2005; Römkens 2010; Johnson and Ferraro 2000). According to Römkens, these opposing views can be explained by methodological and also ideological differences between the two fields. The intimate partner violence often studied by qualitative studies taking into account the context and revealing patterns of violence and control is not the same kind of violence studied in large-scale quantitative population studies in which violent incidents are studied outside of their context. Studies of the first kind reveal that women are more often the victims of severe partner violence; studies of the second kind show that women and men use partner violence on an equal basis (Römkens 2010: p. 14–17). Johnson has developed a typology of different forms of violence in intimate relationships. *Intimate terrorism* is part of a systematic pattern of control, in which one partner attempts to exert general control over the other. *Situational couple violence* or common couple violence is less coherent and consists of separate conflicts escalating into violence. This typology does not describe the level of violence; both forms can range from relatively innocuous to severe and from infrequent incidents to regular assault (Johnson and Leone 2005: p. 322–325; Johnson and Ferraro 2000).

Control being the main factor, intimate terrorism is closely connected to power relations in the marriage. Anderson proposes analysing violence as a way of doing masculinity:

> Gender theory proposes that violence is a resource for constructing masculinity, and thus the use of violence will have different meanings for women and men. […] The integrated theory proposed here suggests that these elements of the structural environment may influence violence because they also influence resources for power within inter-personal relationships. Higher reported rates of violence among young, cohabiting, and non-White men with low levels of education and income may reflect their limited alternatives for demonstrating a masculine identity. When they have fewer status resources than their female partners, some men may rely on violence as a means of gaining power and establishing masculine difference. (Anderson 1997: p.658–659)

As discussed above, transnational marriages sometimes include inversions of or changes to the gendered division of work in marriage. In such cases, violence may be an alternative resource of power. Jewkes et al., for example, found that the wives of unemployed men and migrant workers in South Africa had a greater chance of being abused (Jewkes et al. 2002: p. 1607). Anderson (1997) found in an US study that status differences between spouses can have a gendered effect on the risk of domestic violence. When women earn more than their husbands, those men have a 3.5–5.5 times higher chance of perpetrating violence compared to men with equal earnings. Similarly, odds were up to 40 % lower when men earn more than their wives (Anderson 1997: p. 664).

Aside from the added risk factors in transnational marriages, statistics on intimate partner violence in all three countries are mostly about still-married couples or about all violence ever experienced, regardless of marital status. It could very well be that amongst divorcing couples, violence is more common, as marital conflict is a risk factor for domestic violence (Jewkes et al. 2002: p. 1604). Additionally, a Dutch study on divorce found that in 20 % of divorces with minor children and 10 % of divorces without minor children, physical violence was a reason for the divorce (Clement et al. 2008: p. 43).[8] As most respondents who had experienced domestic violence in their transnational marriage did not label it as the reason for divorce, this might indicate that the actual prevalence of domestic violence in Dutch divorces might be higher than the 10 % or 20 % who considered it a reason for divorce as well. Below, I will show the diversity and complexity of the presence of violence in the divorce cases in this research. After this, I will further discuss how these experiences and accusations of domestic violence played a role in the court cases of the interviewees.

Forms of Violence

R: Well, then I spent my holiday here [in Morocco] and also some really bad things just happened with that man. Because of course, in a certain way, he just claimed me. I'm from [North-East Morocco], and then [place], that's a smaller village, even far more conservative. And that man claimed me. He also was, right away, like, he just hit me once. He just, just really, well, not beat me up, I mean that just doesn't happen to me. I just got a solid blow. And nobody in the family said anything or stood up for me. (Naima, Dutch-Moroccan woman divorced from Moroccan husband)

R: He hit me. Even after the wedding [of former husband and another woman, the end of their marriage] I still had, I was still covered in bruises. […] That was the last time he completely beat me up. I went to the hospital. I was admitted to the hospital. I even still got the papers. I was completely covered in bruises. […]

I: Did he do it before? Hit you?

R: It was always like that. If I opened my mouth like: [ex-husband], your mother said this to me, or [ex-husband] I'm tired. It was always, you know, like, shut up. I always had bruises. But I never dared show them. He always said to me like: you can never tell anyone about our private life, about our marriage. (Samira, Dutch-Moroccan woman divorced from Moroccan husband, living in Morocco)

[8] For men in both cases 1 %.

The use of violence in relationships can take many forms and degrees, ranging from a single push to a pattern of battering. The partner violence mentioned by the interviewees in this study varied widely with regard to severity and how often it happened. Three women mentioned having sustained physical injury because of violence used by their (former) husbands. However, on closer examination, nearly all incidents mentioned by female respondents were related to a pattern of domination and control. Even when there was just a single incident of violence, like in the quote from Samira at the start of this section, the story was recounted as a symptom of an ongoing effort of the husband to gain control over his wife, and one of the reasons she broke off the marriage before the couple ever started living together. Similarly, when a Dutch woman recounted her experiences with her Moroccan husband, she described an incident of violence as part of an ongoing story about control.

> R: It was all small things, but together they weighed incredibly heavy. He always tried, like, even when he was gone things should go in his way. [...] So also when he was absent, he tried to keep control. [...] So you constantly tread on eggs, and even that's not good enough. Something's always happening. He thought that [the floor] should be mopped down more often. Right, I said, there's the mop and there's the floor, go ahead. But that wasn't what was wanted. I said: 'I'm already working my ass off. I've got a full-time job, I have to do those children and you are whining to me about the floor that needs to be done.' I said: 'whenever am I going to do that?' [...]
>
> I remember it really well. [It was] the third day [after son was born], when the baby blues start. He was so angry that the child kept crying. And I was sitting there, on the nursery floor, crying, like, I did not know what to do anymore either. And then he pushed me against the wall, so I got something of a blow, saw a flash of light. Well, that was not the main issue, but it stayed like that. And he demanded that I go on dragging the child around. (Ingrid, Dutch woman divorced from Moroccan husband, living in the Netherlands)

In this quote Ingrid dismisses the push against the wall as not important; it was the pattern of control and the distribution of labour that bothered her in the relationship. In the interview, she did not explicitly label this incident, or her relationship, as being violent. Another Dutch woman described how she learned from a women's empowerment training to label what happened in her relationship as violence.

> When he went to Schiphol [airport] he always drove full speed, on purpose, you know? I was incredibly afraid. Even if I said: don't do that, I'm afraid, he just kept on driving full speed. Villainous. He just did not want to show consideration to me. That's psychological abuse. I learnt that in that course. (Margriet, Dutch woman divorced from Egyptian husband, living in the Netherlands)

Looking back on her marriage, which was characterised by recurring patterns of intimidation and control (but not mentioning any physical violence), Margriet now labels her husband's behaviour as violent, even though she did not do so at the time. This had effects on how she felt and behaved in her marriage.

> R: Well, all those years, you get into a kind of pattern, right? If you've been oppressed in your marriage for such a long time, you get into a pattern that everything revolves around him, you know? He's coming home. Oh, is everything tidy, do we have food he likes. You're constantly complying to his wishes, and with his likes. You don't think about yourself anymore. (Margriet, Dutch woman divorced from Egyptian husband, living in the Netherlands)

In this quote, Margriet illustrates Komter's second dimension of power, latent power. In her married life, she tried to anticipate the wishes of her husband out of fear for his reactions and to avoid conflicts. After divorce and participating in a women's empowerment course, Margriet learned to see this normally invisible second dimension of power in her own marriage. These stories show how, through a pattern of control, intimate terrorism took place in some of these marriages even in the absence of (severe) physical violence.

Stories of situational or common couple violence were limited to one Moroccan husband's defensive narrative. Farid admitted having used violence during arguments a few times, but not in the degree his former wife claimed. Moreover, he claims she was violent and aggressive as well, especially to their child. Her older children from an earlier marriage had already been taken from her by the child welfare system. During this confusing interview, an overall picture of a couple using mutual violence in escalating fights arose, making this more a story of common couple violence than of intimate terrorism, as references to a pattern of control were absent.

It is remarkable that there is only one story of common couple violence, told by a Moroccan man, and so many stories of intimate terrorism told by women of all backgrounds in this study. Like in the literature divide mentioned above, I think this is at least partly connected to methodological issues. As I did not systematically ask respondents about domestic violence, its presence often only came up as an illustration of what was 'wrong' with the marriage or their former spouse, generally a pattern of control. It is therefore possible that I 'missed' less severe cases of common couple violence. It is also possible that respondents who have been involved as perpetrators rather than victims may be less willing to speak about that in the interviews.

Domestic Violence and the Divorce Procedure

How can these issues of domestic violence be linked to the divorce procedure? In Morocco and Egypt, fault-based divorce on the basis of harm, and arrangements for the *mut`a*, as discussed in the legal chapter, make violence an important issue in divorce procedures, although proof is needed to back a claim. However, no-fault divorce, introduced in the 1970s in the Netherlands and more recently in Morocco and Egypt, does not provide space for discussing wrongs in the relationship in the divorce procedure, as they have become irrelevant. Only in disputes over child care or child access and—in rare cases—Dutch spousal maintenance, can domestic violence play a role, especially if one of the parents has been violent to the children. However, claims of the mother that the father has abused her are in itself not sufficient to block contact between the father and the children. Especially if a mother does not have proof, such claims might even potentially threaten her chances of having child residence, as speaking negatively about the father can be seen as a disqualification of her parenthood.[9] In this research, none of the women who had been the victims of domestic violence used this as an argument in a court case. Two fathers, on the other hand, told how they had been falsely accused of domestic violence and child abuse by their former wives in a court case on child contact:

> Then there was another court case. And it turned out that she, that her lawyer was arguing that I should not see the children, because of all the things I did to them. 'See, see!' So he came with a rubbish story, that I pushed him [son] down a slope, on purpose, and that he had broken his hip, or I don't know what. He did not have anything whatsoever with his hips, it was all bizarre rubbish. And another story, I had threatened them with knives. And she had a few more of those stories. (René, Dutch man divorced from Egyptian wife, living in the Netherlands)

After his wife had left with the children, René found her notes for preparing the court case and instructing their children what to say to social workers and judges:

> She wrote 'sexual abuse?' 'Not to mention but to imply' she wrote below.[10] Later, I found all kinds of things she told social workers from all sorts of agencies who came to help, or supportive agencies who came to take care of her, she had also sent them all kinds of reports. [...] She claimed I abused [son], that I sexually abused [daughter] as well. But those things were never specified. She sent things to social workers and kept copies, and I found those, in her things. It was all the order of the day, those stories, those claims. A report, notes about what [son] should tell the judge, because he was 12 and allowed to come to the judge and say what he thought about it. It was all completely prepared. (René, Dutch man divorced from Egyptian wife, living in the Netherlands)

In appeal, René gave these notes of his wife to the court to prove his innocence, and they were accepted as supporting his case. However, his

[9] A few lawyers I interviewed for this research also mentioned that if there had been violence in the marriage they generally advised mothers not to mention this fact in court unless they had proof, such as a criminal conviction of the father.

[10] When quoting from his former wife's notes, René uses English instead of Dutch.

wife had already left the Netherlands with the children, and his attempts to a contact arrangement failed again.

Farid, a Moroccan father, was also accused by his former Dutch wife of committing domestic violence. She had him prosecuted and started a court procedure having him blocked from having access to their child because of the violence and because she was afraid he would abduct the children to Morocco. Because of language difficulties, I did not manage to get a clear picture of whether he was convicted for the violence or not, and whether he was accused of using violence against his wife or also against the children. However, it was clear that he appealed all decisions up to the highest courts but lost. As a result, Farid was expelled from the Netherlands and was no longer able to see his child informally as before.[11] In this marriage, the Dutch wife acted as a gatekeeper, effectively blocking her husband from both access to their child as well as the Netherlands.

Family law is not the only part of law applicable on domestic violence. It can, in all three countries, also be punished under criminal law. In this study, four interviewees, three women, and one man went to the police to report violence. Driss, the Moroccan husband of a Dutch-Moroccan wife, reported a violent housebreaking by his family-in-law. A Moroccan woman living in the Netherlands, a Dutch woman returned to the Netherlands from Egypt and a Dutch-Moroccan woman living in Morocco also tried to have their (former) husband prosecuted for abuse. However, in all three cases, the police did not want to file their reports:

R: You have to report to the police. I did that at the police station. I was covered in bruises. But from the doctor, I got a form which said 'seven days'. And at the police station, it turned out that seven days was not enough to punish him. I thought it was very weird.
I: Right, so seven days in hospital?
R: No, seven days on the form was not enough. Not enough. They said: the law won't punish unless there are 21 days on the paper from the doctor. Only then he will be punished. And 21 days on the paper you only get

[11] As their marriage had not lasted long enough to grant him independent residence and because there was no contact arrangement, he could not claim residence on the ground of the presence of his child in the Netherlands.

> when it is bleeding or if you've got a broken hand or something is broken. But covered in bruises is only seven days. (Samira, Dutch-Moroccan wife divorced from Moroccan husband, living in Morocco)

The interviewee and I both failed to understand at the time the fact that the Moroccan penal code discriminates between different kinds of violence based on the result of the violence, instead of the act itself. This misunderstanding could be related to the migration background of the employee, as I later understood these rules are considered general knowledge in Morocco. The injury is measured in days of disability. Only severe injuries, more than 20 days of disability, qualify as high-level misdemeanour. According to a Global Rights report, the police will generally only respond to claims of domestic violence for such severe injuries (2011: p. 8). Malika had a similar experience in the Netherlands. The Dutch police at first refused to take her report. She blames this on the influence her Dutch husband has in their small village. Only after she threatened to file the report in another city did the local police record her statement. Both husbands were never prosecuted however. In the last case, Manon, a Dutch woman, left Egypt to flee from her violent husband. After her return to the Netherlands, she tried to report him to the Dutch police and immigration officers, hoping to block his future entrance to the Netherlands. Her attempt failed, as she did not have sufficient evidence and the violence had been committed outside of the Netherlands.

Two husbands also told how their (former) wives had reported them to the police, although both denied being violent. Farid's case ended in losing his rights to child contact, as has already been discussed above. In the other case, Latif, an Egyptian man, told how he was suddenly summoned to the police station after spending a day with his Dutch wife in a wellness resort in a final reconciliation attempt to save their marriage:

> In the end we had sex. It was the first time in ten years. And the next day she reported me to the police, for abuse. [...] She had asked me to come for dinner, but nobody was home. So I called her: 'where are you?' 'We are reporting a crime. Here the police on the phone'. [The police officer said:]

> 'Are you coming? Your wife is hysterical'. I wanted to come the next morning, but I had to come right away, or they would arrest me. I told everything, in the lobby. I could talk or wait for a lawyer. Next day I called the police for ten minutes and then I was free. It was very clear. I was in Egypt at the moment of the accusation. [...] I've got all the evidence, even photos. We were in a wellness resort, I've got the tickets. At the date of the 'rape' she was working at [employer], there are cameras there.[12] I can prove it was a false report. (Latif, Egyptian man separated from Dutch partner, living in the Netherlands, two children)

In the end, the case was never brought before a judge. According to Latif, the police did not believe his wife. He was disappointed, as he wanted to go to court to tell his side of the story and have his name cleared. He kept calling the police for news about the case, and did not give up:

> I'm still collecting evidence. I hope she lets her tongue run away with her. In all those years of marriage I pushed her once. That's all. Still, I'm registered at the police. I've been a good man; I never hit her, never. (Latif)

In the end, this incident never played a role in any court case. The couple informally decided to share the parenting equally in a co-parenting arrangement.

It is difficult to balance these stories of false accusations by men with the stories of abuse and control by women. Allegations of domestic violence, and especially of child abuse, first uttered in the context of divorce, child contact or custody cases are sometimes seen as suspect, forged weapons in a struggle over the children. However, several studies on child abuse allegations in divorce cases have shown that, contrary to public belief, forged accusations are rare (Geurts 2009; Brown et al. 2001; Jaffe et al. 2003). In this research, I have chosen to analyse the stories and narratives of respondents. I do not aim to question whether these stories are 'true' facts. Instead, these stories about divorce give valuable insights in how spouses experienced their marriage and divorce and, moreover, in the norms and images that inform their conceptions of proper behaviour between spouses and the way they deal with law.

[12] Quotation marks gesticulated by interviewee.

Conclusions

Marital power relations are complex and manifold. In this chapter, I focussed on two power-related themes which were important in the interviews: the marital division of labour and domestic violence. Due to this focus on the division of labour and domestic violence, this chapter mostly discussed issues of dominant men and vulnerable women, with gender taking a central position in marital power relations. This does not mean, however, that power relations are always one-dimensional and the same in all aspects of marriage. As was demonstrated by several stories of female breadwinners, the relations between the gendered division of labour and marital power were not as clear as they would seem based on resource theory. Wives gaining more financial resources because of paid employment did not necessarily gain the marital power connected to these resources.

In this chapter, I have hinted at some connections between marital power relations and the law. On the one hand, most respondents kept their issues of unequal power relations and domestic violence outside of their divorce procedure. No-fault divorce does not provide a space for discussing the wrongs of the marriage, nor do laws regarding financial matters after divorce take into account the actual division of labour during the marriage. On the other hand, Dutch migration law was used as an instrument of power, for example, when lack of child contact can also mean a deportation from the Netherlands. Some spouses also tried to involve the law in domestic violence cases, by reporting to the police, but all failed to mobilise the law in such a way. Moreover, because of legal arrangements like maintenance and child care, power relations connected to financial dependency and violence can continue after the divorce.

It is difficult to draw conclusions on marital power relations on the basis of a research on transnational divorce. In this chapter, I recounted stories *about* power, and thus mostly about decision-making, Komter's first dimension of power. Still, some latent dimensions of power, the second dimension of power in Komter's division, become visible after divorce ends the marriage. Looking back on their marriage, some women told stories of control and violence which they had not recognised as such when they were still married to their former husbands. As most stories which deal with marital power deal with attempt by the other spouse to exercise power, they are stories about powerlessness, resistance, and agency. These stories of victimhood can in themselves also carry a certain power, which is also related to gender, ethnicity, and social class. As we have seen in discussions of the *Bezness* frame in Chapter 4, not all interviewees have equal possibilities to claim a position of victimhood. Further research, including both (former) spouses, is needed to unravel the influence of other status inequalities specific for transnational marriage, such as residence status, ethnicity, social and cultural capital, and their intersections with gender and migration.

References

2011. Morocco: Challenges with addressing domestic violence in compliance with the Convention Against Torture. 47th Session of the Committee Against Torture (31 October–25 November, 2011). Global Rights/The advocates for Human Rights.

Anderson, K.L. 1997. Gender, status, and domestic violence: An integration of feminist and family violence approaches. *Journal of Marriage and the Family*: 655–669.

Bartowski, John P. 1999. One Step Forward, One Step Back: "Progressive Traditionalism" and the Negotiation of Domestic Labor in Evangelical Families. *Gender Issues* 17(4): 37–61.

Blood, Robert Oscar Jr., and M. Wolfe. 1960. *Husbands & wives: the dynamics of married living*. Glencoe: Free Press.

Brown, Thea, Margarita Frederico, Lesley Hewitt, and Rosemary Sheehan. 2001. The Child Abuse and Divorce Myth. *Child Abuse Review* 10(2): 113–124.

Buitelaar, Marjo. 2000. Het liefst gewoon een Marokkaan? Over de partnerkeuze van hoogopgeleide vrouwen van Marokkaanse afkomst in Nederland. In *Liefst een gewoon huwelijk? Creatie en conflict in levensverhalen van jonge migrantenvrouwen*, ed. Kristel Luyckx, 139–180. Leuven: Acco.

Clement, Christine, Corine van Egten, and Saskia de Hoog. 2008. *Nieuwe Gezinnen. Scheidingen en de vorming van stiefgezinnen*: E-Quality.

Diop-Sidibé, Nafissatou, Jacquelyn C. Campbell, and Stan Becker. 2006. Domestic Violence Against Women in Egypt—Wife Beating and Health Outcomes. *Social Science & Medicine* 62(5): 1260–1277.

Gentry, James W., Suraj Commuri, and Sunkyu Jun. 2003. Review of Literature on Gender in the Family. *Academy of Marketing Science Review* 2003 (1).

Geurts, Edith. 2009. Omgaan met signalen van ex-partners over kindermishandeling. *Jeugd en Co Kennis* 3(2): 8–18.

Helmers, Dini. 2002. *Gescheurde bedden.* In *Oplossingen voor gestrande huwelijken, Amsterdam, 1753–1810.* Hilversum: Verloren.

Jaffe, Peter G., Claire V. Crooks, and Samantha E. Poisson. 2003. Common misconceptions in addressing domestic violence in child custody disputes. *Juvenile and Family Court Journal* 54(4): 57–67.

Jewkes, Rachel, Jonathan Levin, and Loveday Penn-Kekana. 2002. Risk Factors for Domestic Violence: Findings from a South African Cross-sectional Study. *Social science & medicine* 55(9): 1603–1617.

Johnson, Michael P., and K.J. Ferraro. 2000. Research on Domestic Violence in the 1990s: Making Distinctions. *Journal of Marriage and Family* 62(4): 948–963.

Johnson, Michael P., and Janel M. Leone. 2005. The Differential Effects of Intimate Terrorism and Situational Couple Violence. *Journal of Family Issues* 26(3): 322–349. doi:10.1177/0192513x04270345.

Komter, Aafke Elisabeth. 1985. *De macht van de vanzelfsprekendheid in relaties tussen vrouwen en mannen.* Leiden: University of Leiden. Proefschrift.

———. 1989. Hidden Power in Marriage. *Gender & Society* 3(2): 187–216.

Korvorst, Marjolein, and Tanja Traag. 2010. De verdeling van arbeid en zorg tussen vaders en moeders. *Bevolkingstrends* (2e kwartaal 2010).

Lukes, Steven. 1978. *Power: A radical view.* London: Macmillan.

Luyckx, Kristel. 2000. *Liefst een gewoon huwelijk? Creatie en conflict in levensverhalen van jonge migrantenvrouwen.* Ed. A. De Munynck, M.C. Foblets, B. Hubeau, A. Martens and S. Parmentier, *Minderheden in de samenleving.* Leuven:Acco.

McDonald, Gerald W. 1980. Family Power: The Assessment of a Decade of Theory and Research, 1970–1979. *Journal of Marriage and the Family* 42(4): 841–854.

Pyke, Karen D. 1994. Women's Employment as a Gift or Burden? Marital Power Across Marriage, Divorce, and Remarriage. *Gender & Society* 8(1): 73–91.

Römkens, Renée. 2010. Omstreden gelijkheid. Over de constructie van (on) gelijkheid van vrouwen en mannen in partnergeweld. *Justitiële verkenningen* 36(8): 11–32.

Speelman, Gé. 2001. *Keeping Faith. Muslim-Christian Couples and Interreligious Dialogue.* Meinema: Zoetermeer.

Tichenor, Veronica. 2005. Maintaining Men's Dominance: Negotiating Identity and Power When She Earns More. *Sex Roles* 53(3/4): 191–205.

van der Velde, F., D.A. Albers, and K.D. Hekkert. 2009. Mannen in zorgberoepen en kinderopvang. Onderzoeksprogramma Arbeidsmarkt in Zorg en Welzijn.

van Dijk, Tom, and Erik Oppenhuis. 2002. *Huiselijk geweld onder Surinamers, Antillianen en Arubanen, Marokkanen en Turken in Nederland : aard, omvang en hulpverlening*. Hilversum: Intomart.

Verwijs, Rianne, and Katinka Lünnemann. 2012. *Partnergeweld. Achtergrond en risicofactoren*. Utrecht: Verweij Jonker Instituut.

Vogler, Carolyn. 1998. Money in the Household: Some Underlying Issues of Power. *The Sociological Review* 46(4): 687–713.

6

Taking Care of the Children. Organising Child Care After Divorce

> Meanwhile I have tried to convince [ex-wife] about what happened. What she has done to the children. That it really won't do, and that it's just very bad for the children. And that something needs to be fixed. I tried talking to her, on the phone, in conversations, emails. And she keeps refusing, she maintains she's the best mother in the world, and so on. Because that's how she sees herself. But not to my liking. (René, Dutch father divorced from Egyptian mother, living in the Netherlands)

René, a Dutch father, was involved in a series of court cases against his Egyptian ex-wife on their children, involving legal issues such as the residence of the children, child contact, and maintenance.[1] René blames his former wife for harming the children by keeping them away from him and by involving them in conflicts between their parents. His story is framed

[1] In Morocco, Egypt, and the Netherlands, a multitude of legal, semi-legal, and non-legal terms are used to describe child care arrangements after divorce. These terms do not always translate easily into—legal—English, because of the differences in legal culture. In this chapter, I have chosen to use the term residence and residential parent to describe the place and the parent with whom the children live. The term residence as used in this book describes a de facto situation and is not necessarily connected to the legal position of the parents. Child contact is the contact between the non-residential parent and the child(ren). Again, this is the actual contact taking place, regardless of there being a formal agreement or contact order by a court.

I. Sportel, *Divorce in Transnational Families*,
DOI 10.1007/978-3-319-34009-8_6

completely in terms of the best interest of the children. He presents himself as a good father, trying to protect his children from the effects of divorce while his ex-wife acts as a bad mother who took the children away from their father. In this chapter, I explore parenthood after transnational divorce. How did participants arrange the care for their children after divorce? How did they deal with cross-border disputes? And what was the role of the law in taking decisions on children and child care after divorce?

Like René, many parents told stories of 'good' and 'bad' parenthood after transnational divorce. In this chapter, I will demonstrate the importance of gendered notions of good and bad parenthood for how parents talk about care for children after divorce. I will draw on the work of Kaganas and Day-Sclater (2004) who have demonstrated how, in UK contact disputes, parents and the court share a 'welfare discourse', constantly trying to present themselves as good parents, acting in the best interest of their child. According to Kaganas and Day-Sclater, this welfare discourse includes certain implicit images of good and bad parents, which are voiced in gender-neutral language in the law and in court, but are strongly gendered in practice. The good mother puts her own interest below that of her children and actively enables contact with the non-resident father (Kaganas and Day-Sclater 2004: p. 13). The bad mother obstructs that contact and uses her influence with the children to alienate them from their father, influencing them to refuse contact (Kaganas and Day-Sclater 2004: p. 20–21). Because of the crucial importance the welfare discourse attaches to contact between children and their fathers, the qualifications for being a 'good' father are not very burdensome (Kaganas and Day-Sclater 2004: p. 18).

Below, I will draw out in more detail these notions of good and bad parenthood after divorce, and how these impacted actual arrangements and disputes over child residence, contact, and maintenance costs.

Stories on Good and Bad Parenthood in Transnational Marriage

Many parents in the interviews presented stories of good and bad parents. Often these stories took a prominent place in the interview, especially if there had been conflicts over the children, and they regularly came up without any questions or prompting. One Moroccan father already started making his point about parenthood after divorce the minute after I entered his car, heading towards the home of his parents where the interview was agreed to take place.

It must be noted that analysing the interviews with divorced parents as stories in which they construct images of good and bad parents does not necessarily mean that these parents are consciously manipulating their narrative to make themselves look good or their former spouse look bad by talking about the best interest of their children. As has been said before, high-conflict cases involving domestic violence, child abduction, or deceit may be overrepresented in this study. Analysing these interviews in terms of images is not meant to lessen the impact of these stories, as interviewees may very well be right if they claim their children have been harmed by the behaviour of their former spouse. But analysing their stories can reveal underlying norms on good and bad parenting.

From the interviews in this research two stories emerge about 'bad parents', both during the marriage and after divorce. First of all, there is the absent parent, who fails to meet the needs of his or her children. Secondly, there is the parent who involves the children in the conflict with the other spouse or uses them to pressure the other parent. On the other hand, the 'good' parent is involved in child care both during the marriage and after divorce and takes the best interest of the child as a starting point. Many interviewees consider it necessary for children that both parents, or at least both a female and a male caregiver, are involved in the raising of a child.

The absent parent, both during the marriage and after divorce, is a strongly negative image that comes up in several interviews. Three mothers, for example, volunteered stories of being alone with a crying baby while their husband would not be disturbed:

> When he had a late shift, the little one should not cry at all. [he said:] 'Get your child and get out!' It was a small apartment. Not a place where I could go upstairs or downstairs. It was my child and not his child. 'It's your child, go to sleep!' I really was surprised and disappointed. (Rabia, Moroccan woman divorced from Dutch-Moroccan husband, living in the Netherlands)

> He was very concerned during the pregnancy and all, so that was ok. But once the child was there and I laid in bed more dead than alive, then things had to... [Son] was a fussy baby. It was just a terrible disaster, because he thought that the baby should not cry. But he also thought that I was better at it than he was, because if he walked around or whatever with the child it just kept screaming. So that was my job. [...] But right, I just gave birth, the child was five days old and I kept dragging it around. And it kept crying. He [husband] lay in bed like, well, that's arranged fine, and I had to.... (Ingrid, Dutch woman with a Moroccan husband)
>
> Also when [name daughter] was born. The first year he slept in the attic. Because he did not want to wake up from her crying. So I had to get out of bed every night to take care of her. He said: 'well, I need to be on the road the next day, and I can't concentrate if the child keeps me awake half the night'. Well, have I been dragging those children around on my own to get them to be quiet. No, I raised the children all by myself. All those years till now. (Margriet, Dutch woman divorced from Egyptian husband, living in the Netherlands)

The crying babies in these quotes were already adolescents or even adults at the time these interviews were held. Though the choice of examples given by these interviewees might have been related to my own position as a researcher—I carried out all of these three interviews either visibly pregnant or as a new mother—being 'left alone' at such a time obviously is taken as a strong token of being an absent and therefore 'bad' husband and father. In the last quote, Margriet used the phrase: 'I raised the children all by myself.' Other mothers, from different backgrounds, have made the same remark. Elizabeth, for example, 'He almost never came home anymore. He arrived at 11pm, midnight. I raised the children by myself' (Dutch woman divorced from Egyptian husband, living in Egypt). In another interview, Halima said, 'I had to do everything on my own in the home. I had to stay inside all day and take care of my sister-in-law and my son. He was working all day' (Halima, Moroccan woman married to Dutch-Moroccan husband, living in the Netherlands).

A few of the interviewed parents included specific elements of transnational marriage in their story about absent and involved parents. For example:

> They have a father from abroad who taught them nothing. No Arabic, nothing. All they hear are nasty things. 'You're not allowed to'. Especially [daughter] she's allowed nothing. If she would have lived in Egypt she would have been allowed nothing at all. [...] Then I tried to get an Arabic teacher into our house. But then he heard that there was quite a lot of beating going on. And anyway, if such a man came to our house he had to be there, and he did not have time for that. He could not leave his wife alone with such a man, no that's not possible. Well, and if he was here, for a few days, on Fridays he took [son] to the Mosque in [city]. But [son] did not know how to pray. He never taught him that. And it isn't my job to do that. Because I know how to pray. I even married as a Muslim. I know how to pray. But it wasn't my job to teach that to my children. But [ex-husband] thought so. Yes, you should teach your children that. Well, and then he left again and they just didn't want to. (Margriet, Dutch woman divorced from Egyptian husband, living in the Netherlands)

In this quote, Margriet blames her husband for being an absent father, leaving his wife and their children for long periods of time to do business abroad. He does not just fail the standard of being an involved father; he failed to be an involved *foreign* father. Margriet refused to teach their children how to pray, as she considered this to be the responsibility of her former husband. As an Egyptian father in a mixed marriage, he should have taught his children about his language and religion.

In another story, René, the Dutch father divorced from an Egyptian wife, who did not have contact with his children after his former wife took them abroad without his consent, explicitly countered his ex-wife telling this story of the absent father in court:

> [I told the judges] about how it went in the past, with the children. And that it was absolutely not true that I did nothing for the children. On the contrary, I did quite a lot, in spite of working elsewhere. I took care of swimming lessons, and on Wednesday, when I was there, I dragged them to all kinds of things. From creative things, sports, after-school child care, language lessons, doctors, those kinds of things. The dentist. And that I did a lot on weekends, that it wasn't true I did nothing, on the contrary. And that I could take care of them very well, no problem. (René, Dutch man divorced from Egyptian wife)

In his story, René counters the argument of his former wife that he should not be allowed a contact arrangement because he was a 'bad', absent father. He positions himself as being an involved, 'good' father by recounting the things he did for the children and his capacity to take care of them.

The stories recounted above are highly gendered. Mothers complained about their marriage, 'raising their children all alone', whereas fathers countered such narratives by showing their involvement in the upbringing of the children during the marriage. Furthermore, they are remarkably similar across the wide diversity of cultural and religious backgrounds of the parents interviewed. While a few stories have distinct transnational elements, many narratives share a strong resemblance in content and wording, raising questions on how 'different' transnational families actually are when it comes to the issue of absent parents. The cultural frames so common in explaining the end of the marriage are remarkably missing in these stories on absent fathers.

In the second story of the 'bad parent' after divorce, parents use the children in the conflict with the former spouse, acting in their own interest instead of that of the children. In the interviews, this story is reflected especially in cases where there was a high level of conflict between the parents on the residence of the children, including two cases where one of the parents has taken the children abroad. René, the Dutch man divorced from an Egyptian wife, speaks at length about how his former wife estranged their children from him and involved them in their dispute:

> She said things to me like 'me and the children are one'. That meant that I just shouldn't ask anything with regard to the children. She really sees it like that. Maybe that explains the fact that she involves the children in all the ugliness. And that they just have to play a role, like a kind of child soldiers. They are trained to deal with jobs for her. Well, the more I became aware of this, the harder it was for me to ask anything at all, because if I asked something, or if I did something, the children were given hell about it. (René, Dutch man divorced from Egyptian wife)

The mother of the children is pictured as a bad mother because she involves the children in conflicts between the parents, and even punishes them for what their father does. In contrast, René positions himself as a good father, that is, a parent that puts the best interest of the children before his own and leaves them out of the conflict. Elsewhere in the interview he recounts:

> I have always, in any subject, taken the position that I do not want to get in a situation where she is pulling the children from one side and I on the other. [...] The last thing I want is for things to go through them. But that did not work out. If we had a fight, for example, I always wanted to just freeze it until we had absolute time for it, to talk about it quietly, away from the children, but she never wanted that. Fights were always solved on the spot, with a lot of shouting. When I had left the house, in these kind of situations, when she was screaming again—she did that during fights—well then I said; 'let's take it easy. Do not scream, be quiet, the children are upstairs.' And then she just shouted the children downstairs, to come and join us, etc. It was just unbelievable. (Ibid)

In his story, René tries to protect his children by keeping them out of the conflict, as a good parent should do. He fails, however, because his ex-wife insists on involving them. She is described as the paradigm bad mother, putting her own interest above that of her children and keeping them away from their father. An Egyptian father also referred to this image of good and bad parents when discussing his former partner's behaviour:

> Here [in the Netherlands] everything is more individual. Here, a woman can leave, breaking everything behind her, without showing consideration for others. It's always me, me, me. We do things differently. We don't put elderly parents in a nursing home. Here is egoism. That's also positive, not just negative. But unfortunately not humanitarian. [...] If the children are with me they always can go to her. Because of their pets. It's always allowed, she's their mother. At first they kept asking me for permission, slightly nervous. Now they just tell me. But if they're with her, it's much less. They're a little bit afraid of her. There's no contact [between interviewee and ex-wife], only a text message if necessary. (Latif, Egyptian man separated from Dutch partner, living in the Netherlands)

In this quote, Latif puts an ethnic label on this archetypical bad mother, by relating it to an individualistic and egoistic Dutch society. He goes on with an example to describe himself as a good father and his former partner as a less-than-good mother in this same welfare discourse. Even though they have a co-parenting arrangement, proposed by the mother, she blocks contact between him and the children in the time they spend with her. Latif himself always facilitates contact between the mother and the children, putting their interest above his own 'it's their mother'.

Most of these stories are, again, highly gendered, with 'bad' mothers blocking the access of fathers. However, there were also cases in which mothers invoke this discourse against fathers. For example Karin, a Dutch mother divorced from an Egyptian husband recounts how her former husband decided to stop paying maintenance and change the residence of the children:

> Then suddenly I got an offer from [employer], to work. Then I got a whole different life. [...] But well, if there are holidays, they need to go to him [ex-husband]. He did not like that. And she [new partner] also did not like it. Until last summer. The school added another month to the holiday. And I told them; 'well, the children have to go to you.' Well, I did not get an answer. Nothing at all. But I knew he was home. So I called our taxidriver. Because I had to go to work, I could not leave the children on their own. And [taxidriver] brought them to him. Well, then he exploded. Then he said: 'you're not getting any money anymore. Nothing. The children stay with me. And I'll pay the rent for one more month, it's your problem.' [...] But it's simply all about the money. And it's like that with most Egyptians. I think if you hear most of those stories. It's absolutely only about the money. The amount of money they can take from you. Really, it's always a horror. It's about nothing else. It's horrible but it's true. Well, it's also how they are raised, right? (Karin, Dutch mother divorced from Egyptian husband, living in Egypt)

In this quote, Karin blames her former husband for changing the residence of the children, just for money instead of their best interest. Moreover, like Latif, she ethnicises the conflict by relating it to the fact that he is Egyptian and thus all about the money. In this, she even seems to refer to the *Bezness* frame of Egyptians trying to take away your money. If so, this again illustrates the particular strength of this frame that it can even be used when discussing child maintenance paid by the Egyptian husband to his former Dutch wife.

Thus, in two of these stories on parenting after transnational divorce to be a good parent is to make the best interest of the children central and above one's own interest. In these stories, the best interest of the child is framed using two main criteria. First of all, both during the marriage and after divorce, both parents should be involved with the child. A few parents mention involvement specific to the transnational context, for example, the transmission of 'foreign' skills, such as language or religion. Secondly, the child should not be involved in conflicts between the parents; ideally the parents arrange child care during and after divorce in harmony, or at least without the children's presence. Other than in the frame of absent parents, spouses used cultural explanations more often when accusing their former spouse of involving the children in the conflict.

Arranging Child Care After Transnational Divorce

After a divorce, parents need to arrange how they will provide the necessary care for their children, including issues like—where will the children live (residence) and how and when will they see their other parent (contact), and paying for the costs of their upbringing (child maintenance). In transnational families, where divorce may involve (return) migration, these issues can become both legally and practically complicated. In what follows, I will describe how parents have arranged for child care after their divorce, and how they have taken such decisions.

Considering the differences in legal context between Morocco, Egypt, and the Netherlands, as discussed in the legal chapter, the arrangements parents made for the residence of their children after divorce are remarkably similar for former couples living in the three countries. In the research group, 17 out of 26 interviewees had children with their former spouse.[2] In most cases, the children had lived with one of the parents after the divorce. In ten cases this was the mother; in five cases this was the father, and in two cases, both of Dutch-Egyptian mixed couples, they

[2] A further three interviewees had children from another relationship at the moment of the divorce. In all cases, these stayed with their original parent after the divorce.

lived with both parents. That in one-third of cases the children are residing with the father is rather remarkable considering the strong preference for residence with the mother in Moroccan and Egyptian law and general practice in Dutch society.[3] While the limited number of participants and the design of this study do not support generalisations to the entire population of transnational families, some reasons can be seen to relate these possible differences between transnational and non-transnational families in care arrangements to migration. For example, in some cases, either the father took the children away to another country without the consent of the mother, or the mother abandoned the father with the children and departed to her country of origin. In other cases, however, this was a friendly agreement between parents of older teens who preferred to live with their father, and was thus not connected to the divorce being transnational.

A central point in the stories of transnational couples is that these private arrangements were generally not the result of active bargaining. Rather, the proposed arrangements were often implicit, for example:

> I: And the children came to live with you?
> R: Yes, then, at the moment of the divorce, they came with me. They also had enough of him. Both of them. At first they kept contact, but it broke off after a while. (Sofia, Egyptian woman divorced from Egyptian husband, living in the Netherlands)

> I: And did you arrange anything for the children or the division of property after your divorce?
> R: No, as I said, the eldest already left. He was almost 19, and the youngest turned 18 shortly afterwards. So he stayed with his father for a while. But we all live nearby, so we see each other regularly. [...] We did not make any formal arrangements, everything went in harmony. (Claudia, Dutch woman divorced from Moroccan husband, living in the Netherlands)

In these quotes, the interviewees present their solution as natural and logical, regardless of whether it was the father or the mother who

[3] In the Netherlands, between 2000 and 2007, in about 10 % of the divorces, the children had their main residence with their father, whereas in a further 20 % of divorces the children had their residence with both parents, travelling back and forth (CBS 2009: p. 21).

became the resident parent. As such, this can be seen as an aspect of *latent power*. There is no open conflict, as the situation is considered natural, necessary, and unchangeable (Komter 1989). Only a few interviewees explicitly explained why they chose a certain care arrangement, even though there had been no discussion over the residence of their child. For example:

> R: […] Well, basically he was there [at his father's house] every other week.
> I: You agreed about that from the beginning?
> R: Yes, because he worked on weekdays. He had to get up early and could not have a small child about the house.
> I: And did you then discuss that [name son] could live there?
> R: No, no. In any case I do not consider a man alone to be a good situation for a child, and I arranged everything properly with child care and things like that, so I just let it go.
> I: But would your ex-husband have wanted him to have lived with him?
> R: In theory he would have liked to, but how he would have dealt with everything practically he did not know yet, so, well... Of course, things like pre-school child care exist, but you need to make additional arrangements for that. Actually, he was all right with it. (Ingrid, Dutch woman divorced from Moroccan husband, living in the Netherlands)

Ingrid mentioned both practical reasons as well as ideological reasons. She thought small children should stay with their mother, or at least not with a single father. At the moment of the interview, the now adolescent child was living with his father, who had by then contracted a new marriage. There were a few more interviewees using this explicitly gendered discourse in which small children belong with their mother. It can also be seen in the story of Amar, a Moroccan father. His wife had abandoned him and the children when she unexpectedly returned to the Netherlands after having an affair with one of his relatives. Because she had been the main breadwinner, he was left with their children but without an income to support himself or the children. He then moved to live with his mother. He was quite unhappy with his situation. Even though when his wife had left them, and he had been the major caregiver during their marriage, in his opinion his wife still had more rights—and the duty—to have the children, because she is female:

> If she does not come back and I get my money from the Netherlands.[4] I would like a new wife for the children. And my own house. There has to be a woman for the children. Tomorrow my mother will die, and then what? (Amar, Moroccan man with Dutch wife, living in Morocco)

In this quote, Amar specifically refers to his children needing a female caregiver. Regardless of being the main caregiver during the marriage, Amar would have preferred the 'usual' arrangement, with the children living with their mother and him having the right to visit them one day a week: 'She is free. I have to take care of three children all day. [...] I should never have started a family. She wanted children, ok, and then we make children. Now I am left with them, always on my hands (Amar).' In this last quote, taking care of the children is more of a burden than of an asset, even though the father had already been the main caregiver during the marriage.

Amar represents a second situation in which there has been no discussion over the residence of the children: one of the parents taking and enforcing a unilateral decision. In these decisions, which can be seen as a form of *manifest power* (Komter 1989), power is more visible than in those situations where no open conflict was present. If one of the spouses left the marital home or even the country without making any arrangements for the children, the spouse that was abandoned has little choice but to continue taking care of the children. A rather similar story was told by Rabia. After several years of marriage her Dutch-Moroccan husband left for another European country to start a business there, intending to move the whole family when the business was successful. When his wife and children came to visit, however, they found out that he had found a new partner.

> Then I decided to stay here [in the Netherlands] after all and go on with my job. I had good employment, but I did have six children. It was a very tough job.
> I: Six children?

[4] This interviewee was involved in a dispute concerning social security from his former Dutch employment.

R: Yes, it was his wish to have six children. But in the end I was left with them. [...] I had some patience, hoping that he would miss his children after all. And that he would come and visit us, but it did not happen. He did not call; he did not come to visit. He left everything behind him and forgot it all. (Rabia, Moroccan woman divorced from Dutch-Moroccan husband)

Like the Moroccan man in the previous quote, Rabia refers to having children because her husband wanted to [have so many]. By leaving their children behind with their former spouse and leaving the country, both ex-partners left them little choice but to continue caring for the children. However, it must be noted that not all spouses had similar possibilities to undertake such actions, had they wished to do so. For example, the Dutch mother who left Amar and their children behind in Morocco made use of the mobility connected to her Dutch nationality which ensured her husband and children could not follow her to the Netherlands.[5] Amar, a Moroccan citizen and unwanted migrant in the Netherlands, would not have been able to take similar actions.

These issues of residence disputes involving national borders and, thus, migration and residence law are specific to transnational marriages. In other cases, parents have also made use of state borders and Dutch migration law to take one-sided decisions over their children's residence but in different ways. Some Dutch-Moroccan fathers had not abandoned their former spouse but kept living in the marital home while they made both their wife and the children leave the country. Other spouses took the children with them, leaving the other parent behind.

A situation specific to Dutch-Moroccan migration marriages residing in the Netherlands is the involuntary abandonment (*gedwongen achterlating* or 'leaving behind') of women and children in the country of origin. In these cases, Moroccan women and children who have been living in the Netherlands are taken to Morocco, for example, for visiting relatives or a family holiday. During their stay, the husband takes away the Dutch passports or residence papers and returns to the Netherlands alone,

[5] Legally, the children should have had Dutch nationality, as they had a Dutch mother. However, as explained above, there were some problems with their situation and they did not yet have Dutch passports to travel with.

leaving his wife and children behind in Morocco (Bakker 2008, Bartels 2005, Smit van Waesberghe et al. 2014). For example:

> Suddenly he said 'let's go on holiday, because last time was not pleasant at all.' [...] I did not bring enough clothes. He said I would not need them because we were only going for two weeks. I also did not bring enough clothes for our child. It was all just normal. He acted kindly, so I would not notice anything. We stayed with his family for a night and then he said I could spend a nice holiday with my own parents, and he with his parents. But after a few days he did not call. And he did not answer my calls. (Halima, Moroccan woman with Dutch-Moroccan husband)

In this quote, Halima blames her husband for deceiving her about going only on a short holiday, emphasising how she was asked to only to pack a small number of things, which was not just a problem for her, but also for their child, implicitly blaming her husband for neglecting to keep his child's interest in mind. As the story continues, the husband's family kept providing different excuses to account for his absence and reasons to prolong their visit until Halima found out that her papers were missing.

This story of involuntary abandonment contains an element of deception and discovery similar to those in the *Bezness* stories described in Chapter 3. Halima finds out that she has been deceived, and that what should have been a nice holiday in which the couple could reconcile their differences was in fact an intentional attempt to return her and her son to Morocco. By abandoning his wife and child in Morocco while returning to the Netherlands, this father did more or less the same as the parents who abandoned their spouse and children, thus unilaterally enforcing child care after divorce. However, instead of migrating himself, he made his wife and child leave their country of residence, the Netherlands, and return to Morocco.

As it is far more difficult to return to the Netherlands on a Moroccan or Egyptian passport than it is to return to Egypt or Morocco on a Dutch passport, abandonment is almost exclusively a problem for migrating spouses from the Global South, mostly women (see also: Smit van Waesberghe et al. 2014). It is this difference in nationality and migration laws, what Castles has called hierarchical citizenship (Castles 2005: p. 690), which provides certain transnational parents with the powerful means of involuntary abandonment in the country of origin without legal documents. Furthermore, this citizenship interacts with other resources of power, such as access to financial means, care, and (legal) knowledge. Since 2004, considerable attention has been paid to this phenomenon. Several NGOs have lobbied to alter Dutch immigration policies to enable these women to return to the Netherlands, at least temporarily, to deal with their affairs in the Netherlands. Abandoned women can now report to the Dutch embassy in Rabat or to the Berkane office of NGO SSR, where they can get assistance to return to the Netherlands.[6] Through this assistance, Halima was enabled to return to the Netherlands and formally divorce her husband.

The opposite of leaving one parent behind to take care of the children is so-called international parental child abduction. This means one of the parents takes the child away from the usual place of residence and the other parent to another country, taking the child out of the reach of the other parent. In these cases, children and child care are seen less as a burden, and more as a benefit that can be stolen away.[7] International child abduction is a well-known phenomenon, especially with regard to mixed marriages, and in all three countries such cases have received media coverage. Some divorced spouses, especially Dutch partners in mixed marriages, considered international child abduction an important risk of divorce. For example, Margriet, a Dutch mother, was very much afraid of her husband taking the children away to Egypt and therefore chose to postpone her divorce:

> Because I had witnessed that abduction of our close friends. I was pregnant with [Son] when it happened. They were twins. Oh, oh. I always thought about that when I wanted to divorce. [name Daughter] was four when I

---

[6] I will further discuss the SSR and the Dutch embassy in Chapter 7.

[7] Legally, child abduction has been arranged in the *Hague Convention on the Civil Aspects of International Child Abduction* of 1980 and the *Convention on Jurisdiction, Applicable Law, Recognition, Enforcement and Co-operation in Respect of Parental Responsibility and Measures for the Protection of Children* of 1996. Morocco and the Netherlands are party to the Child Abduction Convention, Egypt is not. In practice, the regulation of international child abduction means that parents in a transnational marriage who share custody legally cannot leave the country of residence with their children without the permission of the other parent or a judge. See for a thorough discussion of transnational child custody disputes: (Carlisle 2014).

> first thought about divorce. But I waited until they were grown-up. [...] Because I did not want the fuss, I did not want things to happen, like him abducting the children or something. (Margriet, Dutch woman divorced from Egyptian husband)

Of the 17 divorce cases with children in this research, there were 3 cases which could be classified as parental child abduction; one of the parents had taken the children away from the other parent without their consent, crossing national borders. A Dutch-Moroccan and an Egyptian mother both took their children away from the Netherlands and in one case a Dutch-Moroccan father took the child from Morocco to the Netherlands. Interestingly, both mothers did not take the children to their countries of origin, but to third countries of which they did not have the nationality. Unlike the parents that abandoned their spouse and children and broke off contact, parents whose children were taken away did not make that choice themselves. In all three cases, there was no, or only very limited, contact between the abandoned parents and the children. In the other interviews as well, transnational elements played a role in the enabling or impeding of contact between non-resident parents and their children.

Contact with the Non-resident Parent

As most of the children stayed with one parent after divorce, contact with the other parent was no longer as self-evident as when parents and children were living in the same household. Sometimes, parents and children had no problems keeping contact:

> My youngest son went his own way, but he regularly came to me for dinner or to bring his laundry. From a distance, I have kept an eye on things for a few years afterwards. On Saturday, or at weekends, when there was time, I went there to do some housekeeping. That's how things developed. (Claudia, Dutch woman divorced from Moroccan husband, living in the Netherlands)

Claudia described no conflicts whatsoever surrounding her divorce and the contact with the children who stayed with her former husband.

However, this situation was an exception among the participants in this research. Of the 17 divorce cases with children in this research, in 9 cases there was no contact at all between the children and the other parent. Furthermore, in half of the 8 cases in which there was contact, it was a source of dissatisfaction or conflict.

In all but one of these no-contact cases, one of the parents had migrated to another country after the divorce, with or without the children. Although regular contact between parents and children after divorce is of course far easier when living in the same country, this does not mean that the transnational context is always the *cause* of severing contact between non-resident parents and children. For example, René, the Dutch father whose children were taken away by their mother, already lost all contact with his children before their mother took them abroad, despite many attempts to establish contact, including several court cases. All no-contact cases involved either one of the spouses abandoning the other parent with the children, child abduction, or leaving mothers and child(ren) behind in the country of origin. These no-contact cases are thus better explained from being high-conflict divorces, than from parents living in different states.

In some cases, such a lack of contact between non-residential parents and children can also have consequences for the residence status of a dependent foreign spouse. Taking into account Dutch residence law and immigration procedures, contact with a child can be closely linked to the possibilities for a foreign spouse to remain living in the Netherlands after divorce. If a divorce takes place while the Moroccan or Egyptian spouse is still on a dependent residence permit, without having spent enough time living in the Netherlands to be allowed to stay independently, this might mean that he or she has to leave the country.[8] This gives the resident parent power over their former spouse; by blocking contact—even if there are important reasons to do so—the former spouse will lose the right to stay in the Netherlands. In one case in this research, Farid, a Moroccan father, did not have access to his child because of Dutch migration procedures, losing his dependent residence permit after his former wife arranged a

[8] For the cases in this research this was generally after three years of marriage, since 2012 it has become five years.

court order to block contact. His forced return migration abruptly ended the existing informal contact arrangement, which had continued despite the court order (Farid, Moroccan man divorced from Dutch wife).

On the other hand, several parents whose children lived with them complained that the other parent of the children did not keep in contact:

> The children are fed up with it. My daughter keeps asking 'is that my mother?' about women she meets. My eldest son is very angry with his mother. I tell the children that their mother will not come back. I do not want to give them false hope. I never get a reaction to my emails. They are your children, please contact them, they want to see you! But we never saw anything. (Amar, Moroccan man with Dutch wife, living in Morocco)
>
> She [daughter] does not even want to go with him [the father]. He hurt her a lot. He thinks that life is only money or whatever, but he does not know that his daughter needs her father. She sometimes talks about her friends in school. Their fathers hold them on their laps or cuddle them. She does not have that. [...] She tells me: 'mama, I am afraid that, in the future, you may also get married and leave me behind all alone'. (Samira, Dutch-Moroccan woman divorced from Moroccan husband, living in Morocco)
>
> And when my son calls his father, his father says: 'we will see each other on Saturday'. But many Saturdays go by and he does not come. He has not seen his father in five months. (Majda, Moroccan woman with Dutch-Moroccan husband, living in Morocco)

These parents also frame their stories in the welfare discourse. Speaking from the perspective of their children, they blame their former spouse for not being present when their children need them. Although in the cases of the last two quotes there actually was contact between the non-resident parent and the children, it did not run smoothly and the mothers still felt that their ex-spouses failed their children by disappointing them and not meeting their children's needs before their own. Conflicts about child contact were regularly accompanied by conflicts about child maintenance. In these conflicts, similar reproaches about non-resident fathers not meeting the needs of their children were made. I will discuss this further below.

Child Maintenance

Raising children can be expensive, while family income may go down after divorce, as two households need to be sustained instead of one. Thus, financial responsibilities can be an important part of child care after divorce. It must be noted that many participants did not make a distinction between child maintenance and spousal maintenance, combining both to a female right of mothers and wives to be maintained by their former husband. I will go further into these aspects of maintenance in Chapter 7 on financial issues. Below I will limit my discussion on child maintenance to the context of child care after divorce.

In total, 11 out of 17 parents in this study reported that some form of maintenance had been determined or agreed upon, 7 in the Netherlands, 2 in Egypt and 2 in Morocco. All of the receiving parents were mothers. In half of the cases, this was the result of a court procedure, while in the others it was arranged privately. When it was arranged privately, most couples did not mention a lot of explicit bargaining when determining the amount. Similar to child residence agreements, this either was described as natural or as the result of one-sided decisions forced by one of the parents. For example:

> I: Did you also just arrange an amount for maintenance or did the judge do that?
>
> R: I said 125 *gulden*, and he did not object. We even forced it up a bit. Because you could only deduct [the maintenance paid] from the taxes from 150 gulden. So he paid me a little bit more officially, and then I returned it underhandedly. Back then I still received tax rebates, so we tried to arrange everything as neatly as possible. At least, as advantageous as possible. (Ingrid, Dutch woman divorced from Moroccan husband, living in the Netherlands)

This couple had made private arrangements without consulting a judge or a lawyer on the matter. While Ingrid determined the amount, she even helped the husband to gain tax advantages for maintenance. In another example, the amount of maintenance was decided one-sidedly by the paying father:

> Here in Morocco they have a law that he has to give a small amount for his daughter. And how much did he leave for her? 120 euro. Per month.
>
> I: Well, that's not much.

> R: What's that for such a small child? She pays 70 euro per month for school. A private school. What's left to live by? He arranged all that. (Samira, Dutch-Moroccan woman divorced from Moroccan husband, living in Morocco)

Samira considers the amount of maintenance paid by her husband to their daughter to be unfair, as it is their only source of income and they cannot both live by such a limited amount. In her story, her husband arranged their divorce without her knowledge, leaving his former wife no further options to defend her own or her daughter's financial interests in court or in private negotiations.

Instead of giving money to Samira if their daughter needed something, he bought it for her, but only after she pressed him to do so. The child maintenance paid thus does contribute to schooling, but not to basic needs like food and housing. Moreover, because Samira needs to ask each time, and only receives goods instead of money which can be spent freely, the dependency on maintenance also gave her former husband power over her. She feels like she should be careful around her former husband, in order not to upset him and endanger her child's schooling.

For other respondents in this research, maintenance was also often a source of conflict. There were only two cases in which the maintenance payments were actually made as agreed upon or ordered by the court. For some of the interviewed mothers who were dependent on this income, this was a serious problem, forcing them to look for additional sources of income or support. The issue of maintenance can also be symbolic for larger conflicts. Two interviewed men stopped or delayed maintenance payments because of other conflicts with their former spouse over their children, using maintenance payments as a resource of power:

> R: Because I refuse to pay, as my children have been abducted. It's a matter of principle. Moreover, the fact that she has taken away the children completely from me, well, then she also has to take complete responsibility. Moreover, she has the means to do so, so it's not like the children lack anything. Now it's like, if I would pay child maintenance, it's just a bonus for her. Considering the pay she gets. So I just refuse [to pay]. (René, Dutch man divorced from Egyptian wife, living in the Netherlands)

René stopped the child maintenance payments at a symbolic moment after he had reported to the police that his children were missing. He considers it to be unfair that he should still pay child maintenance to his former wife when she has taken the children from him. Moreover, he claims that his wife has more than sufficient means to support the children herself, so that they will not suffer if he does not pay. With this statement he counters the welfare discourse argument that he pays maintenance for the interest and upkeep of his children, regardless of the behaviour of his former wife or his contact with the children. This is also implied in the popular Dutch statement '*alimentatie is geen kijkgeld*', meaning that maintenance and contact between children and non-resident parents should be unrelated and the interest of the children should be central.[9] Similarly, another man also refused to pay maintenance until his other demands regarding the children were met:

> She doesn't get a penny from me. She won't consent to passports for the children, for a holiday to Egypt. She would only cooperate once I pay all the overdue maintenance. 350 euro a month, that's 10,000 euro in all. But maintenance was only item number six [on their agreement]. I wanted to arrange all other points first. 1. Custody. 2. Last name. [...] I'll only pay once the passports are here. But when [daughter] was in hospital, I was informed. I really appreciated that. If there is normal contact [between interviewee and ex-wife] I'm willing to do something extra. (Latif, Egyptian man separated from Dutch partner, living in the Netherlands)

Even though Latif has a co-parenting arrangement with his former Dutch partner, he has an ongoing struggle over the last name and parental authority over their children. When they separated, both parents bargained over an agreement, and Latif refuses to pay maintenance as long as those demands he considers most important have not been met, using the money as a bargaining tool while his former wife uses her control over the passports of the children with similar effect. While both spouses could go to court over

[9] A popular saying in Dutch media and online discussion forums, which even sometimes appears in court documents, for example, ECLI:NL:RBDOR:2012:BX0572, Rechtbank Dordrecht, 2012. In this case, a private agreement detailing that the children would not have contact with their father if he did not pay the agreed maintenance was considered by the court to be conflicting with public policy.

these issues, they avoided doing so. When describing child maintenance, Latif does not refer to the welfare discourse or the best interest of the child. Instead, he introduces the contact and communication with his former partner as a factor, mentioning his appreciation of her texting him when their daughter was admitted to hospital. If their relationship could improve, he would consider doing 'something extra'. Again, this demonstrates how Latif sees maintenance payments as a payment to his former partner, unrelated to his children's welfare but related to their relationship and contact, and as a gift instead of an obligation. While Latif and his former partner, like most respondents, resolved their conflicts out of court, a minority started court cases over issues related to their children such as child maintenance, residence, or contact. I will go further into these procedures below.

Legal Procedures on Child Care

In most transnational divorce cases in this research, the residence of children after divorce was arranged privately between the parents, without any legal procedures. This is in line with what scholars have written about divorce procedures in the Netherlands (Griffiths 1986), Morocco (Mir-Hosseini 2000), and in Egypt (Sonneveld 2012a). Only a minority of the spouses in this research went to court over issues related to child care after divorce, mostly regarding child maintenance. Although some of the interviewees were quite unhappy about the arrangements for child care after their divorce, only in a few cases there had been actual court cases regarding custody, visitation, or residence. This was mostly in cases where the court was the only option left, including in all three child abduction cases, and in cases were the state was involved, such as the Moroccan father Farid, for whom child contact and residence in the Netherlands were related. Remarkably, all three fathers involved in court procedures demanded contact, whereas the one mother involved in a court procedure wanted residence. This pattern is clearly gendered and probably related to earlier care arrangements during the marriage.

All respondents started court cases relating to child care in the country where they lived, which was not necessarily the country of residence of their former spouse or children. In some cases, legal consciousness played an important role in this decision. René, for example, did not consider starting a court case in Egypt, even though his former wife and children had been staying there for some time before she took them to another country:

> I: Did you ever consider starting a court case in Egypt?
> R: No, absolutely not. I think the legal system in Egypt is really horrible. Far worse than in the Netherlands. And the lawyers are even worse. Then you're so vulnerable for, say, dirty play, corruption, those kinds of things. I absolutely don't want to expose myself to that. Nor the children. The stories I hear [laughs]. It's just unbelievable. I think that, if you've got the cash and you're aggressive, meaning you're going for it, entirely, well, then you can gain a lot over there. The results are very unpredictable. (René, Dutch man divorced from Egyptian wife, living in the Netherlands)

Through his experiences, René has lost some of his trust in the Dutch legal system, but he also developed competence in handling it, developing a perspective of situational justice. His perspective on the Egyptian legal system are far more negative and distrusting, informed by his experiences with corruption in Egypt, of which he told some anecdotes during the interview. As has been outlined in Chapter 4, this illustrates how legal consciousness is closely related to personal experience with a certain state, in which a wide range of experiences with the law and state bureaucracy can shape legal consciousness. However, different than the examples relating to the divorce procedure discussed in Chapter 4, legal consciousness was a factor in choosing where to start a child contact procedure.

Another Dutch respondent, living in Egypt, displayed strong confidence in the Egyptian court:

> R: But he's not allowed to take the children. Not at the age of seven. According to the law, they should just be with me. My daughter now can choose.[10] She will appear before the Judge and he will ask: do you want to live with your father or with your mother? Well, they're both fed up with being with their father during the week. During the weekend they're with me. It's always tears when they leave. But he just knows I haven't got the

[10] Anna does not seem to be aware of the legal reform of 2005, which grants women the right to *hadana* for children up to 15 years of age; while her children were 14 and 7 at the time of the interview.

> money to take a Judge. (Anna, Dutch woman divorced from Egyptian husband, living in Egypt)

Anna cannot afford to start a legal procedure ('take a judge'), but fully trusts that an Egyptian judge will award her the custody over her children once she starts a procedure, showing a strong adherence to what Merry calls an ideology of formal justice (Merry 1986: p. 257). As her divorce in Egypt was an administrative one, she has not yet had any actual contact with the Egyptian legal system, nor does she say much in the interview regarding negative experiences with Egyptian bureaucracy or institutions. It is legal costs rather than legal consciousness which keep her from starting a court procedure on the children, and which enable her former husband to use his control over money and maintenance to determine the residence of their children.

Conclusions

The stories in this chapter reflect two main stories about good and bad parents after transnational divorce. These are remarkably similar to the welfare discourse which also influenced family law in all three countries, centring on the best interests of the child. Firstly, involved good parents share the burden of child care, whereas the bad parent is absent during the marriage or deserts his or her children after divorce. Secondly, the good parent puts the best interests of the children before his or her own and does not involve the children in the conflict with the former spouse. The bad parent, on the other hand, uses the children in ongoing conflicts. Both fail to put the best interests of the children before his or her own, which makes them fail to be 'good parents'.

In this study, the child welfare discourse seems to be nearly universal, present in all three countries and in all interviews with parents. This is a remarkable finding, as writings on the welfare discourse so far have mostly focussed on the West, and especially Anglo-Saxon countries. As discussed before, academic writings on Muslim-majority countries and Islamic family law focus almost exclusively on the rights of women and mothers, rather than how and why they arrange parenting after divorce and the role of the law. As such, this raises questions with regard to the universality of some parenting experiences as well on how discourses and norms on parenting after divorce travel transnationally.

However, there are also some elements specific to transnational families. First of all, in a transnational setting, contact between children and non-resident parents can be complicated by state borders and travel distance. Migration law can be a powerful tool for parents in transnational divorce, made visible in issues such as international child abduction and involuntary abandonment in the country of origin. In some cases, these issues even prevented respondents from applying for divorce. Secondly, especially in mixed marriages, frames of deceit and *Bezness* inform the perspectives of some parents. Thirdly, some of the stories also contain elements of cultural difference. Being a 'good transnational parent' in some stories by spouses from mixed marriages entailed the transfer of culturally specific skills. Lastly, in only half of the cases in this research was there any contact between the non-resident parent and the children. In many no-contact stories, the other parent lived abroad. Many of these cases were also characterised by high levels of conflict, including international child abduction.

The welfare discourse can be qualified as what Merry calls a moral discourse, focusing on guilt and obligations in relationships, not legal rights or laws (Merry 1990: p. 112). In the interviews, there are very few references to law when discussing child care after divorce, and most parents make arrangements outside of the court. Also, none of the interviewees made use of faith-based arbitration, as in many British studies of legal pluralism. Even though some parents were quite unhappy about the way things were organised, this did not mean they would start a court procedure or turn to formal alternative dispute resolution institutes. Moreover, even when arranging child maintenance, child residence or contact privately with the non-resident parent, this was generally not the result of explicit bargaining 'in the shadow of the law' (Mnookin and Kornhauser 1979). Instead, the outcome was either taken for granted, or one of the parents took matters in his or her own hands, which made both latent and manifest forms of power an important factor. Thus, despite increasing state interventions in divorcing families aiming to protect the 'best interest of the child', such as the Dutch obligatory parenting plans (introduced in 2009), the law only seemed to play a limited role in arranging child care after divorce.

However, this analysis is complicated by the fact that, as discussed in the legal chapter, a welfare discourse is also important in recent—attempts for—legal reform in Morocco and Egypt and has for some time been the central ideology in the Dutch legal system with regard to child care after divorce. These reforms made the best interest of children a legal norm. Thus, there seems to be a widely shared moral discourse in which the best interest of the child is the most important principle regarding child care after divorce for both parents and the law.

References

Bakker, Sanne. 2008. Achtergelaten Vrouwen. De weg terug van Marokko naar Nederland. Master Scriptie, Mediterrane studies, Radboud Universiteit.

Bartels, Edien. 2005. Onderzoeksnotitie over migrantenvrouwen en kinderen die gedwongen zijn achtergelaten in landen van herkomst. In *Voorstudie*. Den Haag: Adviescommissie voor vreemdelingenzaken.

Castles, Stephen. 2005. Hierarchical Citizenship in a World of Unequal Nation-States. *PS: Political Science and Politics* 38(4): 689–692.

Carlisle, J. (2014). "That Hurt Me, That Hurt My Family": The Role of Migrants' Families During Transnational Parental Child Custody Disputes. In: T. Geisen, T. Studer and E. Yildiz. (eds.). *Egypt. Migration, Familie und Gesellschaft: Beiträge zu Theorie, Kultur und Politik*. Wiesbaden, Springer Fachmedien: 279–298.

CBS. 2009. *Jaarrapport 2009. Landelijke Jeugdmonitor*. Den Haag: CBS.

Griffiths, John. 1986. What do Dutch Lawyers Actually do in Divorce Cases? *Law & Society Review* 20(1): 135–175.

Kaganas, Felicity, and Shelley Day-Sclater. 2004. Contact Disputes: Narrative Constructions of 'Good' Parents. *Feminist Legal Studies* 12: 1–27.

Komter, Aafke Elisabeth. 1989. Hidden Power in Marriage. *Gender & Society* 3(2): 187–216.

Merry, Sally Engle. 1986. Everyday Understandings of the Law in Working-Class America. *American Ethnologist* 13(2): 253–270.

———. 1990. *Getting Justice and Getting Even. Legal Consciousness among Working-Class Americans*. In *Language and Legal Discourse*, eds. William M. O'Barr and John M. Conley. Chicago- London: The University of Chicago Press.

Mir-Hosseini, Ziba. 2000. *Marriage on Trial. A Study of Islamic Family Law*. London-New York: I.B. Tauris.

Mnookin, Robert H., and Lewis Kornhauser. 1979. Bargaining in the Shadow of the Law: The Case of Divorce. *Yale Law Journal* 88: 950.

Smit van Waesberghe, Eliane, Iris Sportel, Lisanne Drost, Esther van Eijk, and Elja Diepenbrock. 2014. *Zo zijn we niet getrouwd. Een onderzoek naar omvang en aard van huwelijksdwang, achterlating en huwelijkse gevangenschap*. Utrecht: Verwey Jonker Instituut.

Sonneveld, Nadia. 2012a. *Khul' Divorce in Egypt: Public Debates, Judicial Practices, and Everyday Life*. Cairo: The American University in Cairo Press.

7

Financial Aspects of Divorce

Apart from legally arranging the relationship between spouses and their children, marriage, and divorce are also—maybe even foremost—financial matters, entailing rights, and obligations for the spouses as well as the household property. Laws concerning the financial consequences of marriage and divorce recreate certain ideas about the household and the family as an economic unit. In the legal chapter, I have demonstrated how Dutch, Moroccan, and Egyptian family law regarding the financial effects of marriage and divorce are based on similar ideas and assumptions about the family in gender-based roles of homemaker and breadwinner. However, the legal systems provide different solutions for arranging the financial consequences of this gender-based division of labour. For transnational couples, these differences in law can have severe negative consequences, but also provide options for strategic behaviour.

Therefore, financial matters are especially suited for so-called forum shopping, both because of the great differences in legal arrangements as well as the tangibility and easy transportability of money. However, even though financial matters are at first sight 'simply about money', issues such as maintenance and alimony are infused with moral matters such as fairness. Merry (1990: p. 112–115) and Sarat and Felstiner (1995: H2)

I. Sportel, *Divorce in Transnational Families*,
DOI 10.1007/978-3-319-34009-8_7

have described the dominance of moral discourse in describing marital problems and divorce in the American context. Studies on Muslims in the West and family law often depart from a perspective of legal pluralism, where multiple norm systems interact with official state law. In these studies, it is often assumed that immigrants bring their 'own' family law and norms to Western legal systems. To my knowledge, no similar studies have been made of Western migrants to the MENA region. Transnational families, who, to some extent can choose the legal systems applicable on their marriage and divorce, therefore provide an especially interesting case to test such assumptions.

This chapter will start with an analysis of discourses used by participants about financial arrangements in transnational marriage and divorce. As many financial issues are decided at the moment of marriage, I will then address marriage contracts and prenuptial agreements in a transnational context; how and why the participants in this research have arranged their marriage contracts and how these arrangements turned out at the moment of divorce. After that, I will discuss maintenance and marital property arrangements after transnational divorce, paying special attention to the gender roles inscribed in the legal systems and their effects on transnational marriages.

A Fair Deal? Images on Proper Financial Arrangements

Coming from different regional, class, and ethnic backgrounds as well as legal systems, spouses may have quite different perceptions of what financial arrangements during and after transnational marriages are fair or proper. Although these perceptions were, of course, informed by respondents' positions and interests, three general lines of reasoning can be found. First of all, people are arguing from a moral perspective of earning and deserving, based on a balanced division of work and its rewards, both paid and unpaid. Central in these stories is the earning of certain rights by working for them and losing them by 'bad' behaviour. Secondly, there is the moral principle of need and capacity, of sharing wealth. These two perspectives can be described as different moral discourses. Thirdly, there is a perspective of—actual or perceived—legal rights. These perspectives are not exclusive and respondents regularly shift between them during the interview.

In the first moral discourse, the sharing of financial means during marriage and after divorce is framed as something which can be deserved or lost with proper or improper behaviour. For example, René, a Dutch father refused to pay spousal maintenance after his ex-wife took their children abroad without his consent:

> R: It was just a matter of principle. I think that it's strange if in child abduction cases the parent who stays behind should still pay these kinds of things. I'd think that this really is a typical example of a poignant situation. Not because of the money, I can afford it. But, like, it's just insane. Similar to those criminals who run abroad, while social service continues to pay their benefits, you know, it's really odd. (René, Dutch man divorced from Egyptian wife, living in the Netherlands)

In this quote, which is rather similar to his remarks about child maintenance, René's ex-wife no longer deserves to be maintained after taking the children away from him. Even though the court did not agree, he did manage eventually to convince the LBIO of his views when his wife's lawyer transferred her claim to them. Similarly, Rabia, a Moroccan woman living in the Netherlands, was shocked when, years after their divorce, she was approached by the municipality in which her former husband had just applied for social security:

> R: He returned to the Netherlands to apply for social security. The first time, he went to live in [small town]. The local government of [small town] contacted me because of the maintenance. I had to pay maintenance to him.[1] Because of the law, we were bound to each other for ten years. I was out of my mind then. Because I had to pay him 300 *gulden*, 300 euro, something like that. No, it was before 2002, so I had to pay 300 *gulden*.[2] I completely lost my cool. I wrote a very angry letter to the *wethouder* [local administrator]

---

[1] It is standard procedure in the Netherlands that municipalities try to cover part of social security paid to divorced people by claiming maintenance from the former spouse.

[2] 300 *gulden* is about 135 euro.

to explain my situation. My brother also took steps to check where he was living, what he was doing and so on. And then we managed to arrange that I did not have to pay maintenance. (Rabia, Moroccan woman divorced from Dutch-Moroccan husband)

Rabia was outraged at the thought of having to pay maintenance for her former husband. She felt that her husband did not deserve to be maintained by her after abandoning her and six children in severe debt, contracted to fund his business abroad, without any support or contact after his departure. Furthermore, she had been the main breadwinner in their relationship as well as the main caregiver, and she still resented him for not providing his share of the work. In a last example, Sofia, an Egyptian woman felt treated unjustly when her former husband refused to pay maintenance:

R: Yes, it has been a long while. It doesn't matter anymore to me. The only thing is how he played it. I never received any maintenance from him in the Netherlands.
I: Not at all?
R: He played it in a way. He ran up debts. So he had to pay his debts. And he kept the house. Would you believe it, he was cheating on me, I was a housewife. I was given the brush-off, I got nothing at all. And he got everything. But now he is living like a dog, alone. Nobody wants him. (Sofia, Egyptian woman divorced from Egyptian man living in the Netherlands)

As Sofia had been a housewife, providing care and housework, and, moreover, since her husband had cheated on her, she feels she should have gotten her share of the marital property as well as her husband's income, instead of her former husband keeping everything. Only when she applied for social security did the local government manage to have the former husband pay maintenance for a while.

In their narratives, all these respondents focus on moral obligations in relationships, for example, in sharing work in a fair manner and keeping contact between parents and children. Proper financial arrangements are seen as a consequence of those moral obligations, and rights can be lost by behaviour not fitting with these norms.

The second moral discourse centres on the concepts of need and wealth. In this discourse, resources should be equally shared during the marriage and after divorce, without major differences between the partners. Many interviewed spouses expect (former) husbands to maintain their wives during marriage and after divorce if they need it, regardless of actual legal provisions in this respect.

> R: He did not want to give anything, right? That's why they go abroad [to marry], not to give anything to their wives. And I think it's unfair. Very unfair. 'You came from Morocco; now go back to your country, because you won't get a thing from me. Everything is mine.' But this house is also my house. I lost my house [in Morocco], I don't have another home. But they don't think about that. Yes, you're coming to share their life. But they don't want to share. Nothing at all. [...] He knew everything about my finances. Because I have a principle. We are partners, we need to share everything. But from his side, his life is his. He is taking decisions without consulting me. He is determining things for me. Without my knowledge. I find that regrettable. I think it's awful. Because I'm a human being too. (Malika, Moroccan woman divorced from Dutch husband, living in the Netherlands)

As Malika sees it, marriage is about sharing. She was sharing her life and possessions with her husband and considers it to be unfair that he would not let her participate in financial decisions or share his wealth with her and her daughter when she ran out of money. Looking back on her marriage, Malika now suspects that he did this on purpose, that he went abroad to find a Moroccan woman that would not demand sharing, like other men of 'his kind'.

Interestingly, Malika's and Sofia's ideas about sharing did not relate well to the Moroccan and Egyptian legal systems they grew up in, but were closer to the Dutch system of communal property during the marriage. Their Egyptian and Moroccan backgrounds alone thus cannot explain the conflict with their Dutch and Dutch-Egyptian husbands.

The last discourse is a legal perspective, the claiming of—real or perceived—rights by referring to the law:

> R: I mean, at some point it should just stop. I gave him back everything. His house, everything that was his. I returned everything. I just did not want to have it anymore. According to the law, he should have bought me another house. I did not ask for it. And still, trying to make life difficult for

> you, trying to hurt you. In any way possible. (Elizabeth, Dutch woman divorced from Egyptian husband living in Egypt)

In her story, Elizabeth uses a mix of moral and legal discourses. In her anger about her former husband's behaviour, who changed the children's residence to force a stop to maintenance payments, Elizabeth refers to both her legal rights as well as her own good behaviour in renouncing some of these perceived rights. Another mother also referred to the Egyptian legal provisions about children's maintenance:

> You know, there are certainly things of which I think they just have to be done. Because the boys now need braces. And then I think [ex-husband], you can handle that. Normally the man has to take care of everything, tuition, clothes, medical costs, everything. I think that's going too far. (Janneke, Dutch woman divorced from Egyptian husband, living in Egypt)

Even though she does not agree with the Egyptian legal principle of fathers being responsible for all costs of their children, and therefore also participates in maintaining the children, Janneke does refer to this legal principle when determining her position on which costs she does and does not pay. As such, she is actively relating herself to a 'shadow of the law' (Mnookin and Kornhauser 1979), in which her contributions are voluntary. Again, these Dutch women living in Egypt are referring to *Egyptian* legal norms rather than wishing to have their 'own' Dutch cultural or legal norms recognised in Egypt.

Other Dutch women in mixed marriages also referred to this Moroccan and Egyptian legal norm of men providing for the family regardless of the wife's means. Related to the *Bezness* frame of false love, this norm of male providers is sometimes used as a kind of test to determine whether their potential spouse is a good man and not just pursuing their money or a residence status:

> Then he had bought something and asked me for money. And from that moment I had the idea that this did not feel right to me. […] In the Islam, it is absolutely not permitted that a husband asks his wife for money, right, to make a certain purchase for himself. So that did not feel right to me.

> I gave him the money; it was 300 euro; so it did not run into thousands right away. It was very strange for me. I asked him: is something wrong? You never asked me for money. You have always provided for yourself. We are trying to build something together, and this is very unfortunate. It just did not feel right to me. (Inge, Dutch woman divorced from Moroccan husband, no communal residence)[3]

Inge felt her former husband's request for money was improper. She refers to an 'Islamic' notion of men not being allowed to ask their wives for money, possibly based on the idea that in Islamic family law and also in Moroccan law, husbands are responsible for maintaining their wives and children, keeping the wife's property separate. What is remarkable about this strategy is that, once her Moroccan husband would have migrated to the Netherlands, Dutch law would have become applicable to their marriage, meaning that they would have been married under communal property, as they had made no prenuptial agreement in the Netherlands. In her story, Inge recounts several more incidents in which her husband asked for money. Looking back on her marriage, she now considered these incidents to be the first signs of her husband's false love, marrying her only for her wealth or for a visa to the Netherlands. In the powerful *Bezness* frame, attempts of less wealthy Egyptian or Moroccan men to share in their Dutch wife's wealth are easily suspect, as in the romantic image of marriage informing this frame 'true love' excludes any other motives for marriage, including financial gain.

Like the discourse of female entitlement to maintenance, these moral discourses contain gendered elements. All three perspectives are related to care and the division of labour in marriage, and as such are all gendered but in different ways. First of all, the discourse of deserving and earning has close ties to the child welfare discourse. As we have seen in Chapter 6, the concept of the best interests of the child is of paramount importance in the stories of divorced parents. Secondly, the discourse of need and sharing is remarkably absent in the *Bezness*-related stories, where Egyptian or Moroccan men, despite their lesser wealth, are blamed for financially benefiting from their Dutch partners, making them suspect of false love.

[3] This case is discussed in more detail in Sportel (2013).

None of the participants blamed a wife for financially benefiting from her husband or being in the marriage only because of the money. Below, I will describe in more detail how the interviewees arranged the financial consequences of their marriage and divorce using these three discourses, starting with the issue of conditions upon marriage.

Preparing for a Transnational Marriage: Conditions Upon Marriage

Most financial aspects of divorce are already arranged at the moment of marriage. As has been discussed in the legal chapter, in all three countries there are possibilities to include conditions in the marriage contract or in a prenuptial agreement. There are three types of financial conditions: a *mahr*, arrangements with regard to marital property, and a choice of law. The first type of financial agreement, the *mahr*, was included by participants the most often, as it is obligatory for the validity of an Egyptian or Moroccan marriage. The *mahr* or *sadaq* (dower) is an amount of money paid by the husband to the wife, and her personal property. In this research, a difference could be seen between marriages conducted in Morocco and marriages conducted in Egypt. In most marriages concluded in Egypt, the *mahr* did not seem to be an important issue. For example:

> I: Was there something like a bride price in it [the contract], for example?
> R: Yes, yes, and everybody just says something. Maybe we had one pound or something. [We] just did not discuss it.
> I: It was never an issue at the divorce?
> R: No. That one pound? I don't even remember what it was [laughs]. No, and I did not do it in my second marriage either. (Conny, Dutch woman divorced from Egyptian husband, living in Egypt)

Conny did not consider the *mahr* a serious issue in her marriage or divorce, and even considered my questions regarding the *mahr* to be funny. Of the eight couples that married in Egypt or at an Egyptian embassy abroad, most of them between Dutch women and Egyptian men, five Dutch women had only a symbolic amount in their contract whereas one Dutch woman claimed not having any *mahr* at all in her marriage contract.[4] In the one marriage between an Egyptian woman and a Dutch man, however, there was a more substantial deferred *mahr* in the marriage contract. The wife in this marriage insisted on a high deferred *mahr* in the Egyptian marriage contract, befitting the status and norms of her family:

> R: She said, 'well, it's customary here [in Egypt] that you have to sign for a dowry. That's how it's done; it's also a case of family honour and the like. Well, we're a pretty prosperous family, so we cannot just fill in a very small amount. But it's something I would never demand, say, I would never claim it in case [the marriage] would go wrong. But would it be all right if you would just fill in,—what was it, I believe it was 100,000 *gulden* or something, such an amount—that would be, like, acceptable for the standard of living we have.'[5] Well, if you won't claim it anyway. I mean, I didn't have that money, because back then I was just an employee at [company], say, then fine, I'll fill it in, no problem. (René, Dutch man divorced from Egyptian wife, living in the Netherlands)

Later, however, René found out that this was not as normal in her family as his former wife claimed it to be.

> I told her sister and she said: 'I married my husband for a dowry of one euro. Symbolic. So it's really nonsense that it isn't an option in our family. If you want I could send you our marriage contract.' So in those days she was also just telling things that aren't true. So well, apparently it was already in her. (Ibid)

René relied on his wife's explanation for the meaning of the marriage contract he signed, including the very high deferred *mahr* she claimed he would not really have to pay. As it was a transnational marriage, he had little knowledge of Egyptian family law or customs regarding the *mahr*. However, he later found out that his former sister-in-law did not actually share his wife's perception of the customs in their family; he interpreted

---

[4] In a last case, it did not become clear from the interview whether a *mahr* had been part of the marriage contract.

[5] 100,000 *gulden* is approximately 45,000 euro.

the issue as yet another sign that his wife had been lying to him, a pattern which he saw as being very persistent in this highly complicated and discordant divorce case.

In the Dutch-Moroccan interviews, the amounts of *mahr* paid or received were generally higher than those in Egypt, although one Moroccan woman divorced from a Dutch husband mentioned not having any *mahr* at all in her contract. Respondents mentioned amounts ranging from 5000–10,000 DH (Moroccan Dirham).[6] The content and spending of the *mahr* also differed. Almost all of the interviewees described the *mahr* paid or received in their marriage to be 'normal', including the one woman who did not receive a *mahr*. The differences could thus possibly be related to some regional or class differences in *mahr* practices. For example, in some cases the *mahr* was used to buy furniture for the future marital home, either by the husband or by the wife, which would then become the private property of the wife. Other women received gold or were instructed by their parents to buy gold from the money they received.

Looking back on their marriage, some of the interviewed women were not happy about the *mahr* they received.

> I: Was there something like that in your marriage contract, do you remember what was in [the contract]?
>
> R: Yes, there was an amount in there, indeed. Off the top of my head it was an amount of 1,000 *gulden*. Yes, he was [paying] 1000 *gulden*.[7] Because I know enough stories in which [the husband] was really exploited. He was lucky with my parents; there were also parents who were really conscious of their value, so to say. And who let that be heard in the amount they asked for. Because my parents wanted [laughs] they just wanted to get rid of me as soon as possible. [...] just imagine, that's 500 euro nowadays, that's nothing. Nothing at all. (Naima, Dutch-Moroccan woman divorced from Moroccan husband)

---

[6] About 500–1000 euro. However, out of 13 interviews on marriages concluded in Morocco, in five cases I did not get a clear answer on the *mahr*, either because the interviewee did not know or remember what had been in their contract or did not seem to understand the question. One Moroccan interviewee, although she reluctantly answered the question, remarked that it was a sensitive issue to ask questions about. This may be part of the explanation of such a high number of unclear answers, which did not happen with any other subject in this research.

[7] About 450 euro.

Naima links the *mahr* she received to the value her parents attached to their daughter; the 'cheap' *mahr* reflected her parent's wish to marry her off as soon as possible, even though they could have claimed more because of the migration opportunities accompanying the marriage to a Dutch-Moroccan girl. Malika, a Moroccan woman who did not have any *mahr* in her contract, also felt that her family might have been too easy on her Dutch husband. Even though she claimed elsewhere in the interview that it is not general practice to have a *mahr* in a Moroccan marriage contract and that it was not necessary in her marriage, she feels her family should have demanded a high [deferred] *mahr*:

> I: What did your family think about you getting married to someone from the Netherlands?
>
> R: Well, it was my own responsibility. If it would go wrong, I would have to take responsibility myself. That's what they said. It was a very easy family. Yes, it was lucky for him, right? I would have wanted them to be really warlike. Because back then he would have done anything to have me. Anything. But my family was so easy on him. I would have wanted my family to say: sir, if you ever want to get a divorce, we want [you to pay] this. He would have accepted. But we did not do that. I regret it. Yes, because people, those Dutch, or at least this man, thinks that if he asked me, I'm his thing. A very easy thing. No family, no nothing. I have no choice, just saying: yes and that's it. (Malika, Moroccan woman divorced from Dutch husband, living in the Netherlands)

Malika felt that, without the support of her family, she was powerless against her husband. She felt that she would have been more protected from his later misconduct if she at least had had a high deferred *mahr* in her marriage contract, even though the protection of a high *mahr* would have probably meant little in a Dutch divorce case.[8] Even though this protective quality of the *mahr* is regularly mentioned in the literature on this topic (Mehdi 2003, Mehdi and Nielsen 2011), in none of the other interviews such a protective quality was ascribed to the *mahr*.

[8] For a further discussion of *mahr* in Europe see also the volume edited by Mehdi & Nielsen (2011) and (Jansen 1997).

Another Moroccan woman was disappointed as promises made at the moment of marriage with regard to the *mahr* were not kept:

> [...] he did not keep his promise. He brought a bouquet. He had been to the hairdresser [laughs]. No, really, he did not [pay]. Though in Islam he should have given something, but he only paid for the ring. [...] Let's see, besides the furniture being mine. But that was of no use to me. We still had to buy it. It was of no use to me. He put in the contract that he paid something like 500 euro to me as a dowry, [and that] he bought furniture from that money. And the furniture was in my name. (Rabia, Moroccan woman divorced from Dutch-Moroccan husband, living in the Netherlands)

Rabia was severely disappointed when she came to the Netherlands and it turned out that her husband did not have any money and did not even buy a bed for them. The promised furniture of her *mahr* was eventually bought from her own salary after she found a job. This pattern continued throughout her marriage and divorce narrative, which ended with him abandoning her with severe debts and six children to take care of. This case clearly has transnational elements; if the marital home would have been in Morocco, or she would already have had family members living in the Netherlands, they could have checked the existence of the promised furniture and the financial affairs of the husband. Now his limited funds came as a surprise to her only after she migrated to the Netherlands.

Although a *mahr* is normally not a part of a Dutch marriage contract, one Dutch-Moroccan couple aiming to make their Dutch prenuptial agreement valid in both countries also included a *mahr*:

> In the [marriage] contract there should be mentioned, at least according to the Moroccan norms of that time, whether a dowry is involved. [Former husband] had bought an encyclopaedia from a colleague. It had cost him an arm and a leg and he was very fond of it. [...]. He was the one who bought it from a colleague, it was his. But he thought it would be a good, symbolic dowry for me. Because it then would not be about the money, but just about, well, a symbolic value, highlighting my scientific side. (Eva, Dutch woman with Moroccan husband, living in the Netherlands)[9]

[9] This quote is also used, and the case is discussed in more detail in Sportel (2013).

In an attempt to reconcile Dutch and Moroccan norms on *mahr*, the Moroccan husband creatively chose a present for his Dutch wife-to-be that pleased her and would be acceptable legally as well as socially in both countries, as receiving money would have been awkward for Eva.

The second type, arrangements with regard to marital property, was only used by mixed couples getting married in the Netherlands, and by one Dutch-Egyptian couple planning to move to the Netherlands after their marriage. Of the three interviewees who married in the Netherlands (all of them mixed marriages), only one did *not* sign a prenuptial agreement. She had very clear reasons not to do so, directly related to her marriage being mixed:

> [...] We celebrated a large wedding, and everything in communal property, so everyone knew that it wasn't for a residence permit. He already had a residence permit for his business. He had a [business]. So communal property, sharing everything, so he could show everyone that it was serious. (Margriet, Dutch woman divorced from Egyptian husband, living in the Netherlands)

Margriet was afraid people would consider their mixed marriage a marriage of convenience, referring to the powerful Dutch discourse on marriages of convenience, marriages intended only to provide a residence status present in the Netherlands (de Hart 2003: p. 127–129). In the context of this discourse, she did not have a prenuptial agreement. Without a prenuptial agreement, all property and debts, including the husband's business, became communal at the moment of marriage. In this way, the couple aimed to prove that the husband was serious. Apparently, this was only something the husband had to prove, not the Dutch wife. Similar to the *Bezness* frame of one-sided love, it is only the Moroccan or Egyptian partner who potentially faces accusations of false love.

The other two couples marrying in the Netherlands and a Dutch-Egyptian couple marrying in Egypt but intending to settle in the Netherlands all made an agreement at a Dutch notary's office. Although one Dutch woman could only vaguely remember what she agreed on, only that they separated the property, the other two respondents took quite some effort to draft a contract which would be valid in both legal systems, consulting with legal experts in both countries.

> Then she also wanted *huwelijkse voorwaarden* in the Netherlands. Because the marriage would also be registered here, so you need the prenuptial agreement in the Netherlands. Because of the amount of property her family owned in Egypt. It was all shared property, and she did not want it to dilute, that wasn't acceptable for her family. So we just had to put clearly on paper that it would remain separated. Moreover, according to her own customs, in Islamic law property remains separated if you marry. So that's what we agreed on. [...] For the rest it was nothing out of the ordinary, just because we kept everything separated. (René, Dutch man divorced from Egyptian wife, living in the Netherlands)

In this example, the couple made arrangements in the Dutch prenuptial agreement that their Dutch financial situation closely resembled Egyptian (Islamic) law, at the initiative of the Egyptian wife in order to protect the property of her family. René complied with his future wife's wishes; he did not seem to consider it a particularly important aspect of their marriage or a reason for bargaining.

Contrary to the marriages conducted in the Netherlands, none of the interviewees that married in Morocco made use of the possibility to change the default arrangement of marital property. However, several interviewees did refer to the possibility when asked about the conditions in the marriage contract:

> I heard it happens now. For example if someone gets married, they usually say, everything in half. If they divorce, the wife gets half and the husband gets half. But he, oh no, he never would have done that. And I never actually asked about it. I never paid attention to such things. It was the last thing on my mind. [...] Neither in the beginning. Maybe I was too young and did not think about it. And it also was because, well, because I did not work. What could I put in my half? (Samira, Dutch-Moroccan wife divorced from Moroccan husband, living in Morocco)

Samira seems to refer to the new possibilities to include arrangements on the division of property in an appendix to the marriage contract, possible since the introduction of the new *Moudawana* in 2004. However, she also suggests that she was not in the right position to get her husband and family-in-law to agree on such conditions, even if she would have known about the possibilities.[10] Some of the respondents who have married recently recalled that the *adoul*, or notary performing their marriage, mentioned that they had the right to attach an arrangement on the division of property to the marriage contract. However, none of them had actually made use of or even seriously considered this option.

The third type of financial agreement, choice of law, was used only by one couple in this research. Their entire Dutch prenuptial agreement was an effort to have their legal situation arranged similarly in both countries, even though they never actually registered the Dutch marriage in Morocco:

> I: Did you have the contract acknowledged or registered at the consulate?
> R: No. We made a French contract *onder huwelijkse voorwaarden*, in which it was clear that my father was the *wali* [marriage guardian] and I would have a dowry, yes, that looked like the phrases in Moroccan style.[11] But we particularly married for the Dutch law. [...] In the end we did not need it [the contract], because we divorced in the Netherlands. But even then we thought, there is a difference in law between Morocco, and the Netherlands, and we did not want to agree on something here that would be interpreted differently there. And the other way around as well. We did not want to agree on something that would be interpreted negatively in the Netherlands. So we did what was possible, necessary, to make something valid in Moroccan law at that time, and we integrated that in this French-language contract. With separated property, my father was *wali*. It just missed mentioning I was not a virgin, you know, those kinds of things. But it did mention that I had a right to travel to my parents, travel to Europe, and a right to work. You can see that there, each spouse had their own private property, while in the Netherlands we pretend you always automatically have to add everything and go half.[12] (Eva, Dutch woman divorced from Moroccan husband, living in the Netherlands)

---

[10] As she married before 2004, this was not yet possible.

[11] Eva uses the term *onder huwelijkse voorwaarden* here meaning a prenuptial agreement with separated property. A *wali*, or marriage guardian, giving permission for the marriage, used to be obligatory when concluding a Moroccan marriage.

[12] This quote is also used in Sportel (2013).

The most important aim of their prenuptial agreement seems to be the reconciliation of the two legal systems, not leaving any room for misinterpretation or conflict afterwards. Eva seems to consider Moroccan family law not so much as a threat or something to protect herself against as some of the other interviewees. Instead, she aimed to reconcile their legal situation in both countries, aiming at a contract which would be acceptable in both legal systems. Like René, the Dutch man married to an Egyptian wife, these couples used the Dutch prenuptial agreement to create a legal situation which reflected Dutch and Moroccan legal and social values, as well as—in the case of Eva—interpersonal conditions that were important to her, such as the right to work. However, these two mixed couples, both highly educated and mobile professionals, were the only two that invested money, time, and legal knowledge in creating such a legal situation.

Conditions Upon Marriage: Consequences After Divorce

As described above, in all three countries, couples have included financial conditions in the marriage contract or in a prenuptial agreement. What then becomes of these conditions in case of divorce? Are conditions agreed on in one country claimed and awarded in the other? I will now first discuss *mahr* after divorce and then prenuptial agreements, including choice of law. First of all, in all but one case in this research, the *mahr* agreed upon in the marriage contract was a so-called prompt *mahr*, paid at the moment of marriage. Only one of the interviewees mentioned any relevance of this prompt *mahr*, in her case money used to buy bedroom furniture, at the moment of divorce:

> I: Did you get those things back when you divorced?
> R: No, I did not get anything back. My bedroom is still there, my belongings are still there.
> I: All your things are still there?
> R: Yes. I locked my room, but I think they opened it. I wasn't even allowed to take my room, my belongings. I had just some clothes, I took my clothes. Other than that, he has everything. (Samira, Dutch-Moroccan woman divorced from Moroccan husband, living in Morocco)

Samira felt treated unjustly as her former husband kept her and their child's personal belongings and the bedroom furniture that was bought from her *mahr*, even though it should have been hers, both legally and socially. But as her husband arranged the divorce secretly, having her sign documents she could not read, she might have unknowingly renounced these possessions in her divorce contract. In the one case in which a deferred *mahr* was written in the contract, this also became an issue at divorce. In this case, René and his Egyptian wife were living in the Netherlands. A large deferred *mahr* was included in their marriage contract, but the wife had promised not to claim it at divorce. However, when they eventually divorced she claimed it in a Dutch procedure. The court of first instance ruled that René had to pay the *mahr*, and he did. However, the court of appeal took another course:

> R: So later, in the court case, the divorce was in court then, she did claim that dowry. And then I just said in court like; well, she promised she would never do that, so that's what I presumed. But well, it's on paper, it was a signed piece. So then the judge decided, then she first had asked some text from some expert somewhere, from Islamic law here in the Netherlands. [...] If I remember correctly he wrote about it being a kind of maintenance.[13] Anyway, besides that he did not know what to do with it exactly. And ex [wife] claimed it was promised, it was put in writing. In the end the judge decided that was decisive, so it was awarded. Later, on appeal, it was dismissed. The argument of the court was that it wasn't mentioned in the Dutch prenuptial agreement. Apparently, we did not presume that stipulation would be executed. If we would have presumed that, it would have been in the prenuptial agreement. And the stupid thing was that I did not think about that. It was true, but I did not think at all about that plea, nor did my lawyer. [...] But I can say goodbye to the money, at least, that's what her lawyer told me, that she does not intend to ever return the money. (René, Dutch man divorced from Egyptian wife, living in the Netherlands)

Interestingly, here the court of second instance found a legal argument, the *mahr* not being in the Dutch prenuptial agreement, that supported

[13] *Van alimentatierechtelijke aard* in Dutch.

the social argument of the husband, a promise made not to claim what was in the marriage contract.

Similar to these agreements about *mahr*, a Dutch woman had a prenuptial agreement with her Moroccan husband in which they kept their property separate. During the marriage, they decided to buy a house. Hoping that her husband would feel more responsible for the communal household, she put the house in both their names. He promised not to claim his half if they divorced:

> R: And then he claimed his money, even though he promised he would not do so, so well. [...]
>
> I: And then you had to arrange the division of property?
>
> R: No, as such that wasn't a problem. Actually, he took very few things. And by mutual agreement. Can I take that? All right, take it, doesn't matter. Only the house, that was communal. And in the end it was arranged for. No, apart from that he left the whole business, and well, of course that was also because we made that prenuptial agreement, so he did not have much right to anything. (Ingrid, Dutch woman divorced from Moroccan husband, living in the Netherlands)

In this quote, Ingrid refers to both formal and informal agreements made during the marriage. On the one hand, she acknowledges her ex-husband's right to claim part of the value of the house, as it had become communal property, on the other hand, they had an informal agreement that he would not actually claim this right, and she was disappointed that he did. In dividing property after divorce, the couple was really bargaining 'in the shadow of the law' (Mnookin and Kornhauser 1979), both being aware of their legal rights and obligations. Even though Ingrid does not agree with her former husband claiming half of the house, she does not refuse, as she knows he is entitled to it and will win when going to court.

Similarly, in the case where the Dutch woman, Margriet, had decided to marry under the Dutch default system of communal property to avoid accusations of a marriage of convenience, she also regretted this choice afterwards. During the marriage, she had not actively participated in the financial management of the household, and she had no idea of the state of her former husband's affairs. Though there were substantial possessions in Egypt and the Netherlands she could have laid claim to, Margriet was afraid that, as she knew nothing about their financial situation, she would be confronted with even higher debts, which she did not want to pay. She thus decided not to take the risk and formally relinquished all her claims to the property.[14]

In another way, Eva, who had arranged their marital property in the Netherlands to resemble Moroccan family law, including a strict separation of property, also did not keep to their earlier agreement. After divorce, they decided to split the property equally:

> R: We divided the property. It was clear he needed this, I needed that. [...] We could quite easily separate the things. We had agreed together like, you will get this many chairs, I will get that many, I'll get this many tables, you'll get that many, I'll take the *Friese* clock, you'll get the little bible... The photo's we divided equally, agreeing that we could always get copies of each other's photos. (Eva, Dutch woman divorced from Moroccan husband, living in the Netherlands)

Thus, their carefully drafted prenuptial agreement, reflecting Moroccan separated property standards, was never actually put into action, except for the *mahr*. To Eva's surprise, after their divorce, her former husband insisted that she kept the encyclopaedia he wrote in the marriage contract as a *mahr*:

> And well, it was in the contract, so when we separated I suddenly got the encyclopaedia. And I thought he could use it far better than I could, but no, he insisted; 'this is yours'. And it was a nice thing to have, of course. (Ibid)

However, as her *mahr*, it became hers at the moment of marriage, though she feels it only became hers when her former husband gave it to her at the moment of divorce. Eva does not refer to the formal arrangements made earlier, including the choice of law they made in their marriage

[14] Art. 1:103 BW. Relinquishing claims to the marital property only works when debts are made by the other spouse; not when both spouses have signed for them. The spouse relinquishing all claims to the property can only keep her/his clothes and a bed.

contract. Instead, they divided things according to need and personal preference. As can be seen from this and earlier quotes, their divorce was a friendly, harmonious one, making falling back on formal agreements unnecessary.

At the moment of marriage, it can be hard to imagine or foresee a divorce lying many years ahead, let alone in another country and legal system. Most arrangements for divorce made at marriage turned out differently. On the one hand, friendly promises not to claim or to pay what was put in contracts were not kept after a relationship broke down and spouses strategically used arrangements to support their own position. On the other hand, formal arrangements and legal positions were not taken into account in a harmonious divorce where spouses divided property according to need. Using a mixture of moral and legal discourses, spouses navigated problems as they came up, dealing with legal matters such as separated property in a way to best fulfil their needs and worries at that particular moment, such as reconciling two legal systems or trying to fix a failing relationship. With the notable exception of the Dutch wife who received her *mahr*, cultural arguments hardly ever played a role. Below, I will further compare how spouses have dealt with spousal maintenance and the division of property in their transnational marriage and divorce and the possibilities of legal shopping.

The Financial Consequences of Marriage and Divorce

After divorce, not one but two households need to be sustained. Spouses who do not have an independent income, for example, because they have been investing their time in housework or child rearing instead of paid employment, will need some kind of income or financial security after divorce. As has been discussed in the legal chapter, all three countries have made legal arrangements to compensate care work in the division of property and maintenance during and after divorce, based on a similar male-provider and female homemaker model. However, the complex interplay of maintenance and marital property can be an issue in transnational marriages in two ways. First of all, the Netherlands, on the one hand, and Morocco and Egypt, on the other hand, have chosen different, even contradictory, ways to arrange for the financial security of divorced women. When spouses during their marriage migrate from one country to another, the arrangements made in the first country may become invalid, such as a *mahr* in the Netherlands, or communal property in Egypt or Morocco. In theory, these differences can be used strategically by one of the spouses, through forum shopping. However, I encountered very few examples of strategic use in this study and none of those were undertaken by the interviewees. Secondly, as has been discussed in Chapter 5, transnational marriage and migration can lead to gender inversions with regard to the gendered division of household labour, which can disturb explicitly gendered patterns of compensation for care work. I will now go on to discuss how couples arranged financial issues and maintenance after divorce and how this relates to law.

Maintenance After Divorce: A Female Right?

Legally, there are differences between spousal maintenance and child maintenance. However, in the interviews it often did not become clear which form of maintenance was being received or claimed, as many interviewees did not seem to be aware of the difference between the two forms, possibly because in all cases it was the wife who received the maintenance payments for both herself and/or the children. In the research, in ten cases some form of maintenance arrangement had been made by a court or by the divorcing couples privately, including one couple agreeing to share the costs of the children equally. Of these, six were arranged in the Netherlands, two in Morocco and two in Egypt. In 14 cases, no such arrangements had been made, in one interview it did not become clear. None of the respondents interviewed in this research have reported paying or receiving a *mut'a*, or compensation.

Even when spouses were awarded maintenance, the maintenance awarded or agreed upon was regularly not enough to live on. Moreover, as has also been described in Chapter 6, in most cases the awarded or agreed upon maintenance was regularly not paid. This corresponds with the general practice described for the Netherlands and Egypt. Specific for the Netherlands is that divorced spouses without paid employment can apply for social security. If they do, the local government will try to claim maintenance for the former spouse:

> R: So we [interviewee and children] were on social security. But the local government in [Dutch city], they went after him. 'You can tell her [ex-wife] all you want, but not to us.' They [checked] his papers and everything, and they made him pay. For three years. Now the law is that they have to pay for five years. In our case [he] had to pay for two years, to the local government, not to me. (Sofia, Egyptian woman divorced from Egyptian husband, living in the Netherlands)

Sofia felt it was the council, responsible for social security, which had stepped in and made her husband pay, even after she and her lawyer did not manage to get anything from him.[15] However, as the council deducts the received maintenance from the amount of social security, financially, the amount of maintenance paid makes little difference for the receiving women.

As mentioned before, it was in all cases the wife who was receiving maintenance payments from her former husband, for herself or for their children. None of the wives interviewed had paid any maintenance after divorce. This corresponds to Moroccan and Egyptian law and Dutch practice and also seemed the norm in the interviews:

> I: Did you make a maintenance arrangement?
> R: No, no, I declined. I said: 'you also need your money now'. I had my own income and I have not needed him. (Claudia, Dutch woman divorced from Moroccan husband, living in the Netherlands)
> I: Did you both always work during your marriage?
> R: Yes, yes. So I did not need any maintenance.
> I: And you did not have to pay either of course.

[15] This was in the 1980s, when the LBIO was not yet active in claiming maintenance. I have not been able to find the reason why he had to pay for only two years. Since 1994, the obligation to pay maintenance is limited to a maximum of 12 years, before that there was no limitation in duration.

R: No. I mean, we were both. But paying maintenance would have been weird [laughs]. That would *really* be a slap in the face for someone. In the Netherlands, I don't know if it ever happens here [in Egypt]. I cannot imagine. (Conny, Dutch woman divorced from Egyptian husband, living in Egypt)

Both women in these quotes seem to regard maintenance as typically being paid by the husband to the wife, even though they had both been providing in their marriage. Conny even makes an explicit connection between being paid maintenance and male honour, describing being maintained by an ex-wife as a further insult adding to the divorce. In these two quotes, the women spoke about needing or not needing maintenance. They did not so much focus on whether they were actually entitled to maintenance but more as a resource they may or may not need. Claudia, for example, was living in the Netherlands and their children stayed with her former husband. It is therefore very well possible that if they would have gone to court, she would actually have had to pay her former husband child or maybe even spousal maintenance, a possibility which obviously did not occur to her. On the other hand, Conny was living in Egypt and had no children. This means that she could only claim maintenance during the short *`idda* and maybe a *mut`a*. In her quote, she seems to assume she has a right to maintenance, and she only decided to forgo this right because she did not need any financial support from her former husband.

Similarly, Amar, the Moroccan father who had been the main caregiver during his marriage, complained about his financial situation after his Dutch wife abandoned him and their children in Morocco. He could not easily find a job and was completely dependent on his mother and sister for housing and maintenance. Even though he was in a financially dire situation, he never makes any reference to having any right to receiving maintenance from his wife for himself or their children, like many women interviewed for this study do. Still, the wife could be legally obliged to pay child maintenance under Moroccan family law as the father cannot provide for the children (art 199 new *Moudawana*), and she would probably also be required to pay maintenance in a Dutch court case, if she had enough income. Instead of blaming his wife for not maintaining them,

Amar blames the Dutch government for not paying child benefits and the Moroccan government for not taking care of the children: 'The children have no rights in this bloody awful country [Morocco]. [Son] goes to a poor school; it costs 20 euro each month, and 10 euro for transport.' (Amar, Moroccan man separated from his Dutch wife, living in Morocco)

Thus, when analysing how spouses deal with maintenance, gender is the most important factor and not the country of residence or origin. Talk about maintenance is highly gendered. While most female spouses felt a personal entitlement to maintenance from their former husband, none of the interviewed husbands felt such an entitlement, even when they could have legally claimed maintenance from their former wife. This gendered sense of entitlement to maintenance after divorce did not seem to be related to the division of labour during the marriage nor to any actual legal claims.

Division of Property

After a divorce, the property of the spouses needs to be divided. Like spousal maintenance, this is an issue in which there are important legal differences between the Netherlands, on the one hand, and Morocco and Egypt, on the other hand. Above I have already discussed how spouses made agreements about marital property and *mahr* upon marriage and how these agreements often worked out differently at the moment of divorce. I will now go further into how the interviewees who did *not* make such an arrangement handled the division of property after divorce. Some spouses did not have much property to divide, each owning only some personal belongings, and did not tell much about the division. In the cases of interviewees who had been suddenly abandoned, their former husbands or wives often left mostly debts behind.

I will now discuss in some more detail a few cases having distinct transnational elements, in which the oppositions between the legal systems with regard to marital property play a role in the assumptions and conflicts of spouses. Rabia, a Moroccan woman divorcing in the Netherlands, who has already been discussed several times in this chapter, told, for example, how her lawyer informed her about the Dutch legal rules with regard to communal property:

R: I paid for the house myself. And still they told me that, if I sell it, I need to return part of the money to him. And the value is always going up. I'm the only one to work, and the only one to pay for it, so far. He's out of the picture, does not do anything. And still, part of the sum has to go to him.

I: And will you do that, if you ever sell [the house]?

R: I don't know. [laughs]. I don't know. (Rabia, Moroccan woman divorced from Dutch-Moroccan husband, living in the Netherlands)[16]

Rabia was surprised and annoyed to learn that, under the Dutch system of communal property, half of the house she owned was still property of her former husband. She was not familiar with this aspect of the Dutch legal system. However, she does not explicitly refer to the couple's ethnic background or Moroccan norms of marital property, but rather focuses on the fairness of this arrangement, as she was the one who had done all the work in their marriage, both providing and doing the housekeeping and child care work. As her husband had suddenly abandoned her years before the formal divorce took place they never actually divided the property. I suspect, however, that her fear that he still could demand half if she ever sold the house is not necessarily accurate.[17]

In another case, which has already been introduced earlier in this chapter, both spouses had different assumptions about the division of property in their marriage, related to the Dutch and Moroccan legal system:

R: When I was here [the Netherlands] for three years, in [date], he started a divorce case. That wasn't a coincidence. I was three years here and he was afraid I would get my passport, and more rights. […] The local government contacted me; that I could ask for a Dutch passport. The husband got that letter. He was worried and ran to start the divorce right away.

---

[16] This case is discussed in more detail in Sportel (2013).

[17] As it is the property at the moment of the divorce, including the debts the husband left behind, that needs to be divided, not the value after ten years of hard work by Rabia to repay all debts accompanied by a spectacular increase in the worth of houses. Moreover, the former husband could already have claimed the right to half of the property at the moment of divorce or ever since, forcing Rabia to sell the house if necessary, not just at the moment of selling the property.

I: Do you know why he was so afraid that you would get a Dutch passport?
R: He did not want me to get more rights. He wanted me to always stay under Moroccan law. If I became Dutch, Moroccan law would be out of the question. But if I stay Moroccan, only Moroccan, he would always have hope. (Malika, Moroccan woman divorced from Dutch man, living in the Netherlands)

In this case, both spouses had assumed the other's law would apply to the marriage. Malika, as discussed above, acted from a moral discourse of sharing, and freely invested her savings in the communal household, as she could not find enough suitable employment to pay for her and her daughter's upkeep, and spent time doing household and care work.[18] Her husband had assumed their property remained separated. The husband owned a lot of property, including a business, which he did not want to share with his wife. Still, he did not have a prenuptial agreement, something he, being a businessman and it being his second marriage, would most likely have done when marrying in the Netherlands. Apparently, the husband thought that by marrying in Morocco, Moroccan marital property law would be applicable, which would mean their property would remain separate and that this might change if his wife gained Dutch nationality. However, because they did not share Moroccan nationality, and their first communal residence was in the Netherlands, a Dutch communal property regime was already in place. Still, Malika feared that Moroccan law would be applied:

> My daughter cried [when she heard]. I told her, that we cannot be sure to stay here. Because every time, that mister… What should I do? I'm getting divorced. And she said: 'yes, but the cat comes with us. If we are out on the streets, it comes with us, if we leave, it comes with us.' I said all right. […] But the cat is in mister's name. Because mister is in charge here. […] If the Moroccan law would be applied; I would absolutely have hard luck. My own clothes, I would not have them. Because everything is in his name. That would be awful for me and my daughter. And also for the little cat. (Malika Moroccan woman divorced from Dutch man, living in the Netherlands)

[18] The daughter was from an earlier marriage in Morocco.

In her view, Moroccan law would mean that she would end up with nothing at all, not even her own clothes or her daughter's cat. Though this was certainly not the most valuable property in terms of financial value, it was very important to her. If Moroccan law would have been applied in the Netherlands, Malika would have gotten the worst of the differences between the Netherlands and Morocco, without any of the compensations for spouses doing care work provided by the two legal systems in case of divorce.[19] If Dutch law would have been applicable, it would not have mattered who spent or earned the money, as after divorce the couple would equally share the wealth accumulated before and during the marriage. If both spouses would have agreed beforehand on Moroccan family law being applicable to their marriage, Malika would have been entitled to being maintained by her husband during the marriage, and she could have kept her earnings and savings and possibly a *mahr*, as a buffer in case of divorce.

In a similar case, in Egypt, confusion about the Egyptian marital property system also put a Dutch wife at a disadvantage. Although Elizabeth was running a successful business in Egypt before meeting her Egyptian husband, when she became pregnant they married and she stopped working to take care of their children and the household. Occasionally, she still did some freelance work.

> R: I made some money. And I gave it to him. I wish I hadn't done so. Because the law doesn't allow it, officially, right? But well, he did take it. And when we got divorced he said like: 'I don't know' [laughs].[20]
>
> I: Did you have your own bank account?
>
> R: No, nothing. I wasn't allowed anything. [… discussion of controlling behaviour of the husband during the marriage]
>
> I: So everything you earned went to him?
>
> R: Yes, it had to. I mean, you are married together; you have to raise children together. And I never knew that law existed. He never told me. See, the law here is just like, the money the wife earns it just belongs to the wife. The husband is not allowed to touch it. If I had put it all aside, I could have bought an apartment myself.

---

[19] I do not know how the court case ended, but based on PIL as well as Malika's lawyer's opinion, I expect the judge would have applied Dutch family law.

[20] Conversations with her ex-husband were quoted in English by the interviewee.

I: You did well?
R: Yes, but the money is gone. And I haven't got any proof. I never had him sign a paper. So well, you'll never see the money again. That's how smart he was, then already. (Elizabeth, Dutch woman divorced from Egyptian husband, living in Egypt)

Elizabeth, in a similar situation to the Moroccan woman in the Netherlands, trusted her husband to share his income and shared the money she earned with him. Only after divorce she learned that in Egyptian law, the property of the wife is kept separate. Having no *mahr* or savings in her own name, Elizabeth had no capital after her divorce, while the money she earned with the occasional freelance work or her business could have enabled her to buy her own apartment and, combined with the job she took after divorce, keep her children's residence independently of the maintenance from her former husband. Like the Moroccan Rabia, however, Elizabeth does not explicitly refer to Dutch law as the basis for her assumptions. Instead, she uses both a moral discourse and a legal discourse based on *Egyptian* family law. In her view, her former husband was responsible for informing her about Egyptian law and should not have taken the money which he knew was legally hers.

Thus, some spouses who did not make explicit financial agreements about the division of property at the moment of marriage were unpleasantly surprised to discover their financial situation at the moment of divorce. Often, this coincided with a lack of knowledge and control over financial issues and family spending during the marriage. However, none of them made explicit claims to have their 'own' cultural, religious, or legal norms applied to their divorce. Rather, they used moral discourses about need or fairness as well as local family law to argue their position.

Conclusions

Thus, legal arrangements for financial security after divorce may work out differently in transnational cases. While couples can influence some financial issues before or during the marriage, it can be hard to imagine a divorce lying many years ahead, in another country, and most formal and informal arrangements made at marriage turned out differently at divorce. First of all, because of migration, arrangements made in one country for the security of the spouse providing care work at home may lose their validity in the other country. Secondly, migration can also possibly lead to a shift in gendered patterns of work. These differences between the systems also provide clear opportunities for forum shopping. Some of the interviewees in this study could have gained or lost much by acting strategically and aiming for a maximum of financial benefits, especially after divorce. However, none of the interviewees actually made use of these ample opportunities for strategic behaviour. As described in earlier chapters, most interviewees chose to arrange their divorce, including the financial aspects, in their own country of residence and outside of the courts. Instead of strategic action, exploiting the collision of legal systems to maximise financial gain, gendered moral discourses informed the position of the interviewees, while actual legal provisions played only a minor role in their stories.

These moral discourses can be considered a form of legal pluralism, in which multiple norm systems in addition to state law influence people's behaviour. However, contrary to assumptions in much of the legal pluralism literature, these norms did not seem to be very important in how participants in this study dealt with divorce law. Only a few highly educated spouses from mixed marriages wrote prenuptial agreements aimed at reconciliation of the two legal systems or the application of foreign legal norms. Moreover, none of the migrant participants in this study made identity-based claims to have norms from their cultural, religious, or ethnic background recognised in their divorce case. While some interviewees had an unpleasant surprise when being confronted with the legal norms in their country of residence, which did not always fit with the moral discourses they used, this did not mean they would refer to norms from their country of origin, but rather that they blamed their former spouses for treating them unfairly.

In these matters, gender took centre stage in three ways. First of all, in all three countries, laws regarding marital property and maintenance are based on gendered patterns of household labour, compensating women for care work. Secondly, in the interviews maintenance is framed as a female right which can be claimed if needed, without distinguishing between spousal maintenance and child maintenance. This framing is based on a traditional male-provider female caregiver division of labour, regardless of the actual division of labour in the marriage and leaving no room for financially dependent men or men taking care of children after divorce to be maintained by their former spouse. In talking about the financial aspects, respondents mostly referred to two moral discourses, the first of earning and deserving and the second of need and wealth. Although respondents sometimes also used a more legal discourse, referring to rights they were entitled to under one or both legal systems, the actual legal position of the spouses in both legal systems was at most of secondary importance for their evaluation of their own situation. Thirdly, other moral discourses, including *Bezness* stories, on proper financial arrangements after divorce are also related to this traditional division of labour. Only Egyptian and Moroccan men were accused of financially benefitting from their (former) wife or marrying in order to obtain a residence permit, while women, regardless of their ethnicity, means or actual division of care, can more easily claim a moral or legal right to share in the wealth of their (former) husband or to being dependent on his maintenance.

References

de Hart, Betty. 2003. *Onbezonnen vrouwen. Gemengde relaties in het nationaliteitsrecht en het vreemdelingenrecht., Migratie- en Etnische studies*. Amsterdam: Aksant.

Jansen, Willy. 1997. Gouden huwelijksgaven. Symbolen van liefde en strijd. In *Het geschenk. Over de verschillende betekenissen van geven*, ed. Aafke Komter, 207–221. Amsterdam: Amsterdam University press.

Mehdi, Rubya. 2003. Danish law and the practice of mahr among Muslim Pakistanis in Denmark. *International Journal of the Sociology of Law* 31: 115–129.

Mehdi, Rubya, and Jørgen S. Nielsen. 2011. *Embedding Mahr* (*Islamic Dower*) *in the European Legal System.* Copenhagen: Djoef Publishing.

Merry, Sally Engle. 1990. *Getting Justice and Getting Even. Legal Consciousness among Working-Class Americans*. In *Language and Legal Discourse*, eds. William M. O'Barr and John M. Conley. Chicago- London: The University of Chicago Press.

Mnookin, Robert H., and Lewis Kornhauser. 1979. Bargaining in the Shadow of the Law: The Case of Divorce. *Yale Law Journal* 88: 950.

Sarat, Austin, and William L.F. Felstiner. 1995. *Divorce Lawyers and their Clients. Power and Meaning in the Legal Process*. New York—Oxford: Oxford University Press.

Sportel, Iris. 2013. "Because it's an Islamic Marriage". Conditions at Divorce in Transnational Dutch-Moroccan and Dutch-Egyptian Marriages. *Onati Socio-Legal series* 3(6): 1091–1110.

8

Support in Transnational Divorce: Actors, Norms, and Their Influence

During a divorce, there are often more people involved than just the couples themselves. Divorcing couples may receive support and advice from their networks, friends, and family, and they may also get into contact with all kinds of professionals providing legal or social aid. While these statements are true for non-transnational couples as well, certain specific transnational aspects are relevant in the context of this research. First of all, migration may influence social capital, for example, when migrating spouses lose part of their connections to networks in their country of origin or form new ones after migration (Hagan et al. 1996; Zhou and Carl 1994; Coleman 1988; Curran 2002; Portes and Landolt 2000). Secondly, as has been demonstrated in previous chapters, there are some legal complexities and issues related to transnational divorce, such as the recognition of marriage or divorce in the second country and the involvement of migration law and residence status. These issues related to transnational divorce may require specific forms of support from both professionals as well as private networks. For example, specialised professionals can help navigating the complex interactions of two legal systems, and relatives or friends living in the other country can help arrange for documents needed in legal procedures. Which persons and organisations

I. Sportel, *Divorce in Transnational Families*,
DOI 10.1007/978-3-319-34009-8_8

form the social context in which transnational divorce takes place and how did their involvement support or constrain the spouses in the divorce process? In answering this question, I will use the concepts social capital and transnational legal space. While the concept of social capital has strong positive connotations, I aim to demonstrate how the support of private and professional actors can also entail constraints. As will become clear in this chapter, this is due to the production and enforcement of norms on, for example, conducting a transnational marriage or handling the law in transnational divorce. These norms are created in transnational legal space.

Below, I will start with a short theoretical discussion of the concepts of social capital and transnational legal space. Subsequently, I will introduce three types of support: emotional support, practical support, and legal aid and information. For each of these types, I focus on two main sources of support and information during transnational divorce: professional actors, such as NGOs and embassies, and private networks including friends and family members. Afterwards, I will compare Dutch-Egyptian and Dutch-Moroccan transnational legal space, and the effects of differences between the Dutch-Moroccan and the Dutch-Egyptian spaces for spouses in transnational divorce. Lastly, I will analyse the norms produced in transnational legal space, demonstrating how the support of professional and private actors can also constrain people in how they handle the law in transnational divorce.

Social Capital and Transnational Legal Space

The concept of social capital has been used to describe an 'aggregate of the actual or potential resources which are linked to possession of a durable network of more or less institutionalised relationships of mutual acquaintance and recognition—or in other words, to membership in a group.' (Bourdieu 1986: p. 51). Several authors have pointed out that social capital can change as a result of migration (Hagan et al. 1996; Zhou and Carl 1994; Coleman 1988; Curran 2002; Portes and Landolt 2000). Especially in transnational marriages, where one of the spouses has migrated while the other has not (or at a young age), this situation can easily lead to one spouse having more social capital in the country of residence than the other. However, it must be noted that being part of a migrant community also provides access to new social capital, and that even the act of migration itself has been found to correlate with existing social networks (Palloni et al. 2001; Zhou and Carl 1994).

In addition to social capital, Bourdieu distinguishes two other main forms of capital, economic capital, such as property rights, and cultural capital. Cultural capital, especially in its embodied state, can be qualified as *Bildung*, including skills such as language skills and professional behaviour, and it is the product of a substantive investment of time, preferably from a young age (Bourdieu 1986: p. 47–50). Similar to social capital, cultural capital can also be transnationally employed as 'migration-specific cultural capital' in transnational fields of migrants. Moreover, migrants also have agency in transferring their cultural capital from one country to another and forming new cultural capital in the country of residence (Erel: p. 645–648).

Capital is a concept with mostly positive connotations. According to Portes (2000), the concept of social capital

> [...] focuses attention on the positive consequences of sociability while putting aside its less attractive features. Second, it places those positive consequences in the framework of a broader discussion of capital and calls attention to how such nonmonetary forms can be important sources of power and influence. (Portes 2000: p. 2)

Thus, by using the term social capital, the positive aspects of membership of social networks are emphasised as an asset in transnational divorce. However, I would also like to draw attention to the negative aspects of the involvement of private networks. While family members and friends are a source of social capital, they also produce and enforce norms which can limit or constrain spouses in their making use of legal possibilities. Moreover, norms in social fields can also limit the access to social capital by exclusion if such norms are transgressed.

The second concept of importance for my analysis in this chapter is transnational legal space, defined by de Hart as 'a social field across borders, in which individual family members, family networks or NGOs mobilize law, creating and using new norms in response to the interaction or collision of different family law systems' (de Hart 2010: p. 2). By studying transnational legal space, the perspective is extended from individual spouses having access to social capital to the way family members as well as organisations and institutions interact and produce norms on transnational divorce. I will use de Hart's concept of transnational legal space in analysing how spouses in transnational divorce interact with law and with others involved in the divorce process and how these ties and interactions cross not only state but also community borders. However, I think that envisioning transnational legal space as a social field across borders may overestimate the interconnectedness and cohesiveness of the wide diversity of actors and norms active in this space (cf de Hart 2010: p. 20). According to Glick Schiller, 'Transnational social fields are not metaphoric references to altered experiences of space but rather are composed of observable social relationships and transactions. Multiple actors with very different kinds of power and locations of power interact across borders to create and sustain these fields of relationships' (Glick Schiller 2005: p. 51). As I will demonstrate below, some networks of actors in transnational legal space are indeed creating and sustaining social fields across borders, while others are not. Thus, instead of seeing transnational legal space as a single social field, I propose seeing it as a space comprising multiple social fields and networks of actors.

Emotional and Practical Support

Many interviewees felt they needed 'someone to talk to' about the end of their marriage and the divorce process. This first category of support, emotional support, was mostly provided by friends or family members. However, some respondents were in need of emotional support but had only limited access to family or friends, for example:

> I fell into a sort of black hole. I am alone here in the Netherlands. No support from family, friends. Real friends. You could say I've got acquaintances here. But friendship, friendship needs to be built. I only had acquaintances. (Sofia, Egyptian woman divorced from Egyptian man, living in the Netherlands)

Sofia relates her lack of a solid local network to her migration, as building real friendship takes time. Even though she still had some family living in Egypt and other European countries, she had only limited contact with them, as her former husband refused to provide her with the money necessary for visits during the marriage. Instead, she turned to professional help during her divorce; social workers helped her rearrange her life in the Netherlands.[1]

In a similar situation, Rabia, a Moroccan woman, had been isolated by her Dutch-Moroccan husband when she came to the Netherlands after their marriage. She had little contacts outside of the home, as her former husband made her come home right after work, without talking to others. After her divorce, she went to a Dutch social worker:

> Just to talk. Not about the divorce as such, just to have someone to talk to. Because I had nobody. So I went, and there I could cry, I could unburden my heart. [...] Well, she couldn't really help me. It was just someone who listened. I could come up with solutions myself for all problems. [...] I just needed someone to talk to a bit, someone to listen. (Rabia, Moroccan woman divorced from Dutch-Moroccan husband, living in the Netherlands)

Like Sofia, Rabia turned to a professional to talk to about the experience because she had little contact with family or friends. Moreover, she felt she could not discuss her marriage crisis and subsequent divorce with her family because they had not supported her choice of marriage partner:

> My father, I could not talk to him. Because I am not used to talking about such things with my father. And I also had myself to blame. I was the one who chose him. In the beginning. Therefore I have to take the blame. And I need to solve everything myself. That's what I was thinking. (Rabia, Moroccan woman divorced from Dutch-Moroccan husband, living in the Netherlands)

Other respondents, especially from mixed marriages, also mentioned being excluded from their families as a result of their choice of marriage partner:

---

[1] For a more elaborate discussion of transnational ties, distance, and emotional and practical support and care, see also the work of Baldassar (2007).

> Well, at some point my parents said: well once you have that [husband] out of the house, we'll be there for you. At some point he left the house. It was just before New Year's Eve. So I went to my parents for New Year's Eve. And then my father, it was only just after he left, he had only just packed his things, so I was really heartbroken. And my father kept on nagging me: how did things go? Why did it go wrong? You could have known beforehand. That kind of nonsense. So at some point I said: 'Pa, please stop, I really don't feel like it. You have to stop.' My mother got really sad. And I had put the children to bed there. But he kept carrying on. Then I said: 'you know what I'll do? I'll just go back to [home city]. Because I just don't want this bullshit anymore.' So I took the children from their beds, and at about nine thirty I drove back to [home city] and celebrated my own New Year's Eve. It was great, truly delightful. But well, then my father was really offended, so I did not see him for another half year. So much for the help. 'We'll help you if he's gone.' Well, look how they kicked me when I was down, right. (Ingrid, Dutch woman divorced from Moroccan husband, living in the Netherlands)

Again, Ingrid's parents had not supported the marriage. In choosing a Moroccan husband, Ingrid had crossed social norms regarding 'proper' husbands. Her parents' support was conditional on Ingrid's admitting she had been wrong and thus to re-commit herself to keeping to this norm. Like Rabia and Ingrid, other respondents also lost the support of their families because they crossed the social norms for choosing the right marriage partner. When these interviewees broke these rules, their family reacted with partial or complete exclusion from the support they would otherwise have offered at the moment of divorce.

The practical support interviewees received during their divorce differed. Some interviewees were able to arrange things themselves, without mentioning any need of support from others. Having sufficient cultural and economic capital, they did not need to rely on their social capital or turn to professional organisations in practical matters. People who needed practical support in their divorce case received this mostly from family members or friends. This support ranged from friends helping to move furniture to a new house, to cases in which family members or friends mediated marital conflicts, provided shelter for abused spouses, arranged the divorce procedure or contributed financially to the upkeep of interviewees and their children.

In several cases, family members present in the country of residence proved a valuable source of practical support and of great importance in the divorce procedure. For example, Driss, a Moroccan man married to a Dutch-Moroccan wife, had also migrated to the Netherlands because of the marriage. Having had little education, he worked in unskilled labour while his wife ran a business and handled all the accounts. When his wife's business failed, she suddenly took their children and went abroad to escape her creditors, without telling her husband why and where they went. Driss was stupefied and left behind with severe debts, a situation he could not solve himself. He then made an appeal to some family members who had been living in the Netherlands for a longer time and had Dutch education. They helped him gain an overview of all debts, and arranged for subsidised legal aid and a specialised lawyer to start a divorce case, hoping to put an end to the harsh actions of the creditors of his wife's business. They also translated for him when he had to visit his lawyer, the local government or the court. In this case, Driss' lack of cultural capital in the Netherlands was compensated by his social capital. Without the support of his family members, he would probably have been evicted from his home.

In this, there was a difference between migrating spouses in mixed and migration marriages. While many migrating spouses from mixed marriages had no family members in their new country of residence, most migrating spouses from migration marriages had family members already living in the Netherlands or Morocco. This can be explained by the Dutch-Moroccan context which entails certain specific migration patterns, as discussed in Chapter 2, but also other research, which showed a relation between migration and social capital, as the presence of migrants in a person's family increases the chance of that person migrating her/himself (Palloni et al. 2001).

In two cases, both migration marriages between a Dutch-Moroccan woman and a Moroccan husband, the marriage had been arranged by the parents. In both cases, the parents did not support a divorce. Similar to the women who did not follow the norms of their families in choosing a marriage partner, these respondents could not rely on their family for aid in the divorce process. Samira, for example, did not even want to inform her parents about her divorce:

> I'm still living in a story of lies. My parents don't know yet that I'm divorced. And I'm afraid to tell them. [...] What should I tell them? First of all I would get major problems at home. Because, in Morocco, you should return to the home of your parents. You cannot go elsewhere. Now I live here. I have some support from people. So for now I can live in this house. And I have support from friends in the Netherlands. But how long will it stay that way? Because this is just for the short-term. I don't know. I don't have any income. [...] And my father is really strict and orthodox. Then you can hardly leave the house. I know what my father is like. It would be a big shock for him. And he's diabetic. So now I'm thinking, my God, what should I do? How should I start? It would be such a shame for my parents, I'm divorced for a year and they don't know yet. (Samira, Dutch-Moroccan woman divorced from Moroccan husband, living in Morocco)

Afraid of being forced to move back in with her parents and hurting them by revealing that she was divorced, Samira sought support from some of her old friends living in the Netherlands. One of them provided her with a place of residence in Morocco and several supported her financially. However, even though Samira's parents were not informed about the divorce, they were aware that her husband had married another wife, which they felt was not proper behaviour. They thus broke off contact with the husband and his family—to whom they were also related—enabling Samira to hide the divorce. Moreover, her parents provided practical support in the form of child care when Samira resumed her education after the divorce, and she ate most meals at their home. Thus, although this interviewee had broken several social norms by moving into a place of her own after her divorce, her family would probably still have supported her, especially since the divorce was not her own choice. However, in accepting their support, Samira would have to keep to certain family rules about proper behaviour for a divorced woman which would limit her freedom of movement. Therefore, she chose to rely on her contacts back in the Netherlands where she grew up, which had less stringent norms about female behaviour after divorce.

Professional organisations were only involved in providing practical support in a few cases. Most of these were in the Netherlands, and especially for those interviewees which did not have enough social, economic, and cultural capital to arrange such things themselves. As we have seen above, the Egyptian wife who had a limited network in the Netherlands received emotional support from Dutch social workers. They also provided her with practical support in arranging for new housing and by helping her to apply for social security from the local government. Similarly, Samira relied on professional support in arranging some practical matters related to her court cases, such as retrieving documents from another city.

Legal aid and Information

The third category of support, legal aid and information, is the only one in which professional organisations took a more important position than the private networks of the spouses. Only interviewees who had specific reasons for not turning to the legal system to dissolve their marriage used their social capital instead. As has already been discussed in earlier chapters, this happened particularly in the Dutch-Egyptian context, where, especially in Egypt, a court procedure or legal representation was not always necessary. Other interviewees also used social capital in their divorce case, but they used it in addition to legal aid by professional organisations, not as a replacement.

During the divorce process, spouses in transnational marriages may come into contact with a wide range of professional actors. As has been discussed in Chapter 4, the involvement of lawyers is often necessary or even obligatory for arranging the divorce. Furthermore, as we have seen in previous chapters, there are some issues which require legal aid specific to transnational divorce, such as the involvement of migration law, the possible registration or acknowledgement of marriage and divorce in two countries and foreign documents which may need to be translated and legalised. However, it must be noted that only a minority of the spouses in this research considered a divorce in the second country to be necessary or relevant to their situation. Most, therefore, used local legal aid in arranging their divorce.

A network consisting of a wide variety of interconnected organisations is, or rather, was at the moment of research, an important part of Dutch-Moroccan transnational legal space. This network consists of both profit and non-profit actors, including migrant NGOs and lawyers as well as businesses specialising in the legal recognition of Dutch divorces in Morocco. Elsewhere, I have analysed these organisations as a social field in itself, a transnational field of legal aid (Sportel 2011).

Although spouses divorcing in the Netherlands and Egypt have much the same legal issues as Dutch-Moroccan couples, a similar network of organisations providing legal aid in case of transnational divorce is not present in Dutch-Egyptian transnational legal space. There are fewer organisations involved in providing legal aid in Dutch-Egyptian divorces, and there seem to be only incidental shared activities such as lobbying or providing education. Specific for the context of Dutch women living in Egypt is the presence of informal networks of Dutch and other European women living in there, as has been discussed in Chapter 2. Some Dutch interviewees therefore had easy access to the Dutch embassy in Cairo for information regarding their transnational divorce, through these networks. Others used these networks of foreign contacts to find a lawyer who would work reliably for foreign clients. It is also these networks in which the *Bezness* stories circulate, providing a rather negative frame of victimisation for transnational divorce.

Below, I will distinguish four main categories of actors active in providing specific legal support in transnational issues: NGOs, private offices, lawyers, and embassies and consulates and how they were used by the respondents in this research. In this section, I will systematically compare between the Dutch-Egyptian and the Dutch-Moroccan context.

NGOs

The first category of actors in transnational Dutch-Moroccan legal space concerns NGOs. In past years, many NGOs have been involved in providing transnational legal aid, both in the Netherlands and in Morocco. After the introduction of a new Moroccan family law in 2004, actors across Moroccan civil society, ranging from environmental protection organisations to women's rights NGOs, have become involved in educational projects aimed at informing the general public on the new family law. These educational projects have, to some extent, spread to Moroccan communities in Europe.

In the Netherlands, after the introduction of the new *Moudawana* in 2004, many projects were started to inform Moroccans living in the Netherlands as well as professionals working with these groups about the legal changes. These projects were often funded by Dutch local and national governments as well as charity funds. Some NGOs also provided individual advice and support. NGOs involved in these activities have a variety of backgrounds, ranging from so-called 'self-organisations', initiated by migrants living in the Netherlands (e.g. MVVN, Kezban) to women's centres (e.g. Idea or Dona Daria), and a wide variety of other welfare organisations. This involvement of NGOs in providing information about Moroccan (and later also Turkish) family law was fuelled by an initiative of the *Landelijke Werkgroep Mudawwanah* (*Moudawana* working group). In 2010 and 2011, this working group obtained funding for a project in which they increased the number of 'other' NGOs involved by training over 100 representatives (most of Moroccan or Turkish descent) from all kinds of local NGOs and welfare organisations in the Netherlands to give information on Moroccan or Turkish family law.

Since the 1980s, *Stichting Steun Remigranten* (SSR) has been one of the most prominent NGOs active in the Dutch-Moroccan transnational legal space, operating in both Morocco and the Netherlands. In 2008, their office in Berkane handled more than 8000 requests for advice on Dutch social security, Dutch and Moroccan family law and Dutch migration law.[2] The SSR office also had specific projects for women and children who are involuntary abandoned in Morocco, cooperating closely with the Dutch embassy in Rabat. However, after funding was stopped, the main office in Berkane had to be closed in early 2012.[3] Similarly, many of the NGOs involved in projects on Moroccan family law lost their funding after cutbacks in government funding. This means that much of the information on NGOs I gathered during my fieldwork between

---

[2] Annual report (*Jaarverslag*) SSR 2008. The majority of these requests dealt with social security issues of Moroccans who have returned to Morocco after a period of residence in the Netherlands.

[3] The office was reopened later that year, by former employee Mohamed Sayem as an independent office. At the time of writing it was not clear what would happen to the *Steunpunt* after Sayed passed away in May 2016.

2008 and 2011 and which has been discussed in Sportel (2011) is now outdated, and that some of the services interviewees used are no longer available.

Most respondents living in Morocco, both men and women, contacted the SSR office in Berkane for legal aid, or were referred to the SSR by the Dutch embassy or consulates in Morocco. Especially for so-called left-behind women, the SSR had a central role in organising both legal as well as practical aid, working together with the Dutch embassy and specialised Dutch lawyers to facilitate their return to the Netherlands. No other NGOs were as profoundly involved in the cases in this research as SSR, even though during the research period smaller organisations with similar services existed.[4]

In contrast to the many NGOs involved in providing legal aid and advice in Dutch-Moroccan marriage and divorce, I have not been able to find any NGOs providing these services specifically in Dutch-Egyptian divorce cases. The only organisation which does provide some support is *Bezness alert*. This organisation was founded by Noor Stevens, after she had written her book *Kus kus Bezness* on her Dutch-Egyptian marriage and divorce story. The organisation aims to provide support for fellow Dutch 'victims of love fraud' and to warn others about the dangers of *Bezness*. The main focus of the organisation is on providing emotional support, including the organisation of self-help support groups and the publication of stories of 'victims' on their website. Furthermore, *Bezness alert* tries to raise awareness of *Bezness* as a problem and lobby with the Dutch Ministry of Foreign Affairs and Dutch welfare organisations for a more proactive policy in handling *Bezness* and aid for victims. They also offer a translation service. Although *Bezness alert* also has contact with several Egyptian lawyers, and would like to be able to refer to them, at the time of research they had not yet been able to find a 'reliable and competent lawyer' in Egypt.[5]

---

[4] This prevalence of SSR clients might be an overrepresentation as I have approached most—though certainly not all—of these respondents through their office in Berkane. I have also approached several other organisations for help in finding possible respondents for this research, as discussed in the introduction. However, the SSR was the most successful go-between.

[5] Interview Noor Stevens, June 2011.

Market-level Actors

A second category of actors involved in transnational Dutch-Moroccan divorce cases is provided by the market. These businesses, mostly run by translators, offer services related to transnational divorce, such as the translation of documents and assistance with legal procedures. These businesses advertise on the internet, for example, through websites like *talaq.nl*, *echtscheidingmarokko.info*, or even on *marktplaats.nl*.[6] Most are located in the Netherlands, although some also have Moroccan offices, such as a branch of Dutch company *Arabika* located conveniently around the corner from the Dutch embassy in Rabat. Services offered include assistance during the Dutch divorce case to facilitate recognition of the divorce in Morocco, arranging the translation and legalisation of documents, and arranging the procedure for the recognition of the Dutch divorce in Morocco. Most promise to arrange the Moroccan divorce in only a few weeks or months. Fees can go up to several thousand euros, although some organisations also help customers in need pro bono or for reduced tariffs.

For example, the Dutch-Moroccan Samira received extensive help from *NL Services* without cost. She had been forced by her parents to marry in Morocco. After her divorce, she wanted to return to the Netherlands where she was born, but in her absence she had lost her rights to residence. Through her Dutch contacts in the Netherlands she came into contact with NL Services in Morocco. Her return to the Netherlands turned out to be a complicated affair, which she would have been unable to navigate without specialised help:

> I was really happy with her [head of NL Services]. Because when we went to apply, my passport had to be extended. Because it had to be valid for another nine months, or another six months I don't know. [...] In the beginning he [ex-husband] had all my papers. My passport, my identity card. He refused to give them to me.

[6] A quick search on Google [executed March 2016] for '*Marokkaanse echtscheiding*' (Moroccan divorce) reveals at least a dozen options, and there are probably many more without online presence. *Marktplaats* is a major Dutch online auction website comparable to eBay, offering their customers the opportunity to buy and sell used and new goods as well as professional services.

I: all of them?

R: Yes, all of them. I told [director of NL Services], she said to me: I need your passport for the application. Then she said: you need to talk calmly to him first. I kept asking calmly, but he did not want to give me the papers. Then she said: now you need to tell him he has to give you the papers, or you will report him to the police. Your passport is your property. I would never have dared to do that on my own. But because [head of NL Services] knows the law, yes, she knows the rules [...] In the end, it helped. I got my passport. And I brought it to [NL Services] right away. Then she told me: 'oh dear, it's only valid for a few more months. We need to extend it.' And then I had to go for another form. And for my birth certificate I had to go to Rabat. Because I was born in the Netherlands. And it was the first time for me to travel to Rabat. Well, [director of NL Services] arranged it all for me, because I was so scared. She told me, 'it's best if you take the bus, there is a direct line to Rabat. And then you need to go there for information and there for information.' I really wouldn't have made it without her. It's as if you're on the street on your own for the first time. I was alone and I was afraid. [...] Well, and then I went to Rabat. [...] and it turned out there was a problem with my birth certificate. Because my name, our last name, here in Morocco was not the same name as was written in [Dutch city]. [...Explains spelling mistake]. And we had to go to court [to correct the mistake]. It all had to go through, well, it was a big step. In the end I got the passport, and only then we could start the application. (Samira, Dutch-Moroccan woman divorced from Moroccan husband, living in Morocco)

This quote illustrates how even the start of the application process for a return to the Netherlands required specialist knowledge to navigate both the Moroccan and Dutch legal system and procedures and their interactions. Moreover, NL Services also provided coaching and support in undertaking these steps, such as travelling to the capital Rabat, a big issue for Samira who had grown up in the Netherlands and had mostly been contained indoors by her former husband in the years she had been living in Morocco. After NL Services had guided her through the collection of documents, a specialised Dutch lawyer was contacted to take further steps in the Netherlands to start the procedure.

Similar to NGOs, there seem to be no businesses offering to arrange for Dutch-Egyptian divorces, nor for the recognition of divorce procedures in the Netherlands or Egypt. A Dutch translator in Cairo told me she always referred her clients to the embassy, and would not provide information or answer questions regarding Egyptian or Dutch family law as she did not want to take responsibility for the effects of such answers.[7] NGO *Bezness alert* has also been considering starting such a business and in 2012 organised a meeting to test the demand for diverse services like legal aid in divorce cases, legalisations of documents, advice on real estate purchases and contracts in Egypt and mediation in child abduction cases.[8]

Lawyers

The third category of actors consists of lawyers. Although technically also market-level actors, most participants divorcing in the Netherlands made use of government-sponsored legal aid, meaning that people with an income below a certain level only need to pay a nominal amount.[9] The Dutch lawyers in this research were for a significant part of their clients, up to 90 % (based on their own estimates), paid by the Dutch government, especially when handling cases from transnational couples living in Morocco, where income levels are lower than in the Netherlands. However, not all lawyers are prepared to handle complicated and time-consuming cases on a subsidised basis. No similar provisions of legal aid were available in Morocco, which can make the Moroccan divorce more expensive than the Dutch one, despite significant differences in the fees of lawyers between the Netherlands and Morocco. Some Dutch lawyers specialising in Dutch-Moroccan divorce offer their clients the possibility to arrange for the divorce in Morocco as well as in the Netherlands.[10]

[7] By e-mail, January 2011.

[8] March 2012, Rotterdam.

[9] There have been significant cutbacks on Dutch government-sponsored legal aid in 2012, but all of the interviewees in this study were interviewed before these new measures took effect.

[10] It must be noted that such services are not covered by Dutch government-sponsored legal aid, and thus must be paid for separately.

There are also fewer lawyers specialised in Dutch-Egyptian divorces than in Dutch-Moroccan divorces. Like in Dutch-Moroccan divorces, it can sometimes be cheaper to divorce in the Netherlands than in Egypt, because of Dutch subsidised legal aid. This is mostly true for women who want to divorce without the consent of their husbands. In Egypt, men do not need a court procedure or legal aid in order to obtain a divorce. Similarly, if transnational couples agree on a divorce, they can easily arrange their divorce without a lawyer.[11] Without the consent of the husband, women who want to obtain an Egyptian divorce need to start a complicated and possibly expensive procedure at an Egyptian court. However, although a Dutch procedure using subsidised legal aid is cheaper, this will not always be a viable option. As the recognition of a Dutch divorce in Egypt is, as far as I have been able to find, not possible, it would probably still be cheaper and easier to go through a full Egyptian *khulʿ* or fault-based procedure in order to formally end the Egyptian marriage. In Egypt, there are English-speaking lawyers specialised in transnational divorces between Egyptians and Europeans. However, their services can be quite expensive. Lawyers I interviewed in 2010–2011 mentioned prices up to 5000 US dollars for arranging an Egyptian divorce, with extra amounts to be paid for the legalisation of documents. In the Netherlands, there is one Egyptian lawyer's office, offering legal aid in both the Netherlands and Egypt on their website.[12]

Embassies and Consulates

The fourth category of organisations active in Dutch-Moroccan transnational legal space consists of the embassies and consulates of both countries. Embassies are involved in a wide range of legal activities, most importantly the legalisation of documents for use in other countries and visa and immigration procedures.[13] This means that almost all participants

[11] For a more elaborate discussion of lawyers in the divorce procedure see Chapter 4.

[12] http://www.elsharkawi.nl/, accessed on 26 April 2013. From the website it does not become clear whether services similar to those of Dutch-Moroccan lawyers or private offices are offered. Unfortunately, I never managed to interview a representative of this lawyer's office.

[13] The Ministries of Foreign and Internal Affairs of the Netherlands and Morocco may also be involved in the legalisation of documents.

at some point during their marriage or divorce came into contact with an embassy or consulate. While some representatives of organisations were critical about the accessibility of the Dutch embassy in Rabat and its policy to make appointments through the internet—to which not all their clients have access—none of the divorced participants in this study considered this a problem.

While the Dutch embassy can answer questions regarding Dutch-Moroccan divorce, it does not generally provide information on family law unless prompted. As the validity of marriage divorce is connected to Dutch nationality and residence rights, it is mostly in this context that the embassy becomes involved, for example, when transnational couples apply for passports for their children and problems arise with regard to the recognition of an earlier divorce.[14] An exception is made in the context of involuntary abandoned women, who were regularly referred to the SSR office in Rabat for assistance. The Moroccan consulates in the Netherlands can also provide information on request on Moroccan family law and transnational marriages and divorces. The consulates share a legal representative who can arrange some family law affairs directly at the consulate.[15]

Contrary to the Dutch embassy in Morocco, the Dutch embassy in Egypt is more actively involved in providing information to transnational couples, including on their website. This information, while provided in English, is aimed at Dutch citizens marrying an Egyptian partner, and is mostly about Egyptian family law and Dutch migration procedures, not about Dutch family law. This information is mostly given at the moment of marriage, as the embassy is almost never involved in transnational divorce cases or the legalisation of divorce documents. According to an embassy representative, this might be related to many transnational marriages being informal, the time it can take to obtain the actual divorce documents and the suspicion that people might be taking the documents to the Netherlands without the obligatory embassy stamps.[16]

---

[14] Interview head of Consular Affairs, 8 October 2009, Rabat, Morocco.

[15] This legal representative is often described as a 'judge'. This does not, however, mean that court cases are held in the embassy, as in Morocco the concept 'judge' has a broader meaning than in the Netherlands. There are four Moroccan consulates in the Netherlands, located in the cities of Den Bosch, Rotterdam, Amsterdam, and Utrecht. The Moroccan embassy is located in The Hague.

[16] Interview with embassy representative, 5 December 2010.

Not all interviewees were satisfied with the help the Dutch embassy in Cairo provided. The embassy was described as being a 'fortress' where employees did not speak Dutch and were not helpful, which seemed to be more problematic than in the Dutch-Moroccan context. Not everyone shared this view though; some people who had participated in embassy activities or knew Dutch nationals who worked there did obtain helpful information and friendly treatment from the embassy. These differences between positive and negative experiences with the embassy may be related to the ways people used to approach the embassy, through their networks, by formal appointment, or by showing up at the counter where visa applications are handled.[17]

The Egyptian embassy in the Netherlands has more possibilities for legal involvement in transnational divorce cases than just giving information. For example, the embassy can handle the registration of *talaq*. This means that men, both Egyptian and Dutch (a Dutch husband only if he is formally a Muslim), can arrange their Egyptian divorce at the embassy. However, women have no such option; they have to go to Egypt to start a *khul'* case at the court. As in Egypt, the wife does not need to be present at the registration of the *talaq*, the authorities will inform her afterwards by sending a letter. The embassy has no possibilities to recognise a Dutch divorce. The embassy organises some educational activities about Egyptian law, but I did not manage to gain access as the embassy claims these activities are only accessible for Egyptian citizens. I suspect this also means they are not open to Dutch spouses of Egyptians who do not have Egyptian nationality.[18]

Professional Actors Providing Legal Aid and Information

Thus, organisations were far less important in providing legal aid and information in Dutch-Egyptian divorce cases than in Dutch-Moroccan divorce cases. Moreover, the organisations in Dutch-Egyptian

[17] The Dutch ombudsman in 1998 handled similar complaints about treatment at the Dutch embassy in Cairo in a report. The complaints were judged unfounded. De *Nationale Ombudsman*, report 1998/588, 29 December 1998.

[18] Information obtained by e-mail from the Egyptian embassy in the Netherlands in cooperation with my colleague Friso Kulk, July 2011.

transnational legal space do not share the same interconnectedness the network of organisations in Dutch-Moroccan transnational legal space has; they work more independently and on a national level without the transnational ties between organisations present in Dutch-Moroccan transnational legal space.

This difference in institutionalisation between Dutch-Moroccan and Dutch-Egyptian transnational legal space might partly be explained by the fewer numbers of Dutch-Egyptian marriages and divorces compared to numbers of Dutch-Moroccan marriages and divorces, as discussed in Chapter 2. Moreover, the existence of the Dutch-Moroccan transnational network of organisations has been fuelled by all kinds of projects, including several expert meetings, for which NGOs have managed to gain government funding from several Dutch ministries, framing their issues in terms of emancipation and participation of migrant women. As Dutch-Egyptian marriages mostly consist of mixed marriages between an Egyptian husband and a Dutch wife they have fewer possibilities to connect to these frames. However, as funding opportunities have subsided, the Dutch-Moroccan network seems to be weakening and the number of organisations involved in transnational legal space is going down.

What, then, does it mean for transnational Dutch-Moroccan spouses when they make use of legal aid and information from the network of organisations during their divorce? And what might an involvement of similar organisations have meant in Dutch-Egyptian divorce cases or those Dutch-Moroccan divorce cases which were arranged without this involvement? In the interviews, it was especially in the cases that involved Dutch migration law in which the support of organisations was of crucial importance. Without legal aid and information by organisations specialised in transnational cases, these spouses would not have had any chance of return to the Netherlands. The lack of a similar network of organisations in Dutch-Egyptian transnational legal space means that there is little specialised professional help available for these kinds of cases. Egyptians in cases similar to the story of the Dutch-Moroccan woman, Samira, whose complicated case needed an integrated approach by someone competent in both legal systems and specialised in transnational cases, would probably have failed to return to the Netherlands (See also: Bakker 2008; Carlisle 2014). However, as my research included mostly mixed Dutch-Egyptian couples, none of whom had any issues with regard to Dutch migration law, there were no cases in which the availability and use of a transnational network of Dutch-Egyptian organisations would have made such a crucial difference in the results of their divorce case.

Similarly, in Dutch-Moroccan cases without migration law issues, the involvement of organisations was more limited and consisted mostly of providing information which was helpful in making the divorce process run more smoothly, but it was not necessarily crucial for the outcome of the case. Most cases might have turned out rather similar without the involvement of the network of organisations.

However, as discussed above, I see transnational legal space as consisting of individual actors and networks of families, groups of friends, and organisations, some of which may be cohesive enough to be considered social fields. Moreover, these networks overlap with local social fields in both countries. In social fields, norms are produced, informing the kinds and amounts of support provided and excluding those interviewees which did not conform to these norms. Thus, the involvement of the professional organisations as well as private networks did not just provide support for the interviewees but sometimes also constrained them in handling their divorce case. As I have argued in more detail elsewhere, two main norms on transnational divorce are produced in the Dutch-Moroccan network of organisations (Sportel 2011). Firstly, most organisations seemed to consider transnational divorce mostly a women's issue. This framing brings the focus of the participating organisations to protecting women's positions in transnational divorces. Secondly, the organisations share a norm of no-fault divorce. This means that they do not aim to intervene in conflicts between the former spouses, nor do they consider the question of fault with regard to the failing of the marriage relevant. Instead, organisations see their work as assisting people in handling complex bureaucracy and procedures that accompany the interaction of legal systems in some divorce cases, similar to, for example, helping clients in navigating the transnational complexities of social security (Sportel, 2011). These shared norms reflect similar national discourses and frames on family law and the rights of (Muslim) women in Morocco and the Netherlands, as discussed in Chaps. 2 and 3.

Norms in Transnational Legal Space

As discussed above, both social fields of organisations as well as of family and friends produced norms which were a condition for gaining their support. What then are the effects of these norms in transnational legal space for how spouses handled the law in their transnational divorces? I will now present two examples of cases which contain some clues with regard to this question, one in which the norms of organisations impacted the access to legal aid and one in which the norms of private networks influenced the divorce process. In both stories, I will pay specific attention to constraints produced by these norms.

In the first case, Farid, a Moroccan father, was deported from the Netherlands after a prolonged custody dispute in which he eventually was denied access to his child for several years and thus could not gain a right of residence based on the contact with his child. After the waiting period in which his right to child access had been suspended had ended, he wanted to re-enter the Netherlands in order to start a new contact procedure. He went to the SSR office for help but his request was not met with the same level of helpfulness as the requests of abandoned women. To his frustration, Farid first had to convince the SSR representatives that he actually wanted to see his child and that the new contact procedure would not merely be an excuse to return to the Netherlands.[19] This reluctance to help can at least partly be explained by this case not matching with norms by the social field of organisations. Farid did not fit the category of female victims of divorce, especially as there had been allegations of domestic violence, making him more of a perpetrator than a victim. Contrary to the abandoned women, he had to 'prove' that his wish to return to the Netherlands was legitimately inspired by his wish to see his child. Nevertheless, like abandoned women, he needed the help of specialised legal aid in order to have any chance of returning to the Netherlands for contact with his child. Even though he had strong social capital in Morocco, his complicated case required specific expertise on

[19] He was asked to specify and write down the reasons why he wanted contact with his child. None of the mothers in this research who had been separated from their children reported ever being asked such a question.

Dutch family law and the interaction of legal systems local Moroccan organisations could not provide. The norms of this social field of organisations constrained him in gaining easy access to their support.

In a second case, family members from both spouses played an important role. Majda, a Moroccan woman, was married twice to the same Dutch-Moroccan man. He re-migrated to Morocco for the marriage, but he kept spending time in the Netherlands with his first wife, although he had supposedly already left her before marrying Majda. He also had an addiction to alcohol and did not maintain Majda and their child. During his first absence, Majda and their child lived with the father of her husband. Her own father supported her and the child financially. He did not agree with his daughter living with her in-laws while her husband was absent:

> My father told my husband that I should have my own house. And that he had to send money for his wife and child. Otherwise he would go to the police. You know, because my father took care of me and my son. My husband got the child benefits from the Netherlands, but he never sent anything to his son. (Majda, Moroccan wife with Dutch-Moroccan husband, living in Morocco. Interview was held with a translator present)

The father also interfered when the husband was violent to Majda: 'He beat me once. I told my father, and he came and told him: If you ever beat her again, you'll really go to prison.' (Ibid) When Majda eventually wanted a divorce, her father paid for a lawyer. He also was present at the court to support his daughter. As the husband showed up drunk, his father spoke for him. Supported by her father, Majda also arranged for a court order on the maintenance her former husband had to pay for their son. When he did not pay, Majda and her father went to court again to have the debt registered with the authorities and with customs, meaning that Majda's former husband would be arrested if he tried to enter Morocco. However, after a while the husband regretted the divorce. He asked Majda to take him back, and he promised to come back to Morocco to live with her and their son. As Majda wanted her son to grow up with his father, she agreed to marry him for the second time. She talked to her father and he agreed, but he also set some conditions:

> He said: 'my daughter should have a good life with [former husband]. She shouldn't go back just like that. They'll have to go to court and put everything in a contract.' (Majda, Moroccan wife with Dutch-Moroccan husband, living in Morocco. Interview was held with a translator present)

However, it soon turned out that the husband was still addicted and spent all his money on alcohol, 'turning the house into a pub'. Majda tried to hide this from her father by paying the household costs herself, as she owned a small business. But when the monthly instalments of the husband's debt to her father were not paid, her father had her husband arrested; he was sent to prison for five months for not paying his debts. All this time, Majda continued to visit her husband secretly in prison, without informing her father.

At the moment of the interview, Majda and her son had moved back in with her parents. After pressure from her father, she had reluctantly contacted a lawyer and was preparing another maintenance claim.

> I thought it was a bit pitiful for [former husband]. Because he just came from prison. I told my father that, maybe, now he has been to prison he is good, he will become good again. But my father said: 'that's just not true. I know what he's like, it will never be good, he'll stay like this.' [...] Then I realised he has money. His father is giving him money. But he never gave anything to our son. (Majda, Moroccan wife with Dutch-Moroccan husband, living in Morocco. Interview was held with a translator present)

Majda thought this new maintenance claim would put her husband in prison again. She refused to start another divorce case, however, as she still loved her husband and hoped his time in prison would change his behaviour. She also blamed her family-in-law for not supporting her attempts to get her husband to psychiatric treatment for his drinking problems.

In this case, several family members intervened in the marital conflicts and the subsequent divorce and remarriage. While not being migrants themselves, in their involvement they were acting in the transnational legal space, producing and reacting to norms. Especially Majda's father had an important role. This role was not limited to advice and financial support but included using the law to actively intervene in his daughter's marriage by threatening to report her husband after an incidence of violence and actually having him arrested for his debts to the family against the will of his daughter. Furthermore, he pressured Majda into taking several maintenance claims to court, which she probably would not have done otherwise. In this story, the father seems to be enforcing several social norms, some of which are social norms from local social fields, but others have distinctive transnational aspects. First of all, a good husband should maintain his wife and child and provide them with a proper place to live, separate from his family. Furthermore, the husband also should not drink alcohol and not beat his wife. Ideally, he should be present in the same country, but at least he should send money from the Netherlands, especially the child benefits he receives for his son from the Dutch government. The importance of Dutch child benefits returns in several stories from Dutch-Moroccan migration marriages, and the norm that they should be sent to the one taking care of the children, is an interesting example of specific norms produced in transnational legal space. The father used several means to enforce these rules, at first trying to solve conflicts informally but using the law if other means failed. If the husband did not comply, he was punished by exclusion from the family, as the father pressed his daughter for divorce, as well as by invoking outside, state-enforced punishment by having the former husband registered at the border and later imprisoned for not paying his debts. In her story, Majda was thus continually pressured to take legal steps, despite her reluctance to do so out of love for her husband.

Conclusions

In this chapter, my aim has been to map the social context of transnational divorce and describe the actors involved in providing emotional, practical, and legal support in transnational divorce cases. In Dutch-Moroccan transnational legal space, there have been many organisations involved in providing social and legal aid in transnational divorce cases. Moreover, many of these organisations were interconnected, forming a transnational social field of legal aid creating its own norms with regard to transnational divorce. While similar categories of organisations are also present in Dutch-Egyptian transnational legal space, the number and level of services offered is much smaller, and the organisations lack the interconnectedness of a network, let alone a social field. The absence of such a network for Dutch-Egyptian cases can be explained by the differences in the legal and migration context. First of all, there is a relatively small group of Dutch living in Egypt and Egyptians living in the Netherlands compared to Dutch-Moroccan migration. Furthermore, there is a relatively high number of mixed marriages between Dutch women and Egyptian men. Many of the projects produced by organisations in the Dutch-Moroccan network of organisations which enhanced the interconnectedness of this network, forming it into a social field, have been financed because of their focus on migrant women, a frame which is of little use to the context of Dutch-Egyptian marriages. However, this chapter also demonstrated the vulnerability of such networks and social fields. As many meetings and cooperation projects have been financed by Dutch local and national governments, connections dwindle or even disappear after funding is stopped, despite the efforts of the people involved. This means that the availability of adequate legal aid in complex cases present at the moment of research might disappear in the future. Especially for cases involving Dutch migration law, such as women who had been abandoned in their country of origin without legal documents, specialised legal aid has been shown to be of paramount importance in their divorce case, as it enabled them to return to the Netherlands, something which is hardly possible on their own. As such, the involvement of such specialised organisations operating in transnational legal space acted as a counterweight to their husband's privileged position based on Dutch nationality or residence status. However, in other divorce cases the involvement of organisations was less essential for the outcome of the case, even though it provided for a smoother divorce process.

Networks of family and friends, social capital, can also be an important tool in a transnational divorce. Especially family members sometimes provide extensive practical support, being involved in court cases or financially maintaining dependent spouses and children. The examples in this chapter illustrate how different forms of capital can interact in a transnational divorce. On the one hand, a lack of cultural or linguistic capital in a certain country, caused by migration, can be compensated by adequate social capital. On the other hand, this social capital can be disrupted by migration as well. In this, there were differences between mixed marriages and migration marriages. Most spouses from migration marriages already had some family members living in their new country of residence while this was not the case for most migrating spouses in mixed marriages. A few of the interviewed respondents managed to use their social capital transnationally, involving friends or family from the other country for support.

However, the involvement of informal contacts, friends, family members or colleagues as well as professional actors is not neutral. Transnational legal space consists of multiple social fields and networks, in which norms are created and enforced, mostly by exclusion. The main question in this chapter was how the involvement of the social environment constrains or supports the spouses in the divorce process. For some interviewees, knowing they had transgressed these norms by choosing the 'wrong' marriage partner or by divorcing from the 'right' partner, this was a reason not to turn to their family for support. Depending on their stories and positions, some interviewees were also confronted with friction between their case and the norms of NGOs and other organisations when they applied for support. Analysing social capital in the context of transnational legal space has made visible the norms imbedded in such networks, and how transgression of these norms can limit the access to support.

References

Bakker, Sanne. 2008. Achtergelaten Vrouwen. De weg terug van Marokko naar Nederland. Master Scriptie, Mediterrane studies, Radboud Universiteit.

Baldassar, Loretta. 2007. Transnational Families and Aged Care: The Mobility of Care and the Migrancy of Ageing. *Journal of ethnic and migration studies* 33(2): 275–297.

Bourdieu, Pierre. 1986. The Forms of Capital. In *Handbook of Theory of Research for the Sociology of Education.*

Carlisle, J. (2014). "That Hurt Me, That Hurt My Family": The Role of Migrants' Families During Transnational Parental Child Custody Disputes. In: T. Geisen, T. Studer and E. Yildiz. (eds.). *Egypt. Migration, Familie und Gesellschaft: Beiträge zu Theorie, Kultur und Politik.* Wiesbaden, Springer Fachmedien: 279–298.

Coleman, James S. 1988. Social Capital in the Creation of Human Capital. *American Journal of Sociology* 94: 95–120.

Curran, Sara. 2002. Migration, Social Capital, and the Environment: Considering Migrant Selectivity and Networks in Relation to Coastal Ecosystems. *Population and Development Review* 28: 89–125.

de Hart, Betty. 2010. Kin work and Legal Work in Transnational Legal Space. Moroccan-Dutch and Egyptian-Dutch Transnational families. WOCMES Conference, Barcelona, July 2010.

Glick Schiller, Nina. 2005. Transborder citizenship: An outcome of legal pluralism within transnational social fields. In *Mobile People, Mobile Law: Expanding Legal Relations in a Contracting World*, eds. Franz Bender Beckman and Keebit Bender Beckman, 48–81. London: Ashgate.

Hagan, John, Ross MacMillan, and Blair Wheaton. 1996. New kid in town: Social capital and the life course effects of family migration on children. *American sociological review*: 368–385.

Palloni, Alberto, Douglas S. Massey, Miguel Ceballos, Kristin Espinosa, and Michael Spittel. 2001. Social Capital and International Migration: A Test Using Information on Family Networks. *American Journal of Sociology* 106(5): 1262–1298.

Portes, Alejandro. 2000. Social capital: Its origins and applications in modern sociology. *Annual Review of Sociology* 24: 1–24.

Portes, Alejandro, and Patricia Landolt. 2000. Social capital: Promise and pitfalls of its role in development. *Journal of Latin American Studies* 32(2): 529–547.

Sportel, Iris. 2011. Transnational Divorce in Dutch-Moroccan Families. The Semi-Autonomous Social Field of Legal Aid. *Recht der Werkelijkheid* 32(3): 37–51.

Zhou, Min, and L. Bankston Carl III. 1994. Social Capital and the Adaptation of the Second Generation: The Case of Vietnamese Youth in New Orleans. *International Migration Review* 28(4): 821–845.

9

Conclusions

In this final chapter, I will present the conclusions of this study on transnational Dutch-Moroccan and Dutch-Egyptian divorce. In my analysis, I combined law and legal texts with a bottom-up approach in which the stories of spouses divorced from a transnational marriage were central. During the transnational divorce process, the spouses in this research were faced with many choices and decisions: where to arrange their divorce, whether or not to arrange for the recognition of the divorce in the other country, how to deal with children, marital property, and how to arrange for maintenance. How did spouses from transnational Dutch-Moroccan and Dutch-Egyptian marriages handle law in case of divorce, how did they deal with different legal systems and how can this be explained?

In answering this question, I will discuss five main themes. First of all, I will start with an analysis of Dutch, Egyptian, and Moroccan family law; their interactions and consequences for transnational families and how the spouses in this research arranged their divorce in one or both legal systems. Secondly, I will discuss the issue of marital power relations and extend the perspective of power relations between spouses with a discussion of the power of the law in intimate relationships. Thirdly, I present my findings on transnational legal space and the kinds

I. Sportel, *Divorce in Transnational Families*,
DOI 10.1007/978-3-319-34009-8_9

of support organisations and private networks provide in transnational divorce cases. Fourthly, I will go into the meaning of family law in the everyday life of transnational families. As has been demonstrated in Chapters 4–8, discourses, frames, and images on the law, on proper behaviour of spouses and on parenthood after transnational divorce played an important role. Lastly, I will question one of the assumptions of this research by raising the issue of how special transnational families actually are, and if and how they are the same as or differ from 'normal', non-transnational families in the three countries.

Transnational Divorce and the Interactions of Dutch, Egyptian, and Moroccan Family Law

Although the Dutch, Egyptian, and Moroccan legal systems are generally seen as markedly different, especially with regard to gender, my research could not confirm this assumption. Instead, all three family law systems can be seen as based on similar underlying notions of a gendered division of labour between the spouses, in which the husband (mainly) provides the means of living and the wife (mainly) provides care work. However, the three family law systems have each used different mechanisms to arrange for the upkeep of the partner doing the care work during marriage and after divorce. In Morocco and Egypt, the financial position of women and mothers is protected by separating the marital property, a prompt and deferred *mahr* and an obligation for the husband to provide for the family, regardless of the wife's means. The Dutch legal system found a solution in a system of communal property and prolonged spousal maintenance after divorce. With regard to children, Morocco and Egypt give mothers the right and obligation to daily care while fathers have the right to take major decisions about the children and the right to a contact arrangement. In the Netherlands, especially since 2009, the law arranges for a division of care tasks after divorce in which both parents are now equally obliged to care for their minor children. Based on an analysis of parliamentary documents and jurisprudence, however, this norm has been demonstrated to mean a right (and obligation) to have contact, not to equally divided care work. In practice, most Dutch children live with their mother after divorce while they have a contact arrangement with the father. Thus, the legal systems of all three countries are based on a similar image of the family, but the Netherlands, on the one hand, and Morocco and Egypt, on the other hand, have chosen different or even contradictory solutions to protect wives and mothers from the financial consequences of divorce.

A major difference between the legal systems is the access to divorce, especially for women. The Netherlands has no-fault divorce for both women and men since the early 1970s. Since 2004, Morocco has similar no-fault options for divorce for both women and men. In both Morocco and the Netherlands, wives do not lose their rights to financial compensation for care work when they initiate the divorce. Egypt, however, has very easy access to divorce for men and couples who agree on the divorce. For women the access to divorce is far more limited, and it mostly entails renouncing financial rights.

When the Dutch and Egyptian or Moroccan family law systems interact, these interactions can have several effects for transnational families. First of all, they potentially provide spouses in transnational marriages with space for forum or legal shopping, arranging their divorce where it will benefit them most or even trying to gain financial benefits in both legal systems. Forum shopping is especially relevant with regard to financial issues such as the division of property and maintenance (cf Baarsma 2011: p. 96).

A second possible effect of the interaction of two legal systems in transnational divorce is that people can be caught up in interactions, leaving them without any of the measures taken in the legal systems to protect spouses doing care work. For example, in mixed marriages, the absence of a *mahr* can leave Dutch wives without financial means in Morocco or Egypt, where there are only very limited possibilities for spousal maintenance and no communal property. This effect can be strengthened by the shifts which sometimes occur in transnational marriages with regard to gendered patterns of work, as a result of migration. When gendered patterns of work are shifted or inverted, some family law provisions for child care and financial matters can have unexpected effects, such as mothers doing both care work and paid work and having to pay spousal maintenance to a mostly absent father, or fathers taking care of the children full-time but without a claim to spousal maintenance under Moroccan or Egyptian law.

Access to divorce can also be (further) complicated by the interactions of two legal systems. If spouses in a transnational marriage aim for recognition of their divorce in both legal systems, they may need to go through a second divorce procedure. The interactions of legal systems with regard to the acknowledgement of the foreign divorce or a full second divorce have different consequences for spouses based on their gender and nationality. First of all, whereas recognition of the Dutch divorce is possible in Morocco since 2004, this is not the case for Egypt. Egyptian men or Dutch Muslim men living in the Netherlands can easily divorce at the embassy, but Egyptian or Dutch women need to go through a full second divorce procedure in Egypt if their former husband does not cooperate. This makes the recognition of Dutch divorces in Egypt or Morocco, the latter especially before 2004, more of an issue for women, especially if they aim to remarry, as men have easier access to divorce as well as the option of polygamy. For transnational couples divorcing in Egypt or Morocco, the recognition of their divorce in the Netherlands can be problematic. Dutch international private law requires proof that the wife has assented or resigned to the divorce before registering an Egyptian or Moroccan *talaq* divorce, while this is not required for other types of divorce, nor in 'ordinary' Dutch divorce procedures on the initiative of the husband. This means that it can be much harder for men to have their Egyptian or Moroccan divorce registered in the Netherlands than for women, in rare cases even making it impossible for Egyptian or Moroccan men to divorce in the Netherlands at all.

Handling Interactions of Family Law Systems

How then did people handle these family laws and their interactions in transnational divorce? In literature on a wide range of legal issues, litigants making strategic use of the availability and interaction of legal systems by so-called forum shopping is assumed and sometimes condemned, for example, raising issues with regard to the protection of weaker parties in legal conflicts (Ruhl 2006; Bassett 2006; Algero 1999;

Borchers 2010; Foblets 1998; Jansen Frederiksen 2011). However, I have met very few cases in which spouses have actually chosen or tried to strategically choose a forum to maximise their gains from the divorce. Specific laws in one of the two legal systems were almost never mentioned as a reason for choices in the divorce procedure. I have found three possible explanations for this surprising finding. First of all, many spouses in this research project made choices during their marriage or divorce which limit their possibilities of forum shopping, for example, only having registered their marriage or divorce in one country. The possible benefits of forum shopping often were not a factor in these choices, as many spouses were unaware of the possibilities. Secondly, there were also impediments which limited an effective use of forum shopping. For example, judgements made in one country cannot necessarily be used to claim property in the other country. These practical impediments were sometimes judged as being too much hassle in proportion to the possible gains. Lastly, some respondents who were aware of the possible benefits of forum shopping deemed them unfair to use, and they therefore would not make use of these possibilities.

Instead of forum shopping, most interviewees made decisions in their legal procedure as they went along, getting married in a hotel lobby to be able to share a room or randomly choosing a local lawyer to handle their divorce. The law played little part in their choices as they navigated between practical and financial concerns (cf Kulk 2013). Most couples, for example, only registered their marriage in the other country when it was necessary for the migration procedure while others only started a formal divorce procedure when there was a practical, immediate cause to do so, sometimes taking years to start a divorce procedure after the couple had separated.

In explaining these decisions to arrange legal matters in one or both countries, the presence of ongoing transnational ties was an important factor. In the absence of ongoing relationships with the other country, respondents simply had no reason to go through the trouble of a second divorce. These ties differed for mixed and migration marriages, as in migration marriages often both partners had networks of family and friends in both countries; the migration marriage in itself regularly was concluded because of these ongoing transnational ties. However, transnational ties cannot be presupposed based on the background of an interviewee or their marriage partner alone. Partners in migration marriages had sometimes lost their connections to the other country, while partners in mixed marriages had also created and maintained ties to the country of their foreign spouse.

While divorce in itself requires a legal procedure, the accompanying arrangements for child care, maintenance or the division of property after divorce were mostly made outside of the courts. Most respondents only mobilised the law after informal methods of conflict resolution, such as involving family members, failed. Litigation costs, both financial as well as emotional, further limited respondents' willingness or ability to start court procedures. Furthermore, there was often a lack of explicit conflict. Issues like maintenance, child residence, or contact with the non-resident parent were generally not decided in explicit bargaining between the spouses or their lawyers. Instead, outcomes were either taken for granted, or one of the partners took a decision unilaterally. Some Dutch parents managed to use the easier mobility of their Dutch nationality as a powerful tool in deciding the residence of their children or to escape maintenance obligations, for example, by leaving the country, involuntary abandonment in the country of origin of spouses and children or by taking the children to another country. This subject is closely connected to the issue of marital power relations, which I will turn to next.

Marital Power and the Law. The Power of the Law in Intimate Relationships

Looking back on their marriage, some of the interviewees reflected on dimensions of marital power of which they said to have been unaware during their marriage. While not part of the interview topic list, the issue of domestic violence came up in almost half of the interviews. Literature on marital power relations is often based on resource theory (Blood and Wolfe 1960), describing how spouses exchange resources such as money and care in the household, providing them with a certain amount of power. With regard to the marital division of labour in this research, gender turned out to be of central importance. While some of the interviewed women experienced how their former husbands used greater access to money as a means of power and control, other women were the main providers in the household, but they still failed to exercise similar power and control over their husbands. Similar to what Pyke (1994) and Tichenor (2005) have found in the USA, my findings demonstrate that money and labour in marriage are not universal resources to be used in a neutral exchange, but instead they are highly gendered and depend on the meanings attached in a specific context.

While most of the marital power literature looks at the division of labour, there are many more resources of marital power than money or labour. Some of these resources are specific for transnational marriages. First of all, the relatively 'strong' Dutch nationality and the mobility and rights of residence this nationality entails, called hierarchical citizenship by Castles (Castles 2005: p. 690) is one such resource. Through a dependent residence permit, the very right to stay in the country of settlement was linked to the marriage with the partner already living there. As such, the Dutch spouse acts as a kind of gatekeeper (de Hart 2002: p. 98–99) to the Netherlands, both through the structures of Dutch migration law, which put the migrated partners in a dependent residence position as well through his or her knowledge of Dutch society and language, what Bourdieu has called cultural capital (Bourdieu 1986). However, the power of these migration-specific resources is limited in time. Similar to Erel (2010), my findings demonstrate that cultural capital can be newly acquired in the country of residence as well as sometimes be employed transnationally. Moreover, in all three countries partners gain a right to an independent residence permit or nationality after prolonged residence. This meant that the use of the resources of migration law and specific cultural capital were mostly limited to those whose spouse has migrated especially for the marriage. However, in the Netherlands, the waiting period for an independent residence permit has gone up from three to five years, and there is an added demand of passing an integration test (Strik et al. 2013: p. 24–25), which means that the dependency of migrated partners now lasts for a longer period of time.

The question remains how these power relations work out in divorce procedures. First of all, migration law was used as an important tool in arranging the divorce. The involuntary abandonment of women and children in Morocco was used as a way to end a relationship while keeping control over the location of the former wife by preventing her return to the Netherlands, for example, by taking away passports and residence permits. In one case, a Dutch woman used a similar strategy, ending her marriage by abandoning her Moroccan husband and their children in their home in Morocco, departing for the Netherlands where they could not follow her, thus effectively determining the future residence of the children and division of care work. In these cases, spouses used the strict Dutch migration laws and procedures and their privileged position in the Dutch legal system as a means of power to physically separate themselves from their (former) spouses. This resembles the strategic use of migration law described by Liversage (2013) for transnational families in Denmark. Conversely, international child abduction was also used as a means to determine the further residence of the children and stop access arrangements by taking the children away to another country, without informing the other parent. Migration law is a thus very powerful tool in transnational conflicts, demonstrating the interconnectedness of migration law and family law for transnational families (see also van Walsum 2008).

The contrast of the lack of strategic use of family law and the active strategic use of migration law in some cases in this research is striking. Although a full explanation of this difference would require further research, possible factors could be that the strategic use of migration law is better known among migrant and mixed families than the possibilities of family law. In everyday life, transnational families are regularly confronted with their residence status, for example, when travelling back and forth between the countries. Furthermore, migration law is a very powerful 'tool', directly enforced at the borders of the Netherlands.

Secondly, most respondents kept their issues of unequal power relations and domestic violence outside of their divorce procedure. This can be explained by the character of the divorce procedure itself and by laws regarding property division and maintenance. No-fault divorce does not provide a space for discussing the actions of spouses during the marriage. Instead, some spouses tried to mobilise criminal law in domestic violence cases, by reporting their former husbands or family-in-law to the police but none were successful. Furthermore, laws regarding maintenance or marital property division after divorce do not take into account the actual division of labour; they are based instead on a gendered exchange model.

Thirdly, because of legal arrangements like maintenance and child care, financial dependency and the power relations connected to that dependency can continue after the divorce. Some violent or controlling former husbands tried to retain control after divorce through child access or maintenance payments. Legal reforms taken in the Netherlands and proposed in Egypt which extend the possibilities of non-resident fathers to enforce child contact also extend the possibilities for abusive former husbands to continue their control over their former wife and children. The dominant child welfare discourse in which fathers are crucial to children's well-being, regardless of their behaviour during the marriage, leaves little room for the discussion of these risks, as has been illustrated by the unsuccessful lobby of 'concerned mothers' in the Netherlands.

The Power of Law in Transnational Families

When analysing the complex interplay between state law and power relations at the level of the family, Chunn and Lacombe (2000) suggest seeing law as a practice which can both constrain and enable agency, depending on the other power relations involved, including gender, social class, and ethnicity (Chunn and Lacombe 2000: p. 13). In addition to the opportunities and constraints offered by migration law, I have found two ways in which family law constrains or enables the agency of spouses in transnational divorce: first of all, by providing ways as well as limitations to contract and end a marriage (cf Hull 2003). Having all kinds of legal implications, legal, state-registered marriage significantly differs from informal relationships and, to some extent, also from informal marriages, which are conducted especially in the Dutch-Egyptian context, as we have seen in Chapter 4. These legal implications of a state-registered marriage contain enforceable financial obligations such as maintenance during and after the marriage and communal marital property (in the Netherlands) and the status of children. Children born outside of wedlock can have serious problems in Egypt and Morocco, for example, when registering for education (Kulk 2013). One of the legal implications of formal marriage is also court involvement in divorce when the relationship ends (with the exception of Egyptian men who can simply register a divorce in Egypt). Restrictions on women's ability to divorce and leave the family setting have also been found to be a strong predictor of domestic violence (Hajjar 2004: p. 3; Adelman 2000: p. 1231).

Secondly, the law can be mobilised to punish abuse or to back up or enforce claims, if these claims are legally valid, for example, with regard to maintenance of children after divorce. As such, the law has also provided protection to dependent spouses or those who do not succeed in convincing their former spouses to let them access property, maintenance, or children. A strong example of such enforcing powers was the LBIO, a Dutch organisation that claims overdue maintenance payments. However, as we have seen in Chapters 4–8, these powers of the law are not automatically inflicted but need to be called in by the spouses. In other words, for the protection of the law to work in intimate relationships, one of the family members needs to mobilise it, something which not all interviewees in this study (fully) did.

Explanations for this lack of mobilising the law can be found in socio-legal studies. As studies in sociology of law have demonstrated, mental steps need to be taken to transform a conflict of interests into a legal dispute, and people also need a legal consciousness that the law can be of help in their problems (e.g. Felstiner et al. 1980; Merry 1986), and that the law is accessible and welcoming (Hernández 2010: p. 101). Furthermore, adequate legal information and aid is of great importance to mobilise the law successfully, to which not all interviewees had equal access.

My findings thus emphasise the importance of marital power for an analysis of transnational divorce. Furthermore, it also demonstrates the importance of law for the study of marital power, adding a legal dimension not often found in empirical studies on marital power, especially those in Western countries. However, the way I researched marital power relations in a transnational context has its limits. This research has been done in the context of divorce and thus does not include 'successful' transnational marriages (cf Kulk 2013), and I have interviewed only one of the spouses. A more systematic discussion of power relations in transnational marriages based on research in which both (former) spouses are included, following the example of Komter (1985, 1989), could provide further insights in the workings of marital power in a transnational context. Next to marital power relations between the spouses, the social context also played an important role in how people handled the law in transnational divorce. I will discuss these social contexts below.

Social Fields and Transnational Divorce

During divorce, family members from mixed and migrant families act in transnational legal space (de Hart 2010), a space across borders which consists of institutions and networks of family, friends, and organisations in both countries and in which norms with regard to handling the law are formed and enforced. Transnational legal space is formed by state institutions as well as transnational networks of NGOs, lawyers, and other actors. An important difference between Dutch-Moroccan and Dutch-Egyptian transnational legal space is the difference in institutionalisation. In the Dutch-Moroccan context, there have been many interconnected organisations providing social and legal aid in transnational divorce cases, forming a transnational social field of legal aid (Sportel 2011). While there are also some organisations active in Dutch-Egyptian transnational legal space, the number and level of services offered is much smaller, and the organisations lack the interconnectedness of a social field, which makes Dutch-Egyptian transnational legal space less institutionalised and harder to navigate.

As we have seen in Chaps. 3 and 8, these differences between Dutch-Egyptian and Dutch-Moroccan transnational legal space can be explained both by differences in the migration context as well as by differences in the legal context. Compared to the large number of Moroccan migrants in the Netherlands, there is only a relatively small group of Dutch living in Egypt and Egyptians living in the Netherlands, which mostly consists of mixed marriages between Dutch women and Egyptian men. Moreover, as it is not possible to have a Dutch divorce recognised in Egypt, while Egyptian men living in the Netherlands can easily divorce at the embassy, there are few services to be offered by private offices. Furthermore, as discussed above, migration marriages and mixed marriages differ with regard to the presence of ongoing transnational ties after divorce, which informs the need for recognition of the divorce in the other country.

Again, Dutch migration law plays an important role with regard to the necessity of the involvement of such a network of specialised organisations in transnational divorce cases. For example, organisations can help women abandoned in their country of origin return to the Netherlands, something which is hardly possible on their own. As such, the involvement of specialised organisations can counterweigh a Dutch spouse's privileged position based on his nationality and residence and help to get adequate legal aid in their divorce cases. However, this network of organisations has been demonstrated to be vulnerable. Due to declining funding opportunities, and especially, the end of government funding for the SSR office in Berkane, it remains to be seen whether women and men abandoned in Morocco by their former spouse will continue to receive adequate legal aid to support their return to the Netherlands.

The relationship between institutions and organisations and private networks of family and friends in transnational legal space is complex and depends on the kind of support needed and the availability of this support. Institutions and organisations were the preferred source of legal aid, and interviewees only relied on their personal networks in addition to professional legal aid or as a replacement if no adequate professional legal aid was available. With regard to practical and emotional support, the involvement of informal contacts, friends, family members, or colleagues, social capital was the primary source of support, and people only relied on professional aid if they did not have or could not access their private networks.

The relationship between social and cultural capital and migration is complex. On the one hand, a lack of cultural and economic capital in the country of residence, caused by migration, can be compensated by adequate social capital. On the other hand, social capital can be influenced by migration as well, losing ties in the country of origin but also establishing new ties in the country of residence and in local or transnational migrant communities. The effects of migration differed for mixed marriages and migration marriages. Most spouses from migration marriages already had some family members living in their new country of residence while this was not the case for most migrating spouses in mixed marriages. A few of the interviewed respondents managed to use their social capital transnationally, involving friends or family from the other country for support.

However, the involvement of both networks of family and friends as well as professional organisations is not neutral. They enforce local social norms as well as producing and enforcing new norms in transnational legal space on how to deal with transnational divorce. Support from private networks, as well as organisations, was often conditional upon meeting such norms, 'punishing' transgressions with exclusion, limiting the options of spouses in transnational legal space. When analysing the involvement of private networks solely as social capital to be freely employed in transnational divorce, this conditionality is easily overlooked. Studying both private and professional networks as social fields demonstrated how they can support as well as constrain spouses in transnational legal space. While I would not argue for abolishing the term social capital as a factor or tool in divorce, the constraints and exclusionary working of the involvement of both private and professional networks should be taken into account in future research.

Law in Everyday Life

In everyday life, images and perceptions of the law, or legal consciousness, can be just as important as the law in the books in forming and informing the experiences of people. In the stories of the interviewees, a number of moral and legal discourses were found which were of importance in how they experienced and handled their divorce. First of all, in the Netherlands and among Dutch migrants in Morocco and Egypt, there was a negative discourse on Islamic family law. In this discourse, Moroccan or Egyptian law is presented as both very powerful and completely gendered and ethnicity-based, providing Egyptian or Moroccan men with certain, unspecified, rights while taking away rights from Dutch women, a discourse referred to by some authors as legal Orientalism (Kroncke 2005).

Secondly, with regard to child care after divorce, the welfare discourse took central stage. The welfare discourse centres on the best interests of the child, which should be the central concern of parents after divorce. It is present both in the stories of divorced parents, as well as in recent—attempts for—legal reform in Morocco and Egypt and has for some time been the central ideology in the Dutch legal system. Interviewees used two main stories about good and bad parents after transnational divorce, both part of the welfare discourse. While involved good parents share the burden of child care, bad parents are absent during the marriage or desert their children after divorce. Moreover, a good parent puts the best interests of the children before her or his own, excluding the children from conflicts with the former spouse, while a bad parent uses the children in ongoing conflicts. Both types of 'bad parents' fail to put the best interests of the children before their own.

Thirdly, with regard to arranging financial matters after divorce, several competing moral discourses were present. Respondents used a discourse of earning and deserving, in which sharing of financial resources can be lost by showing a lack of proper behaviour, and a discourse of need and wealth, in which sharing during and after marriage is the norm. For mixed marriages, the frame of *Bezness* is exceptionally strong. This frame entails that Moroccan or Egyptian men only marry Dutch women for financial benefits or a residence permit in the Netherlands, faking their love, while the Dutch women in these marriages really love their husbands and are thus deceived. This discourse of false love is connected to the tourist industry and experiences of swindle commonly shared by foreign visitors to Egypt.

A new Dutch discourse can be found in the issue of 'marital imprisonment'. This issue, which has been put on the Dutch political agenda after a very active and successful lobby by Dutch NGO *Femmes for Freedom*, concerns women who fail to get the cooperation of their husband in acquiring a foreign or religious divorce after their Dutch marriage or informal marriage has ended. In Dutch policy frames, it is connected to forced marriages, involuntary abandonment in the country of origin and even female genital mutilation.[1] While at the moment of writing campaigns were primarily aimed at migrant women in migration marriages,

[1] *Kamerstukken II* 2012-2013, 32 840, nr. 8 (amendment Arib-Hilkens). See also Smit van Waesberghe et al. (2014)

this frame could potentially also be used by Dutch women from mixed marriages. Thus, an important part of discourses in transnational legal space is based in victimhood.

Kapur (2002) and Narayan (1997) warn about the use of victimisation discourses, especially when they contain claims of culture, as these are generally based in gender essentialism and cultural essentialism. Both authors point out how culture is central in explaining violence happening to 'Third-World women' or similarly, in the case of *Bezness*, to Dutch women by Moroccan or Egyptian men, while being neglected, when analysing similar violence against women in Western contexts (Narayan 1997, Kapur 2002). Blaming culture for violence disconnects this violence from the much broader issue of domestic violence (Narayan 1997: p. 90), as also happened in some *Bezness* cases in which the interviewees did not connect their experiences to domestic violence, but only to *Bezness*. Furthermore, victimisation discourses construct women as being 'thoroughly disempowered, brutalized and victimized' (Kapur 2002: p. 18). When applying the frame of *Bezness* to their divorce, interviewees reinterpret the entire marriage, recasting former partners as perpetrators and victims. In this process, their own agency as well as their powerful position based on their ethnicity, nationality, and welfare differences between the countries is being downplayed while the image of the 'dangerous Muslim man' (cf Razack 2007) is reinforced. Why the *Bezness* frame is so influential among Dutch women in Egypt, and why it was especially Dutch women from mixed marriages who narrated their divorce stories taking the position of victimhood, needs more research to explain. I tentatively suggest part of the explanation may be found in the complicated interconnection of mass tourism and power relations between the West and the Middle East (cf Bowman 1989).

What then did the presence and use of these discourses mean for how respondents handled the law in their divorce? The importance of legal consciousness for actual (legal) actions taken by the spouses differed for different levels and topics. First of all, images of both legal systems only rarely had an impact on choosing the country or legal system in which to start the divorce procedure. As has been demonstrated in Chapter 4, earlier contacts with the legal systems of one or both countries, including experiences of discrimination or bureaucracy, had an impact on legal consciousness (Merry 1986, cf Hernández 2010). But even when interviewees had a strong negative image of the law in one country and a positive opinion of the legal system in the other country, this was never a conclusive factor in determining where to arrange the divorce. All but a few respondents arranged their divorce locally, in their country of residence, regardless of their opinion of the local legal system.

Secondly, and contrary to the limited influence of legal consciousness to the choice of forum at divorce, at the moment of marriage, legal consciousness in some cases influenced the way spouses handled and experienced law, such as including conditions in the marriage contract or choosing to get married in one or the other country. Some interviewees, especially women, saw Islamic family law as a threat, which encouraged them to protect themselves by seeking legal information or advice on the Moroccan or Egyptian legal system before the marriage. Especially in more recent stories of Dutch interviewees married to an Egyptian or Moroccan husband, the discourse of legal Orientalism was strongly present. Dutch law is either remarkably absent in these fearful stories or presented as a safe refuge, although it is not always as favourable as respondents assumed. Both of these positions do not encourage further investigation of Dutch family law.

Thirdly, while legal consciousness was never a reason to choose the forum or legal system in which to divorce, it was sometimes of importance in the choice made for arranging for child care or financial matters after divorce within one of the two legal systems. When arranging financial matters and child care after divorce, most interviewees used moral discourses when explaining their arrangements. Whereas the welfare discourse was present in all stories of divorced parents, it was, as Kaganas & Day-Sclater (2004) have also demonstrated, used to defend opposite positions, such as going to court or not going to court in the best interest of the children. With regard to financial matters, wives in all three countries assumed they had a right to maintenance, which they could claim if they needed it. This framing leaves no room for financially dependent men or men doing care work after divorce to be maintained by their former spouse or for women paying maintenance. These gendered perceptions of the law fed certain positions of entitlement, which made a few respondents who would have been legally entitled to claim maintenance refrain from doing so. Only a few interviewees used a discourse of legal rights, but their actual legal position was at best of secondary importance for their evaluation of their own situation.

The *Bezness* frame also had an impact on the divorce procedure, as women who felt themselves to be victims of *Bezness* did not only start a divorce procedure but also (tried to) involve the police or the Dutch migration services, hoping to mobilise the authorities to punish their former husband as a perpetrator. Furthermore, women who felt they have been the victims of false love of their former partner also started to warn and inform others in mixed relationships, thus strengthening the discourse.

Thus, while legal consciousness does not necessarily influence legal actions taken during the divorce procedure, and in itself was not enough to induce a choice of forum for the divorce, some discourses were of importance for how people arranged matters after divorce, such as financial issues and child care, and their marriage. This study has demonstrated the interconnectedness between individual legal consciousness as shaped by personal experience with a legal system and bureaucracy, and the social context in which transnational marriages take place, including discourses in transnational legal space. Moreover, it also adds a transnational dimension to the study of legal consciousness, showing how legal consciousness of the same person can relate differently to foreign or local legal systems. In an increasingly mobile world, future research on legal consciousness should thus be aware of the multiple legal systems in which people, including members of transnational families, but also non-migrant families, may have had experiences.

Having discussed these four main factors which can explain how spouses handle the law in transnational divorce cases and the interaction of Dutch, Egyptian, and Moroccan law, the law and ongoing transnational ties, marital power relations, norms, and support in social fields and legal consciousness, I will now raise one final reflective question below: how special are transnational marriages?

How 'Special' Are Transnational Families?

In this research, it has been demonstrated how transnational legal space encompasses institutions, NGOs, and lawyers in both countries and that both migrant and non-migrant spouses can be actors in that space.

However, by singling out transnational divorces, these are automatically set apart from 'normal', national, divorces. As comparable research for each of the three countries, especially the Netherlands, is limited, it is hard to compare transnational families to 'ordinary', non-migrant families and their experiences with the legal system in case of divorce. In many stories of informants, the transnational aspects of their marriage and divorce are limited or even absent. Remarkably, only a minority of spouses in this research aimed at a reconciliation of their legal status in both legal systems, and even fewer tried to exploit the differences between the legal systems strategically. Instead, most interviewees seemed to be indifferent to their legal status in the other legal system and only took action if required or if they had specific reasons to do so, which might be years after the relationship ended. This is contrary to my expectations and also differs from the findings of Kulk who reports that most of his respondents in transnational marriages aimed at arranging their legal status similarly in both countries (Kulk 2013). This raises the question how 'transnational', transnational families actually are in the way they deal with divorce. When spouses are only using the local legal infrastructure to arrange their marriage and divorce, what then sets them apart from other local divorces?

The first aspect which sets transnational families apart from non-transnational families is the possible involvement of migration law. As has been discussed above, migration law is the 'hard line' that sometimes simply cannot be crossed, enhancing or restraining mobility, and as such sometimes used strategically in disputes. Migration law requirements were often the incentive for spouses to take actions which have consequences in family law. Moreover, some marriages failed after the migration process to the Netherlands was unsuccessful or aborted.

Secondly, the fact that one of the spouses in a transnational marriage has migrated while the other lives in his or her native country is also relevant. Migration can influence power positions within the family. Not everyone was able to use his or her social or cultural capital transnationally, which limited the options of some spouses. However, this type of capital can be reacquired or transformed over time. Migration might even be the consequence instead of the origin of power dynamics in a relationship, influencing the decision of who is going to migrate to where. In this respect, this research group might differ from other groups of people who live transnational lives, such as families who have migrated together or the children of migrants and mixed couples.

Thirdly, this research has demonstrated that the contexts in which marriages and divorces take place, including the factors of time, place and distance introduced in Chapter 2, have been of great importance for how people experienced and dealt with the law in their divorce. Specific for transnational marriages between Europe and the Middle East are the public discourses on mixed and migration marriages and on Islamic family law which have been present at certain times and places relevant for this research, influencing how spouses in transnational marriages perceived the cultural, religious, and physical distance between them. Most of these public discourses were highly gendered. Similarly, Nader (1989) has argued that both Orientalist and Occidentalist discourses frequently focus on the position of women. By commenting on the position of women in the other society, both the West and the East obscure similar gender inequalities in their own society, implicitly placing the speaker in a superior position. Gender ideologies are thus also a part of distinguishing between 'us' and 'them' (Nader 1989: p. 323–325, p. 346). Based on her research on the Ontario Sharia debate, Razack has raised the question 'how might feminists have avoided being drawn into the framework of superior, secular women saving their less enlightened and more imperilled sisters from religion and community and still responded to the dangers at hand?' (Razack 2007: p. 16).[2] In this study, I have tried to avoid these pitfalls by analysing Dutch as well as Moroccan and Egyptian family law from a gender perspective, which revealed striking similarities obscured by the emblematic use of gender in general discourses on Islamic family law. Moreover, I presented a diversity of perspectives of both women and men in mixed and migration marriages, demonstrating how some experiences commonly ascribed to culture or gender are shared by interviewees from diverse genders, backgrounds and ethnicities. Recognising the influence of the specific contexts of transnational

[2] The Ontario *Sharia* debate concerned the introduction of *Sharia* law as a voluntary arbitration option for Canadian Muslims in family law (Razack 2007).

marriages, while at the same time acknowledging the diversity of individual experiences of the people involved, is key to understanding this complex interaction.

References

Adelman, Madelaine. 2000. No Way Out. *Violence Against Women* 6(11): 1223–1254.

Algero, Mary Garvey. 1999. In Defense of Forum Shopping: A Realistic Look at Selecting a Venue. *Nebraska Law Review* 78: 79–112.

Baarsma, N.A. 2011. *The Europeanisation of International Family Law*. The Hague: T.M.C. Asser Press.

Bassett, Debra Lyn. 2006. The Forum Game. *North Carolina Law Review* 84(2): 333–396.

Blood, Robert Oscar Jr., and M. Wolfe. 1960. *Husbands & wives: the dynamics of married living*. Glencoe: Free Press.

Borchers, Patrick J. 2010. Punitive Damages, Forum Shopping, and the Conflict of Laws. *Louisiana Law Review* 70(2): 529–555.

Bourdieu, Pierre. 1986. The Forms of Capital. In *Handbook of Theory of Research for the Sociology of Education*.

Bowman, Glenn. 1989. Fucking Tourists. Sexual Relations and Tourism in Jerusalem's Old City. *Critique of Anthropology* 9(2): 77–93.

Castles, Stephen. 2005. Hierarchical Citizenship in a World of Unequal Nation-States. *PS: Political Science and Politics* 38(4): 689–692.

Chunn, Dorothy Ellen, and Dany Lacombe, eds. 2000. *Law as a Gendering Practice*. Oxford: Oxford University Press.

de Hart, Betty. 2002. Slachtoffers of 'gatekeepers': zwarte, migranten-en vluchtelingenvrouwen en Nederlandse vrouwen met een buitenlandse partner in het familierecht. In *Bundel VN-Vrouwenverdrag*, ed. R. Holtmaat, 95–106. Den Haag: E-Quality.

———. 2010. Kin work and Legal Work in Transnational Legal Space. Moroccan-Dutch and Egyptian-Dutch Transnational families. WOCMES Conference, Barcelona, July 2010.

Erel, Umut. 2010. Migrating Cultural Capital: Bourdieu in Migration Studies. *Sociology* 44(4): 642–660.

Felstiner, William L.F., Richard L. Abel, and Austin Sarat. 1980. Emergence and Transformation of Disputes: Naming, Blaming, Claiming. *Law & Society Review* 15: 631.

Foblets, Marie-Claire. 1998. *Marokkaanse migrantenvrouwen in gezinsgeschillen: wat zijn passende juridische oplossingen?* Antwerpen: Maklu.

Hajjar, Lisa. 2004. Religion, State Power, and Domestic Violence in Muslim Societies: A Framework for Comparative Analysis. *Law & Social Inquiry: Journal of the American Bar Foundation* 29(1): 1–38.

Hernández, Diana. 2010. "I'm Gonna Call My Lawyer:" Shifting Legal Consciousness at the Intersection of Inequality. *Studies in Law, Politics, and Society* 51: 95–121.

Hull, Kathleen E. 2003. The Cultural Power of Law and the Cultural Enactment of Legality: The Case of Same-Sex Marriage. *Law & Social Inquiry* 28(3): 629–657.

Jansen Frederiksen, Katja. 2011. Mahr (dower) as a Bargaining Tool in a European Context: A Comparison of Dutch and Norwegian Judicial Decisions. In *Embedding Mahr in the European Legal System*, eds. Rubya Mehdi and Jørgen S. Nielsen, 147–190. Copenhagen: DJØF Publishing.

Kaganas, Felicity, and Shelley Day-Sclater. 2004. Contact Disputes: Narrative Constructions of 'Good' Parents. *Feminist Legal Studies* 12: 1–27.

Kapur, Ratna. 2002. Tragedy of Victimization Rhetoric: Ressurecting the "Native" Subject in International/Post-Colonial Feminist Legal Politics, The. *Harvard Human Rights Journal* 15: 1–37.

Komter, Aafke Elisabeth. 1985. *De macht van de vanzelfsprekendheid in relaties tussen vrouwen en mannen*. Leiden: University of Leiden. Proefschrift.

———. 1989. Hidden Power in Marriage. *Gender & Society* 3(2): 187–216.

Kroncke, Jed. 2005. Substantive Irrationalities and Irrational Substantivities: the Flexible Orientalism of Islamic Law. *UCLA journal of Islamic and Near Eastern law* 4(1): 41–73.

Kulk, Friso. 2013. *Laverend langs grenzen. Transnationale gezinnen en Nederlands en islamitisch familie- en nationaliteitsrecht*. Nijmegen: Wolf Legal Publishers.

Liversage, Anika. 2013. Gendered Struggles over Residency Rights when Turkish Immigrant Marriages Break Up. *Onati Socio-Legal series* 3(6): 1070–1090.

Merry, Sally Engle. 1986. Everyday Understandings of the Law in Working-Class America. *American Ethnologist* 13(2): 253–270.

Nader, L. 1989. Orientalism, occidentalism and the control of women. *Cultural Dynamics* 2(3): 323–355.

Narayan, Uma. 1997. *Dislocating cultures: identities, traditions, and Third-World feminism*. New York: Routledge.

Pyke, Karen D. 1994. Women's Employment as a Gift or Burden? Marital Power Across Marriage, Divorce, and Remarriage. *Gender & Society* 8(1): 73–91.

Razack, Sherene H. 2007. The 'Sharia Law debate' in Ontario: The Modernity/ Premodernity Distinction in Legal Efforts to Protect Women from Culture. *Feminist Legal Studies* 15(1): 3–32.

Ruhl, Giesela. 2006. Methods and Approaches in Choice of Law: An Economic Perspective. *Berkeley Journal of International Law* 24(3): 801–841.

Smit van Waesberghe, Eliane, Iris Sportel, Lisanne Drost, Esther van Eijk, and Elja Diepenbrock. 2014. *Zo zijn we niet getrouwd. Een onderzoek naar omvang en aard van huwelijksdwang, achterlating en huwelijkse gevangenschap.* Utrecht: Verwey Jonker Instituut.

Sportel, Iris. 2011. Transnational Divorce in Dutch-Moroccan Families. The Semi-Autonomous Social Field of Legal Aid. *Recht der Werkelijkheid* 32(3): 37–51.

Strik, Tineke, Betty De Hart, and Ellen Nissen. 2013. *Family Reunification: a barrier or facilitator of integration? A comparative study*. Brussels: European Commission.

Tichenor, Veronica. 2005. Maintaining Men's Dominance: Negotiating Identity and Power When She Earns More. *Sex Roles* 53(3/4): 191–205.

van Walsum, Sarah Katherine. 2008. *The family and the nation: Dutch family migration policies in the context of changing family norms.* Newcastle Upon Tyne: Cambridge Scholars Publishing.

References

Jansen Frederiksen, Katja. 2011. Mahr (dower) as a Bargaining Tool in a European Context: A Comparison of Dutch and Norwegian Judicial Decisions. In *Embedding Mahr in the European Legal System*, eds. Rubya Mehdi and Jørgen S. Nielsen, 147–190. Copenhagen: DJØF Publishing.

Kalmijn, Mattijs, Paul M. de Graaf, I. Marjolein, Broese van Groenou, and Pearl A. Dykstra. 2001a. Oorzaken en gevolgen van echtscheiding: Een landelijk onderzoek onder gehuwde en gescheiden personen in Nederland. *Tijdschrift Sociale Wetenschappen* 44(2): 1–15.

Kalmijn, Mattijs, Paul M. de Graaf, and Anne-Rigt Poortman. 2001b. Werk en echtscheiding: de interactie van economische en culturele invloeden. *Tijdschrift Sociale Wetenschappen* 44(2): 34–52.

Moors, Annelies. 2003. Introduction: Public Debates on Family Law Reform. Participants, Positions, and Styles of Argumentation in the 1990s. *Islamic Law and Society* 10(1): 1–11.

Silbey, Susan S. 2005. After legal consciousness. *Annual Review of Law and Social Science* 1: 323–368.

I. Sportel, *Divorce in Transnational Families*,
DOI 10.1007/978-3-319-34009-8

Index

A

Note: Page numbers with "n" denote notes.

I. Sportel, *Divorce in Transnational Families,*
DOI 10.1007/978-3-319-34009-8

The manufacturer's authorised representative in the EU is Springer Nature Customer Service Centre GmbH, Europaplatz 3, 69115 Heidelberg, Germany. If you have any concerns regarding our products, please contact ProductSafety@springernature.com

Printed and bound by CPI Group (UK) Ltd, Croydon, CR0 4YY

25/09/2026

02222854-0006